CRITICAL ACCLAIM
FOR *TRAVELERS' TALES*

"The *Travelers' Tales* series is al
—Jan Morris, au   *ong*

"For the thoughtful traveler, th
There's nothing like them on th
—Pico Iyer, author of *Video Night in Kathmandu*

"This is the stuff memories can be duplicated from."
—Karen Krebsbach, *Foreign Service Journal*

"I can't think of a better way to get comfortable with a destination
than by delving into *Travelers' Tales*…before reading a guidebook, before
seeing a travel agent. The series helps visitors refine their interests and
readies them to communicate with the peoples they come in contact
with.…"
—Paul Glassman, Society of American Travel Writers

"*Travelers' Tales* is a valuable addition to any predeparture reading list."
—Tony Wheeler, publisher, Lonely Planet Publications

"*Travelers' Tales* delivers something most guidebooks only promise: a real
sense of what a country is all about.…"
—Steve Silk, *Hartford Courant*

"The *Travelers' Tales* series should become required reading for anyone
visiting a foreign country who wants to truly step off the tourist track
and experience another culture, another place, firsthand."
—Nancy Paradis, *St. Petersburg Times*

"Like having been there, done it, seen it. If there's one thing traditional
guidebooks lack, it's the really juicy travel information, the personal
stories about back alleys and brief encounters. The *Travelers' Tales* series
fills this gap with an approach that's all anecdotes, no directions."
—Jim Gullo, *Diversion*

T R A V E L E R S ' T A L E S

CUBA

TRUE STORIES

TRAVELERS' TALES

CUBA

TRUE STORIES

Edited by
TOM MILLER

Series Editors
JAMES O'REILLY AND LARRY HABEGGER

TRAVELERS' TALES
SAN FRANCISCO

Cover design: Michele Wetherbee
Interior design: Kathryn Heflin and Susan Bailey
Cover photograph: © *Angelo Cavalli/The Image Bank. Musician, Santiago De Cuba, Cuba*
Map: Keith Granger
Page layout: Patty Holden, using the fonts Bembo and Boulevard

Distributed by: Publishers Group West, 1700 Fourth Street, Berkeley, California 94710

Library of Congress Cataloging-in-Publication Data
Cuba : true stories / edited by Tom Miller.— 1st ed.
     p. cm. — (Travelers' tales)
  Includes bibliographical references and index.
  ISBN 1-932361-10-3 (pbk.)
  1. Travelers—Cuba—Anecdotes. 2. Travelers' writings. 3. Cuba—description and travel. 4. Cuba—Social life and customs. I. Miller, Tom, 1947- II. Travelers' Tales guides
  F1765.3.C85   2004
    917.29104'64—dc22

                                              2004015117

First Edition
Printed in the United States of America
10 9 8 7 6 5 4 3 2 1

When first in the dim light of early morning I saw the shores of Cuba rise and define themselves from dark-blue horizons, I felt as if I sailed with Captain Silver and first gazed on Treasure Island. Here was a place where real things were going on. Here was a scene of vital action. Here was a place where anything might happen. Here was a place where something would certainly happen. Here I might leave my bones.

—WINSTON CHURCHILL, on visiting Cuba in 1898

For Juan Carlos and Leonardo,
una distinta mirada a su patria

Table of Contents

Part Four
IN THE SHADOWS

Part Five
THE LAST WORD

Cuba: An Introduction

I'm listening to "Cubana Be/Cubana Bop" right now, Dizzy Gillespie's terrific 1947 fusion of traditional jazz and Latin rhythms. Intricate drumming and chanting from Africa via Cuba surround this musical alloy. The mix of American jazz with muscular, other-worldly sounds gave us something altogether fresh, simultaneously rough and sophisticated, captivating and unique—much as foreigners have seen Cuba in the intervening decades.

When the United States government broadened the definition of who can legally travel to Cuba in the late 1990s, an overflow of applications came gushing in. While the number of American tourists ignoring U.S. strictures on travel to the island continued to increase, a whole new breed of "study groups" started to appear. My favorite was a flock of undergraduate English students from an upper Midwest frostbelt college who came to the sunny Caribbean in the dead of winter. They were the usual bunch—unfailingly polite, hair predominantly adolescent orange, and they spoke almost no Spanish. They were in Cuba, they averred, to learn about Hemingway in Havana. And this is how these American college students studied Hemingway in Havana: every morning after finishing breakfast at their hotel's buffet, they returned to their rooms and changed into their swim suits, picked up a towel and a Hemingway paperback or two, descended to the pool, and lay down in a lounge chair to study Hemingway in Havana.

With all due respect to those students, there are better ways to learn about Cuba, even to study a foreign writer's life there a half-century ago. Just before dawn one morning a few years ago along the Malecón, Havana's expansive seaside boulevard, I met Humberto, a 34-year-old fisherman sitting on the seawall. He snapped his line out from a reel his late father had left him; nice wrist action. When I mentioned Hemingway in passing, he abruptly stood up and, unprompted, recited the opening lines of *The Old Man and the Sea* as if it were the Lord's Prayer. "I practically idolized Hemingway for how he identified with Cuban fishermen," Humberto said when he sat down again. "I was raised with a healthy admiration for him."

It's surprisingly easy to sidestep the well-marked tourist trail, to get under Cuba's skin. Spend a peso to ride a city bus. Pass an afternoon walking the streets of La Lisa or La Víbora, two neighborhoods that seldom see foreigners. Late at night drop in at the Cabaret Las Vegas, a decidedly second-rate but wonderful nightclub, and watch musicians, dancers, rappers, magicians, comics, and crooners take the stage in rapid succession in an all-night variety show. Most recently, the Las Vegas has appeared in Pedro Juan Gutiérrez's fiction, *Dirty Havana Trilogy*, but if you stay long enough you may feel like a character in *Three Trapped Tigers*, Guillermo Cabrera Infante's masterful and bawdy 1960s novel set in Havana's decadent pre-Castro years. The book's narrator, who wears many hats but sometimes little else, hangs out at the Las Vegas, where a wide variety of fleshy entertainers whisper bad puns in his ear.

Listen closely to what people on the street call *norteamericanos*. If it sounds like "yuma," you've got good ears. In Cuban street slang, *yuma* means a foreigner, more specifically, someone from a non-Spanish speaking European or North American country, and most particularly, from the United States. When someone asks my brother-in-law where his sister went, he might say, *"Se fue pa' la yuma."* She went to the United States. Or an American tourist strolling down Havana's Prado might hear, *"¡Oye, yuma! ¡Ven acá!"* Hey 'merican, com'ere! Yuma is a word unknown in Mexico or any other Spanish-speaking country that I know of.

Cubans have always liked our Westerns going back deep into the Batista years, including the Glenn Ford classic, *3:10 to Yuma*. The movie, popular in theaters and on Cuban television, was quintessentially American. Based on a 1953 Elmore Leonard short story, it portrayed the nuance of cowboy honor and obligation. In the quirky way that one language absorbs the sounds and images of another, Cuba, which has embraced so many American totems, has taken Yuma if not to its heart, at least to its tongue. The Cuban street-slang *yuma* derives directly from the film *3:10 to Yuma*.

Late one Havana afternoon, hot on the *yuma* trail, I visited Fernando Carr, a word maven whose language column in the weekly *Bohemia* keeps Cubans on the linguistic straight and narrow. It would be tempting to call Carr the Cuban William Safire, but looking north from Havana, I prefer to think of Safire as the American Fernando Carr. He lives in an apartment house on Salvador Allende Avenue, a street everyone calls by its prior moniker, Carlos III, and when I stepped off the elevator on his floor I gave thanks that no power blackout had taken place during the previous forty-five seconds. I brought along a bottle of rum—*de rigueur* for a foreigner visiting a Cuban for the first time—and with some ice cubes Carr retrieved from a neighbor's refrigerator, we climbed a ladder to his building's rooftop. There we sipped Havana Club as my host pointed out landmarks on the Havana skyline: nearby, the old American-owned telephone company; farther away the cluster of buildings at the Plaza de la Revolución where Pope John Paul II—himself a *yuma*—celebrated mass in 1998. I pointed waaay off to the north and a little west, and said, *"La yuma, ¿verdad?"* The United States, right? Carr nodded, agreeing that indeed the word likely came from *3:10 to Yuma*. Moreover, he thought it was reinforced by the similarity between the first syllables of Yew-ma and Yew-nited States. Next time I see Carr I'll present him with "Cubana Be/Cubana Bop," eight syllables that ought to keep the linguist busy for a while.

Most of all, get outside Havana. The people move slower and the air feels more Caribbean. The dollarization of Cuban culture does not yet dominate the countryside, but foreigners have wandered down just about every paved road, slept in farmers' haystacks, and received emergency medical treatment in the most unpopulated regions of the country. One day near sunset years ago

I was trying to find a town near the south coast that I'd heard had available lodging. I carefully followed the back-country roads on a detailed map I carried with me until I arrived at a village at the end of the blacktop. I pulled up to the plaza where an elderly gent wearing a Spanish beret sat by himself. "I thought this road continued through town to the highway," I said, holding up my map. With his cane he pointed back down the road I'd just come to town on.

"You must have that German map," he said with a chuckle. "Every few days someone comes here looking for a road that doesn't exist, and every one of you has that German map." I looked at the fine print in the corner, and indeed the map was produced in Germany. We lost travelers were the fellow's only source of entertainment, and he invited me to sit a spell and chat.

He was known as El Blanco—Whitey—he said, but there were fewer and fewer villagers left to call him that. The town had no industry and farm labor opportunities were shrinking. Many of his neighbors had gone to Havana to try their luck. Officials in Havana, alarmed that their overcrowded city was growing yet further, began checking ID cards and sending easterners back home. It became the buzz of the street, just below the surface, but Los Van Van, the best dance band north of the South Pole, gave the anguish high profile with their song, "La Habana no aguanta más," Havana just can't take any more.

Another of their uptempo songs popular in Havana's overrun barrios tells of the magical carpenters who manage to create yet more space out of already cramped living quarters. "Artesanos del espacio," it's called, Artisans of Space. Los Van Van give sassy voice to those who have the least.

To many travelers, Whitey in the countryside and Los Van Van's audience in the big city have a certain incorruptible integrity. It stems not from what they have but from what they don't: McDonald's, and the world-wide consumerism it symbolizes. With the foreboding that such businesses may well come ashore in the early post-Castro era, and ignoring that many Cubans would welcome such flamboyant and homogenized offerings, most travelers marvel at the opportunity to visit a land in its pre-golden arches era. The U.S. embargo, nasty and reprehensible as it is, has helped isolate Cuban culture from the commercial excesses of our own. After the embargo melts, well, we can all meet to discuss this further at Six Flags Over Cuba.

"Words should be bright as gold," wrote José Martí, father of Cuban independence, "light as wings, solid as marble." I kept those words in mind when I selected the pieces you're about to read. The writers swoon, argue, get frustrated, and fall in love. They are innocents, sophisticates, naïfs, and spirited participants. They're bewildered, up-ended, challenged, disillusioned, and hopeful. Some are gullible, others suspicious. None are passive, and each has a good story to tell. In short, they're all over the map.

If you read between the lines, you'll come to know Cubans and a Cuba far from today's headlines and yesterday's rancor. And if you listen between the lines, you'll hear Dizzy Gillespie's "Cubana Be/Cubana Bop."

—TOM MILLER

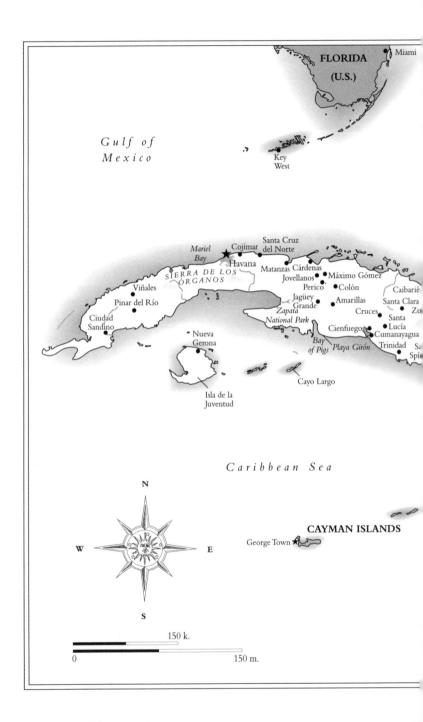

Red
Bay

Nassau

*Atlantic
Ocean*

THE BAHAMAS

*IERRA DEL
SCAMBRAY*

Ciego de Avila

on Júcaro

Camagüey

Cascorro

CUBA

Victoria de
las Tunas

Holguín

Jardines
de la Reina

Manzanillo

Bayamo

Santiago
de Cuba

Baracoa

Guantánamo

Maisí

SIERRA MAESTRA

Niquero

Caimanera

Boquerón

**PICO
TURQUINO**

*Guantánamo
Bay*

U. S. Naval
Base

HAITI

Caribbean Sea

JAMAICA

PART ONE

ESSENCE OF CUBA

★ ★ ★

The Bus

A guagua *named Desire.*

HIS PARENTS HAD FLED TO THE NORTH. IN THOSE DAYS, HE AND THE revolution were both in their infancy. A quarter of a century later, Nelson Valdés traveled from Los Angeles to Havana to visit his homeland.

Every day at noon, Nelson would take the *guagua*, bus number 68, from the hotel entrance, to the José Martí Library. There he would read books on Cuba until nightfall.

One day at noon, *guagua* 68 screeched to a halt at an intersection. There were cries of protest at the tremendous jolt until the passengers saw why the bus driver had jammed on the brakes: a magnificent woman had just crossed the street.

"*You'll have to forgive me, gentlemen,*" said the driver of *guagua* 68, and he got out. All the passengers applauded and wished him luck.

The bus driver swaggered along, in no hurry, and the passengers watched him approach the saucy female, who stood on the corner, leaning against the wall, licking an ice cream cone. From *guagua* 68, the passengers followed the darting motion of her tongue as it kissed the ice cream while the driver talked on and on with no apparent result. Until all at once she laughed and glanced up at him. The driver gave the thumbs-up sign and the passengers burst into a hearty ovation.

But when the driver went into the ice cream parlor, the passengers began to get restless. And when he came out a bit later with an ice cream cone in each hand, panic spread among the masses.

They beeped the horn. Someone leaned on it with all his might and honked like a burglar alarm, but the bus driver, deaf, nonchalant, was glued to the delectable woman.

Then, from the back of *guagua* 68, a woman with the appearance of a huge cannon ball, and an air of authority, stepped forward. Without a word, she sat in the driver's seat and put the engine in gear. *Guagua* 68 continued on its route, stopping at its customary stops, until the woman arrived at her own and got off. Another passenger took her place for a stretch, stopping at every bus stop, and then another, and another, and so *guagua* 68 continued on to the end of the line.

Nelson Valdés was the last one to get off. He had forgotten all about the library.

Eduardo Galeano is the author of numerous works, including Bocas del Tiempo, Open Veins of Latin America, Days and Nights of Love and War, Memory of Fire in 3 volumes, We Say No, Walking Word, Soccer in Sun and Shadow, Upside Down, *and* The Book of Embraces, *from which this story was excerpted. He lives in Montevideo, Uruguay.*

An Elegiac Carnival

Cuba's many enchantments scramble the author's
emotions, and keep bringing him back.

IT IS A MIRACLE OF CALM: ALONG THE WHOLE STRETCH OF EMPTY, brilliant beach, nothing seems to move. There are no hotels in sight, no ice-cream parlors; no radios or holiday makers or amusement parks. Just the transparent blue-green sea, a few thatched umbrellas, the lapping of the waves. In the distance a single white boat mirrors the blinding whiteness of the sand. Yet even at midday there is an early morning stillness here. Everything looks as silent, as flawless, as a postcard.

Cuba is, without doubt, the ultimate getaway, especially if it is the United States, or tourists, or the present tense you wish to get away from; though only ninety miles from Florida shores, Cuba seems to have been totally blacked out from our minds. Think of it today, and you most likely think of army fatigues, Marxist slogans, and bearded threats to our peace; you are liable to forget, in short, that Cuba is a tropical island, a Caribbean place of lyricism and light, with music pulsing through the streets, and lemon-yellow, sky-blue, alabaster-white houses shining against a rich-blue sea. The long, extended claw that is Fidel Castro's home is, as it happens, the largest island in the Greater Antilles, and, very likely, the least visited. Yet everything that made it America's dream playground more than forty years ago is still intact. The water, on a usual day, is eighty degrees; the sun shines an average of more than eleven hours each day. There are 4,500 miles of coastline in Cuba, nearly all of them as tranquil as a private hideaway. Small wonder that Christopher Columbus, laying anchor off this cool-breezed island, pronounced it "the most beautiful land ever seen."

Every time I go to Cuba I come back sounding like a tourist brochure. I bore my friends by counting the ways I love this improbable idyll: a perfect climate (seventy-seven degrees on an average day); a many-colored culture vibrant with bohemian dives, troubadour cafés, and film school partially run by Gabriel García Márquez; and all the warmth of a graceful, passionate, late-night people so openhearted that self-interest and true kindness blur.

Havana days are the softest I have ever seen, the golden light of dusk spangling the cool buildings of the tree-lined streets. Havana nights are the liveliest I know, as dark-eyed, scarlet girls in tight dresses lean against the tail fins of chrome-polished '57 Packards amid the floodlit mango trees of nightclubs like the Tropicana, now after a half century of Vegas paganism.

In Cuba the sophistications of Europe dance to the rhythms of Africa, all in a sun-washed Caribbean setting. There is the savor of rum in the bars that Hemingway haunted; the friendly dishevelment of the sea-worn old Mafia hotels, crowded now with dark-featured tourists from Siberia. There is even, in Havana, a Humour Museum.

> At 21–23 degrees north, Cuba lies on the same latitudes as Algeria, Egypt, India, Mauritania, Oman, Vietnam, and Hawai'i.
>
> —TM

Yet it is something more than the light-filled surfaces that keeps me coming back to Cuba; for there is in Cuba some indefinable air of adventure and possibility. I never want to sleep in Cuba. And when I return home, I find that it still haunts me like some distant rumba: I can still hear the cigarette-roughened voice of the grandma in Artemisa who took me in from the rain and, over wine in tin cups, spun me strange family tales before leading me across puddles to hear Fidel. I can still taste the strawberry ice cream in Coppelia Park, where languorous Lolitas sashay through the night in off-the-shoulder t-shirts. I can still see the round-the-clock turmoil of Carnival, and the Soviet doctor who sat next to me one year, blowing kisses at the dancers. Sometimes, when I go out at night and sit on the seawall alone, feeling the spray of the salt, hearing the faint strumming of acoustic guitars carried on the wind, and seeing the empty boulevards sweeping along the lovely curve of Havana Bay, I feel that I could never know a greater happiness.

In Communist Cuba, of course, the visitor finds shortages of everything except ironies. The Bay of Pigs is a beach resort now, and San Juan Hill is famous for its "patio-cabaret." The Isle of Youth, long the most infamous Alcatraz in the Caribbean, now entices visitors with its International Scuba Diving Center. And one beach near Matanzas (the name means "massacres") has, somewhat less than romantically, been christened Playa Yugoslavia. Cuba, in short, has edges and shadows not to be found in most West Indian resorts: The billboards along the beach offer stern admonitions ("The best tan is acquired in movement"), and the gift stores in the hotels sell such light holiday reads as *The CIA in Central America and the Caribbean*. Many things here take on a slightly sinister air. "Cuba's waiting for you," runs an official tourist slogan. "We knew you were coming."

Cubatur's most intriguing attraction may be its daily four-hour excursion to a psychiatric hospital. But when I asked if I could sign up for the tour, the laughing-eyed girl at the desk looked back at me as if I were the madman. "It isn't happening," she said. "Does it ever happen?" I asked. "Never," she said, with a delighted smile.

The real seduction of Cuba, for me, lies precisely in that kind of impromptu makeshift quality, and in the fact that it feels so deserted; the whole island has the ramshackle glamour of an abandoned stage set. Old Havana is a crooked maze of leafy parks and wrought-iron balconies, where men strum guitars in sun-splashed courtyards. Its singular beauty, unmatched throughout the Caribbean, is that it feels as if it has been left behind by history, untouched.

Here, one feels, is all the quaintness of New Orleans with none of the self-admiration. And the freewheeling gaiety of a Sunday afternoon in Lenin Park, where soldiers twirl one another about to the happy rhythms of steel bands, is all the more intoxicating because it is so spontaneous; here, one feels, is all the spendthrift hedonism of Rio with none of the self-consciousness.

Cuba, in fact, is the most infectiously exultant place I have ever seen: It sometimes seems as if the featureless gray blocks of Communism have been set down on a sunny, swelling, multicolored quilt so full of life that much of the sauciness of the louche Havana of old keeps peeping through. Let polemicists debate whether the exuberance persists because of the Revolution, or in spite of it: the fact is that the Cubans have made an art form of their appetite for wine, women, and song. One young friend of mine in Havana knows only four words of English, which he repeats like a mantra each day, accompanied each time by a dazzling smile: "Don't Worry! Be Happy!" Very often the island reminds me of that famous statement of the eighteenth-century Englishman Oliver Edwards: "I have tried too in my time to be a philosopher; but I don't know how, cheerfulness was always breaking in."

This exhilarating sense of openness hit me the minute I landed in Havana on my most recent trip: The customs officials in the airport were dressed in khaki but winkingly turned the other eye whenever they saw cases piled high with fifteen pairs of new, ready-for-the-black-market jeans; the immigration officials, when not cross-examining tourists, made kissing noises at their female colleagues. Out in the streets I was instantly back inside some romantic thriller, with intimations of crimes and liaisons in the air. Dolled-up *señoritas* looked at me with the sly intimacy of long-lost friends; rum-husky men invited me into their lives.

By the following night, I was sitting along the seawall with a group of earnest young students eager to thrash out Hermann Hesse, Tracy Chapman, yoga, Henry Fielding, and liberation theology. Later, walking through the commercial buildings of La Rampa, I heard the joyous rasp of a saxophone and, following my ears through the video banks and rainbowed portraits of the Cuba pavilion, found myself standing in a huge open-air disco, virtually free (like most museums, concerts, and ball games in Cuba), and alive with teenagers in "We stick to Fidel" headbands and Che Guevara t-shirts dancing to a Springsteenish band. In this way — the government apparently hopes — are party-loving kids turned into Party-loving comrades.

This was at the end of the USSR presence, and when the concert ended, about midnight, I walked over to the ten-stool bar in the Hotel Nacional, where four cheery, red-faced Soviets were singing melancholy Russian ballads to a flirty *mulata* of quick charm. The girl counted off a few figures on her long pink nails, then swiveled into action.

"Iván, Iván," she cooed across at a lugubrious-looking reveler, "why don't you dance with me? Iván, don't you like me?" At which Iván lumbered up, popped a coin into the prehistoric Wurlitzer, and, as "Guantanamera" came up, threw his hands in the air, and began wriggling in place with all the unlikely grace of a bear in a John Travolta suit. This, I realized, was not Club Med.

The country's beaches—289 of them in all—begin just twenty minutes from the capital. At Santa María del Mar, a virtual suburb of Havana, lies one of the loveliest, and emptiest, strips of sand you'll ever see, with only a few old men—salty castaways from Hemingway—standing bare chested in the water, trousers rolled up to their knees, reeling in silver fish. Behind them, across a road, reclines a typical Cuban seaside hotel, filled as always with something of the plaintiveness of an Olympics facility two decades after the games have ended. Next to once-futuristic ramps, bulletin boards crowded with happily crayoned notices invite foreigners to "Workers Shows" ("a very nice activity," offers one board, "where you will see the workers become artists for your pleasure"). Every Monday at 4:30 there are "Cocktail Lessons," and every afternoon "Music, Dance, and Many Surprises." But when I looked at my watch, I realized that it was 4:45, and Monday, and not a cocktail student, not a sign of music or dance, was to be seen; somehow Cuba is always out of season.

The proudest attraction of the tourist office—and its brightest hope for gaining needed dollars—is the string of coral keys that sparkle like teardrops off the coast. One day I took the daily flight to Cayo Largo, an absurdly beautiful stretch of fifteen miles of open beach, graced with every enticement this side of Lauren Bacall. As soon as I got off the plane, at 8:45 A.M., I was greeted with a frenzied Cuban dance band and a lobster cocktail; for the rest of the day, I simply lay on the beach and gasped at the cloudless line of tropical colors—aqua and emerald and milky green, flawless as a Bacardi ad. And as with all the most delectable resorts in Cuba, the place is utterly uncluttered, in large part because locals are not permitted on the beach. (This is no legal fiction: I myself, while walking along the beach one drowsy Sunday morning, was hauled over by a policeman hiding in the bushes, on grounds of impersonating a Cuban.)

One sleepy Sunday not so long ago, I waited for a taxi to take me back to Havana from the beach. And waited, and waited, and waited, for more than three hours in all, under a tree, on a hot afternoon. Finally, just as I was about to lose all hope, up lurched a coughing,   red-and-white

---

Country name: Republic of Cuba

Population: 11–12 million

Major cities (in descending order of population): Havana (capital), Santiago de Cuba, Camagüey, Holguín, Guantánamo, Santa Clara

Size: 42,804 square miles (largest island in the Caribbean)

Highest point: Pico Turquino, 2,000 m. (6,561 ft.)

Annual population growth rate (est.): 0.39%

Life expectancy: 76.2 years

Racial makeup: Mulatto 51%, white 37%, black 11%, Chinese 1%

Voting age: 16

Primary sources of foreign revenue: overseas relatives sending money to Cuban families; tourism

Official exchange: 1 Cuban peso = USD $1

Unofficial exchange: 1 Cuban peso = USD $.05

—TM

1952 Plymouth, with "The Vampire Road" written across the windshield. Seven of us piled into the wreck, and the next thing I knew, the quartet in back was pounding out an ad hoc beat on the seat and breaking into an a cappella melody of their own invention—"*Ba ba ba, we're going to Havana...ba, ba, ba, in a really sick old car....*" For the next two hours the increasingly out-of-tune singers unsteadily passed a huge bottle of rum back and forth and shouted out songs of an indeterminate obscenity while the walrus-mustached driver poked me in the ribs and cackled with delight.

In Santiago de Cuba, the second city of the island and the cradle of the Revolution, I spent a few days in the gutted home of a former captain of Fidel's. From the hills above, where Castro and his guerrillas once gathered, the city looked as it might on some ancient, yellowing Spanish map. Down below, though, in a peeling room that I shared with a snuffling wild pig that was due to be my dinner, things were decidedly less exalted. Every night, in the half-lit gloom of his bare, high-ceilinged room, decorated only with a few black-and-white snapshots of his youth, my host took me aside ("Let me tell you, Pico Eagle...") and told me stories of the Revolution, then delivered heartbroken obituaries for his country. Next door, in an even darker room, his son prepared dolls for a Santería ceremony. And when it came time for me to leave, the old man asked me for some baseball magazines from the States. Any special kind, I asked? "No," he said softly. "I like the ones with Jackie Robinson in them."

That sense of wistfulness, of a life arrested in midbreath, is everywhere in Cuba: In the brochures of the once-elegant Riviera Hotel that now, disconcertingly, offer a "diaphanous dining-room"; in the boarded-up stores whose names conjure up a vanished era of cosmopolitanism—the Sublime, the Fin-de-Siècle, Roseland Indochina; in the Esperanto Association that stands across from a dingy, closed-off building under the forlorn legend "R.C.A.Victor." Hemingway's house in the hills is kept exactly the way he left it at his death—unread copies of *Field* and *Sports Illustrated* scattered across his bed. And the buildings all around, unpainted, unrepaired, speak also of departed hopes. One reason why so many Cubans ask a foreigner, *¿Qué hora es?* is to strike up a conversation—and a deal. Another, though, is that they really do need to know the time in a place where all the clocks are stopped.

It is that mix of elegy and Carnival that defines Cuba for me, and it is that sense of sunlit sadness that makes it, in the end, the most emotionally involving—and unsettling—place I know; Cuba catches my heart, and then makes me count the cost of that enchantment. Cuba is old ladies in rocking chairs, on their verandas in the twilight, dabbing their eyes as their grandchildren explain their latest dreams of escape. It is pretty, laughing kids dancing all night in the boisterous cabarets and then confiding, matter-of-factly, "Our lives here are like in Dante's *Inferno*." It is smiles, and open doors, and policemen lurking in the corners; and lazy days on ill-paved streets; and a friend who asks if he might possibly steal my passport.

In Cuba the tourist's exciting adventures have stakes he cannot fathom. And every encounter only leaves one deeper in the shadows. My first night in a big hotel, a girl I had never met rang me up and asked, sight unseen, if I would marry her. The next day, in the cathedral, a small old man with shining eyes came up to me and began talking of his family, his faith, his grade-school daughter. "I call her Elizabeth," he said, "like a queen." He paused. "A poor queen"—he smiled ruefully—"but to me she is still a queen." When we met again, at an Easter Sunday mass, he gave me Mother's Day gifts for my mother and, moist-eyed, a letter for his own mother in the States. It was only much later that I found the letter was in fact addressed to the State Department, and the kindly old man a would-be defector.

And one sunny afternoon in a dark Havana bar, so dark that I could not see my companion's face except when she lit a match for her cigarette, I asked a friend if I could send her anything from the States. Not really, she said, this intelligent twenty-three-year-old who knew me well. Just a Donald Duck sticker for her fridge. Nothing else, I asked? Well, maybe a Mickey Mouse postcard. That was quite a status symbol. And that was all? Yes, she said—oh, and one more thing: a job, please, with the CIA.

Pico Iyer was born in Oxford in 1957 and was educated at Eton, Oxford, and Harvard. He is an essayist for Time Magazine, *a contributing editor at* Condé Nast Traveler, *and the author of several books, including* Video Night in Kathmandu, The Lady and the Monk, The Global Soul, Sun After Dark, *and the novels* Havana and the Night *and* Abandon.

CRISTINA GARCÍA

✦ ✦ ✦

Simple Life

*Duck fricassee á la cubana, of course, captures
the Cuban's gift for overcoming obstacles.*

IT WAS ABOUT FOUR IN THE MORNING, AND I WAS SITTING ON THE
porch of my aunt's house in Guanabo, a seaside town east of
Havana, catching up on eleven years' worth of family news. The
ocean breeze stirred the fronds of the coconut palms on her modest property as we swayed in our rocking chairs, keeping time with
the rhythm of our stories, interrupting them with frequent bursts of
laughter. Not fifty feet from us, the surf broke against an outcrop of
rocks and a narrow lip of beach.

In the midst of one reminiscence or another, I heard a harsh
buzzing sound, and then all was blackness.

"*Coño, otro apagón,*" my Tía Amada said, referring to the frequent
blackouts of electricity that plagued nearly every town on the island. But just as she was about to launch into her familiar litany of
complaints against what was known as the "special period" in Cuba,
a time of renewed sacrifice and deprivation, Tía Amada noticed my
face. I was staring up at the sky, speechless with wonder. There was
no moon that night, not even so much as a single bulb burning
anywhere in the vicinity, but above us, the heavens looked as if
they would collapse with stars. This was the unintentional gift from
the *apagón.*

✳

To me, that moment represents what I love most about Cuba. *No hay mal que por bien no venga.* This is a quintessential Cuban expression, a kind of mantra. Roughly translated, it means "good comes out of even the worst experiences." I heard it at least a dozen times a day.

Cubans are masters at making the best out of any difficult situation. *Resolver*, to resolve, is probably the most commonly used verb in the language on the island. "*Resolver*" can mean resuscitating a twenty-year-old Russian Lada for a ride to the beach or tracking down a single out-of-season sweet potato for a dessert offering to Yemayá, goddess of the seas.

One Saturday afternoon in Havana, I casually mentioned to my uncle, Tío Jorge, that I was yearning for a piece of cake. About four hours later a prim man appeared at our door carrying an enormous coconut layer cake topped with fluffy pink meringue. It turned out that the delivery man was, in fact, a heart surgeon who bakes cakes on weekends for extra cash. He is in high demand for weddings.

In Cuba "*resolver*" means to survive, to overcome all obstacles with inventiveness, spontaneity, and most important, humor.

Recently my Tía Amada, who rents out part of her beach bungalow to foreign tourists, received a request from her guests, a demanding Canadian businessman and his wife, for a duck dinner. My aunt, unfazed, assured the couple that they could expect their duck promptly at seven o'clock that evening. Need I add that my aunt had never cooked a duck in her life?

That day I accompanied Tía Amada to the farmer's market to track down a duck. There was only one available, scrawny and unsightly with half-plucked quills. She bargained hard and bought it for four dollars.

Back home, my aunt proceeded to wash the creature from her limited supply of freshwater (none was running from her faucets), and then shaved the duck from beak to claw with a antique razor that once belonged to her father.

No matter that Tía Amada's oven has not worked in years. No matter that her pre-Revolutionary pots and pans were now in advanced stages of disrepair. We schemed over how to best cook the beast on top of the stove. Finally, with a blunt knife and a hammer borrowed from a neighbor, we hacked the duck to pieces and opted for fricassee.

The Canadian and his wife got their duck, savory and delicious, served with rice, fried plantains, and a fresh green salad. They said it was the best duck they had ever eaten.

My aunt and I laughed for a long time over the bird, reliving the small adventure, recounting it to relatives in ever more elaborate fashion. By the end of the telling, we might even say we'd gone to Warsaw to "*resolve*" that duck.

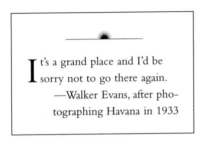

It's a grand place and I'd be sorry not to go there again.
   —Walker Evans, after photographing Havana in 1933

After a long day of such high-intensity resolving, my family would sit around and tell *chistes*, jokes. Cubans turn everything into *chistes*, most of which are aimed at themselves. There are no sacred cows on the island, including *El Jefe*, Fidel Castro. Neighbors might come by and join in on the fun, as the bottle of rum or *marrasquino*, a sweet local liqueur, is passed around.

Often, someone would put a cassette in the tape deck, and the party would be on. Dancing is de rigueur. My uncle has taught me a decent cha-cha, and I can almost make it through a *guaracha* without tripping over my self. Mambos, I'm afraid, the hot ones, the ones that scorch your shoes clear through to your arches, continue to elude me.

I took my daughter with me to Cuba when she was two years old, the same age I was when my parents left the island for good. Over the years nostalgia clouded my parents' memories, bitterness the facts. It was impossible to get a true picture of what we had left behind. To me, Cuba was a beautiful daydream, colored by all that might have been but was not. In fact, I had no direct contact with my family on the island until I visited them for the first time at the age of twenty-five.

At Christmas I took my daughter for her second visit. My relatives continue to go crazy over her. Her great-grandmother Gloria accuses her of not being a girl at all but a *muñequita*, a little doll. Her great-uncle Jorge, an industrial engineer, spends hours entertaining her with handkerchiefs he fashions into a gravelly voiced rabbit named Pepino. Her second cousin Estrella repeatedly demands *un beso rico*, and my daughter happily complies with a kiss.

I know now that I want to go back to Cuba as often as possible. My daughter will grow up knowing the island and her family there. For her, Cuba will not be an abstraction of lost hopes and misplaced longings, but a place of memories, good and bad mingling like any others. Whether my daughter will fall in love with Cuba the way I have, I cannot tell, but the opportunity to do so is one of the greatest gifts I can offer her.

Cristina García is the author of Dreaming in Cuban, The Agüero Sisters, *and* Monkey Hunting. *Her novels have been translated into a dozen languages. She lives in Southern California.*

⋆ ⋆ ⋆

Finding My House
in El Cerro

Some places stand the test of time.

ONE MORNING OTERO SAID: "I SPENT MUCH OF LAST NIGHT WON-
dering where your 1920 house would have been, and I discarded
quite a few possibilities because I understood your need for something distinctive and Cuban, but I failed to identify it. Then, at
breakfast this morning, it came to me, a complete scenario. We're
going to El Cerro." I said: "In all my reading I didn't discover that
Havana had a hill," which was what the word meant, and he chuck-
led: "A slight rise…southwest of the old city…but deliciously cool
in those years before air-conditioning."

As we drove in that direction, he explained: "At the close of the
last century rich families had a big house in town and a spacious
countrylike residence in El Cerro, and they spent money like mad
to make their summer homes works of art. Look as the main street
comes at you!" and as I stared ahead I saw an architectural marvel:
a moderately wide street lined with luxurious houses, each of which
was fronted by a set of six or eight or ten handsome stone columns,
like those before a Greek temple. The effect was almost mesmeriz-
ing, an endless colonnade in various materials and styles marching
backward into the past.

But what added significance to the scene, and brought it within my story, was the fact that behind the lovely façades a number of the old mansions had fallen into total decay. Nothing existed but the shell and as I studied the mournful effect of six magnificent Greek columns hiding a mansion that no longer existed, my learned guide explained in elegiac tones: "The steps went down by decades. 1920s the mansions are in full flower. 1930s the rich families begin to move out. 1940s people grab them who can't afford to maintain them, ruin begins. 1950s ten big families move into each mansion, pay no rent, and begin to tear it apart. 1960s during the first years of the revolution, no housing elsewhere, so even more crowd in, ruin accelerated. 1970s some of the weakest begin to fall down. 1980s many gone beyond salvation." This was exactly the story I had wanted, not to tell but to imply, and as this tremendous visual impact struck, I stood dumbfounded, for it was so much more powerful than I had imagined.

But then a strange thing happened. As I walked down the street with the car trailing behind, I came upon the very house I wanted for my family in the 1920s, very Cuban, extraordinary to see, and not at all ruined. What set it apart was its façade decorated by some four dozen cast-iron swans, each standing tall and slim, its long neck bent straight down in mortal combat with an evil serpent climbing up its leg to sink its fangs. To see two score of these fantastically clever iron castings marching wing to wing and handsomely painted in bright colors was exciting.

My search for a house had ended: "That is it!" I cried, for I could visualize my characters living there. I was so pleased with my discovery that I went to the unscarred door, banged upon it rather rudely, and watched it open to admit me to an adventure I could not have imagined. The Cuban who let me in was a tall, thin man in his fifties with a most engaging smile and naked to the waist. "*Soy norteamericano y tengo gran interés en su casa*," I said, and he reached for his shirt: "*Ay, mi madre, un norteamericano. ¡Venga, venga!*" and he led me into a dark and solemn wonderland, rooms filled with cobwebs and ominous shadows, and he always ahead, calling me to follow.

Slowly I began to see, in the darkness, that the ceiling of the first floor had been removed, and I supposed that this meant the house had fallen into ruin, all except the swan-filled portico. But then I saw looming from the shadows great casks, I mean oaken-staved casks fifteen and twenty feet high, with untold numbers of smaller ones stacked along the walls.

"Contraband?" I asked, and he replied sharply: "*¡No!¡No! La famosa destilería Bocoy, ¡ron!*" and that's what it was, a rum distillery belonging to one of the great firms but tucked away in this unlikely spot because the rents were low or because the Bocoy people had placed it here to serve their hard-drinking customers in the 1890s. It was something out of Piranesi, a ghostly affair with a single unshaded lightbulb shining far in the distance, and as we explored the deep recesses, my guide gave me the ages of the various casks, their wood alone worth a small fortune, and also the ages of their contents. It was an exploration I could not have imagined,

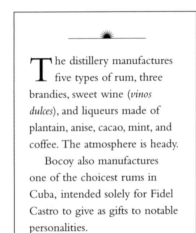

The distillery manufactures five types of rum, three brandies, sweet wine (*vinos dulces*), and liqueurs made of plantain, anise, cacao, mint, and coffee. The atmosphere is heady.

Bocoy also manufactures one of the choicest rums in Cuba, intended solely for Fidel Castro to give as gifts to notable personalities.

— Christopher P. Baker,
Havana Handbook

but there was a keener surprise in store, for when we reached the manager's office he excused himself, then came back proudly, hands behind his back. Almost awkwardly, but with obvious appreciation for this strange visit I had imposed upon him, he brought forth his hands to produce a frail cardboard box in the shape of a pirate's treasure chest and labeled La Isla del Tesoro (Treasure Island). "*¡Ábrete!*" he cried as if he were my uncle at Christmas, and when I did open it I found a large bottle of one of the choicest rums distilled in Cuba.

"We make a little of this each year," he said. "Gifts for important people like generals." He laughed then added: "And today you're a general."

James Michener, who died at age ninety in 1997, had a list of titles that reads like the index to an atlas: Iberia, Alaska, Mexico, Chesapeake, Hawai'i, Poland, *and many others—including* Space. *His far-ranging historical sagas were based on extensive research, and his first novel,* Tales of the South Pacific, *won him a Pulitzer Prize in 1948. So intrigued was he with Cuba during a brief visit while researching his book* Caribbean, *he wrote a nonfiction book about his stay there,* Six Days in Havana, *from which this story was excerpted.*

PHILLIPPE DIEDERICH

* * *

Communism and the Art of Motorcycle Maintenance

Cuba's bikers are neither hellish nor angelic.

CUBA IS A PLACE OF LEGENDS. SOME LEGENDS MOVE FREELY AMONG the wind and palm trees like the words of José Martí while others are whispered with the guardedness reserved for state secrets. One of these legends tells of a time soon after the triumph of the revolution, agents from Castro's government dug a huge hole in the ground—the precise location remains a mystery. Into this hole they dumped hundreds and hundreds of Harley-Davidson motorcycles formerly used by the army and by Batista's feared national police. Flatheads, knuckleheads, panheads, models from the 1930s through 1960. All of them six feet under for eternity, fertilizing the island's sweet cane and strong tobacco. They remain there today, awaiting discovery by some lucky soul.

But outside of legend, the Harley has in fact managed to survive. More than three decades after the closing of Casa Breto, the Harley-Davidson dealership on the corner of Aguila and Colón streets in Centro Habana, the throaty rumble of the mighty hog can still be heard. From Miramar to Regla the thunder resonates from an estimated one hundred vintage Harleys that continue to prowl the broken streets of Havana.

Their proud (some would say fanatical) owners, known as

Harlistas, have had to rely on ingenuity to keep them running all these years; no authentic Harley-Davidson parts are available in Cuba. At least not *officially* available. If you have a foreign friend, and if that foreign friend has access to a Harley-Davidson dealership, maybe that friend will occasionally be kind enough to bring you something you desperately need for your bike. But most of Havana's *Harlistas* turn to a small, nondescript garage in the Luyanó neighborhood, south of Habana Vieja, where a man named Sergio has made Harley-Davidsons his life's passion.

Located directly across the street from his house, Sergio Morales's shop is a cramped space, dimly lit by filtered sunlight and the glow of low-watt bulbs. Motorcycle parts—most of them homemade—are scattered everywhere. The rear of the garage is crammed shelf over shelf with mudguard ornaments, exhaust systems, light moldings, shock absorbers, oil tanks, and various automobile parts and scrap metal waiting to be modified to fit Harley-Davidsons. The distinctive smell of gasoline and oil is pervasive.

Sergio stands amid three partially rebuilt Harleys, a half-smoked Popular dangling from his lips, his fingers permanently soiled with the black grime of motorcycle blood. As dramatic new economic reforms were implemented in early 1994, Sergio recalls, he took advantage of the opportunity to legitimize the work he'd been doing for roughly twenty years—he applied for and received a license to operate a private business, an internal-combustion-engine repair shop. The license cost him ninety Cuban pesos per month, just under four U.S. dollars (since then the price has risen to two hundred pesos per month, about eight dollars). These days he owns the only legal garage in all of Cuba that specializes in the repair and restoration of Harley-Davidson motorcycles.

"The Harleys here are about 25 percent Cuban-made," he says, pointing out that one of his own bikes is equipped with Alfa Romeo pistons. "That's Cuba—*hay que resolver, chico*. Years ago I sacrificed a perfect exhaust system. We sliced it in half to see how it was built. Now we make perfect replicas. We also make Hydra-Glyde shock absorbers, by far the most popular replacement part in Cuba. Older Harleys come with the *frente rígido*, which is very limited at absorbing the deteriorating Cubán roads. We make oil tanks and adapt pistons, the whole timing device with cover, and just about every body detail from lights to ornaments—all made right here."

He picks up a cylindrical piece of metal about the length of a man's finger and twice as thick. "This is the soul of a Harley-Davidson," he explains. "The crank pin. *Hecho en Cuba*, right here in this shop. We take some Russian pressure bearings, open them, and take the ball bearings out. Then we seal them together and grind it to the right specification we got from original crank pins."

Sergio, who is forty-six years old, acquired his first Harley in 1974 while working at a state-run truck garage under the man who is credited with saving Cuban Harleys from extinction and who is also recognized by *Harlistas* as having been the best Harley-Davidson mechanic on the island—the late José Lorenzo Cortez, known to the cognoscenti by his nickname: Pepe Milésima ("Pepe" is the familiar version of José; "Milésima" means thousandth, a reference to the man's reputation for mechanical precision).

"Pepe taught me everything about Harleys," Sergio recalls. "I was his apprentice. He got me started with my first Harley, a troublesome 1946, forty-five-cubic-inch flathead. I got rid of it very quickly. Then I got the '46 knucklehead you see there. There are probably no more than a dozen left in Cuba." He pauses, lost for a moment in the memory. "Pepe was a great man. All the *Harlistas* loved him. He was the best mechanic around. He was incredibly meticulous."

The conversation moves across the street to Sergio's house, where he serves up some *café cubano* for his two helpers, a neighbor, and a *Harlista* who has stopped by to pick up an accelerator cable. "Next Saturday my daughter Miriam is getting married," he says to me. "You ever been to a Harley wedding in Cuba?"

They gather at Sergio's before the wedding—about thirty Harleys and a smattering of old Nortons and Triumphs. The two-wheeled guests are decked out in leather, bandanas, shades, boots, and Harley-Davidson t-shirts advertising U.S. dealerships and motorcycle rallies from years past at Daytona Beach and Sturgis, South

Dakota. When the bride steps outside, an ear-splitting symphony erupts as the bikes rev their engines in unison. The noise—so overwhelming it is tactile—seems to engulf the street, the block, the neighborhood, the entire city. Young *Pioneros* walk by gaping at the strange-looking crowd and the infernal noise. Elderly neighbors cover their ears in disbelief and horror. Some actually smile.

Miriam was supposed to lead the way in her father's three-wheeled knucklehead with a modified rear carriage, but the restoration work was not completed in time. So she rides instead in a '57 Chevy convertible owned by a family friend, perched above the backseat like a homecoming queen, her pristine white bridal gown fluttering in the breeze. The line of motorcycles follows, a spectacular entourage that stops bystanders in their tracks.

After a civil wedding at one of Havana's many *palacios de los matrimonios*, the procession moves to a banquet hall by the sea near Miramar, just west of downtown. The bikers talk, they brag, they argue, and

---

I had two flat tires on my way north to Varadero, and both times, I was reminded of the lengths Cubans would go to help out a stranger. The first flat happened as I passed through the town of Matanzas. I considered myself lucky; I only had to push the motorcycle a kilometer or so to get to the nearest *ponchera*, where I could get the tire patched. I rolled into the station and found two guys napping on wooden chairs in the sunset, their caps pulled down over their eyes.

One of them came forward and stuck his chin out at the tire.

"*¿'tá poncha'o?*" he asked, in that unmistakable Cuban vernacular.

"*'í...*" I answered back, giving it my laziest. It didn't work.

"You're foreign?" he asked me with new interest.

"Yeah, from the States."

"*¿Sí?*" he asked. "*Los Estados Unidos,*" he said, emphasizing the consonants jokingly. "Let's take a look at the tire."

—Tucker Teutsch III,
"Flat Tire"

soon a challenge is set: a Triumph will race a Harley. The Harley wins. Upon returning, the Triumph rider angrily drops his bike on the pavement and rushes his opponent. Fists fly, women scream, men yell, and they are pulled apart. The defeated Triumph owner picks up his broken rearview mirror and hastily departs. The party has just begun.

Guests are served meals in small cardboard boxes Sergio's family had prepared the day before: rice, beans, a bit of pork, and a piece of dessert cake. For liquid refreshment there is a seemingly endless supply of government-issue beer, not Hatuey or Bucanero but that labelless brown brew, half-flat and bitter. The rum is the same burned-molasses-and-raw-alcohol concoction that everyone drinks—not great but not terrible. Amid the food and drink there is much good cheer and Harley talk. And then the power goes out.

But as they say: where there is a Cuban, there is a solution. Someone drives a Willis Jeep into the banquet hall and turns on the headlights. Then the wiring from the Jeep's stereo is rigged to the hall's loudspeakers. The salsa again pulses and the dancing resumes. A beaming Sergio gives me a wink: "*El cubano inventa, chico.*"

As the night wears on, the crowd slowly begins to thin out, each departure announced by the echoing rumble of a Harley heading home.

Havana's *Harlistas* are an obsessive lot. So knowledgeable are they about their machines that they claim to be familiar with every single Harley-Davidson in the capital city. And so devoted are they to the hunt for genuine spare parts (much less the possibility of finding an intact motorcycle) that they will drop everything and travel anywhere at the hint of a possible new discovery.

Just such a hint prompted a quick trip to the town of Matanzas, ninety kilometers east of Havana. Recent rumors had it that a Harley of some sort, in unknown condition, was located there in the possession of some unidentified person. Not much to go on, perhaps, but enough for Sergio, his wife Miriam, his second daughter Mildrem, and his chief mechanic Nelio Acosta to pile into my rental car and head east.

With Nelio guiding the way, we cruise slowly through the seaside town and pull over near a bodega where three young shirt-less men are working on bicycles. "*Compañero*," Nelio calls out the window, "you haven't seen where there's a Harley-Davidson around here?"

The men look over. "A what?"

"*Tú sabes*," Nelio says. "One of those big motorcycles, makes a lot of noise. A Harley."

Then an older man sitting nearby looks up. "Harley-Davidson?" he asks.

"*Sí*."

The old man points in the direction of the water. "*Anda*, go ask around there. There are some kids who work on motorcycles, and I think they know about a Harley-Davidson there."

"*Gracías, puro*," replies Nelio as we drive off.

After asking half a dozen people, we end up at a house that may or may not be occupied by a certain man who may or may not have a motorcycle that may or may not be a Harley-Davidson. Sergio and Nelio walk in while the rest of us wait in the car.

After half an hour or so they return and climb into the car. They say nothing. Miriam is going insane with curiosity. As we pull away from the house, Nelio and Sergio begin laughing hysterically.

"*¿Qué fue, chico?*" Miriam implores. "He's a crazy old man," Nelio says. "It's *perfect*. It looks like it's been garaged since 1958. It doesn't even have 30,000 original miles!"

"*¡Coño!*"

"He's a senile old man," Sergio adds.

"*¿Qué?* Does he want to sell?" Miriam asks excitedly.

"No. *El viejo* has the Harley, a '57 Chevy, and an old Ford. They're all perfect, but he doesn't want to sell anything."

"*Coño. ¿Pero por qué, chico?*" "He thinks he's working on them," Nelio laughs. "He goes into his garage and starts banging on things. He thinks he's fixing them."

"*¡Qué viejo ese!*" Sergio snaps. "We have to be there when he changes his mind. You know one day he's going to decide to sell it—just like that."

"His children want him to sell," Nelio says.

"We just have to keep coming back," repeats Sergio.

What a find! But how frustrating. Nelio, Sergio, and his family will keep this information to themselves, and they'll begin making the trek to Matanzas on a regular basis. In the meantime, we drive to a different house, not far away, in pursuit of yet another rumor.

A Havana neighbor of Sergio's had given him an address along with the tantalizing information that he might find a man there who had Harley-Davidson parts, and that the man might be willing to sell them for the right price. It turns out to be true. For $170 Sergio buys two mudguards, two transmissions, a wheel, one complete gas tank, and one half of another gas tank, as well as a few odds and ends. Not an outrageous rip-off, but no bargain either. Still, Sergio seems pleased and gives a sly wink to signal his approval.

Harlistas with sufficient money engage in a different sort of scavenger hunt. Julio Mérida is one of those people. For months now he has been rebuilding his '56 panhead. Pieces of the bike are laid out like a puzzle in a room of his home in La Lisa, an outlying Havana neighborhood. Under his bed, carefully covered with a white cotton sheet, he stores the freshly painted mudguards and gas tank. Because he is rebuilding the machine using only genuine Harley-Davidson parts (purchased abroad for him by foreigners), it has become a protracted effort. It also has become astronomically expensive. His wife brings *café cubano* as Julio leads a tour of the project. She rolls her eyes: "*¡Está loco!* He spends more money on that thing than the average Cuban makes in a lifetime. Why? *¿Por qué, chico?*"

"Women don't get it," Julio says with a smile and a shrug. "A Harley is like a mistress." Foreign friends have brought him everything from chrome-and-gold gas caps to brand-new piston rings. The paint job alone—using rare, American-made, orange-gold metallic paint—cost $200. "This will be the finest Harley in Cuba when I'm finished with it," he boasts.

Indeed, when completed, Julio's bike will be awesome, a likenew antique that would make most Harley fans drool with envy. But he'll get an argument from Sergio Morales and other *Harlistas* in Cuba. "If it's a question of money, the foreigners will always have better Harleys," Sergio observes. "Julio works for a foreigner and he's spending so many dollars on that motorcycle. You can say money made it, not Julio. How can the average Cuban pay for original Harley parts and American metallic paint? A few weeks ago we had a contest for the best Harley-Davidson and a debate arose: should foreigners be allowed to compete?" In the end, a Harley owned by a German living in Havana won the contest, and Sergio wasn't surprised. Foreigners in Havana, he says, can easily afford to spend a few thousand dollars for a Harley, and a few thousand more to have it restored to mint condition with original parts. In fact, the increasing number of foreigners doing just that has caused the price of vintage Harleys to rise significantly.

Sergio and Nelio are in the shop dismantling the engine of a black Harley that's been leaking oil. Fernando Pérez, a sixty-two-year-old retired health worker who comes by to help and simply pass the time, works on a classic Harley sidecar. Another assistant is busy grinding and hand-sanding mudguard ornaments recently arrived from a foundry.

Despite the din, the men can hear two Harleys ap-

Havana! I can't wipe the grin off my face. After three hours of methodical officialdom oiled by charitable dispensations of cigarettes and beer, I coax the immigration officials into helping manhandle the BMW onto the dock. Cubans gather reverentially. One volunteers to hose down the bike, and I take him up on it for a few dollars. Then I get to work with elbow grease and metal cleaner, removing the rust that has already started to show on the disc brake and chrome.

I had imagined it would take all day to clear the Beemer through Customs, but in no time at all I'm issued a permit that grants me seven days to register with the police and receive a *chapa* (license plate). Four hours after arriving in Cuba, I wheel through the gates of Marina Hemingway and turn east for downtown Havana.

—Christopher P. Baker,
Mi Moto Fidel: Motorcycling Through Castro's Cuba

proaching from almost three blocks away. Their unannounced arrival for a repair (one bike's timing mechanism isn't working properly) is typical. Also typical is Sergio's response. He asks Nelio to investigate the timing problem and then invites everyone else across the street to his house for some *café cubano*. While his wife uses household scissors to cut engine gaskets from a sheet of rubberized material purchased from a peddler, the men settle in the kitchen for coffee and Harley talk. When the discussion turns to tools, Sergio produces an oddly shaped wrench. "There is a wrench just like this one that is special for the Harley-Davidson," he says. "It's very particular, it has this strange curve. This one is *soviético*, for use on a tractor. It is exactly like the one we need for the Harley."

The coffee break is brief. Nelio has fixed the balky timing mechanism without charge, and the two bikers roar off. Only later does Sergio inform me that one of the men, the one known as Ernestico, is the son of Ernesto "Che" Guevara, the late revolutionary hero and avid motorcyclist.

Sergio pulls out his log book. In the last four years he has been keeping a record of all the Harley-Davidsons that come to his shop, as well as their repairs and parts modifications. "This way," he explains, "we can keep a tab on the Creole parts we make and see which ones are working better than others."

In the afternoon, as Sergio's wife begins cataloguing the parts scheduled to be chrome-plated the next day, a new Nissan rental car pulls up. Two men get out and approach Sergio. One of them, a Spaniard whose Harley Sergio has been restoring, remains quiet. The other, a Cuban, wears a spiffy green Izod shirt and has a cellular phone strapped to his thin leather belt. The Cuban argues with Sergio about the slowness of the work.

Once they are gone, Sergio complains: "You know, I don't mind the Spaniard, but there's nothing worse than an arrogant Cuban who thinks he's better than everyone just because he's got money."

Adds Nelio: "Cuba teaches us all one thing: Patience."

"And that Cuban, of all people, should know what it's like to get work done here," says Sergio's wife Miriam, gesticulating wildly. "It takes time to get the parts, to take them to get chromed, to grind a piston for a perfect fit, fine-sanding the parts by hand. We didn't work most of last week because there was no electricity."

"That guy acts like it's *his* Harley," Sergio continues, "but he's only the employee of the Spaniard."

"It's like those people who work the dollar stores," observes Miriam. "They treat you like you're dirt, giving you bad service and acting superior toward you."

Father's Day is a very important occasion for any *Harlista* in Cuba, for on that day in June the bikers pay homage to the late Pepe "Milésima" at Colón Cemetery. As the clock nears eleven, Harleys begin to gather at a prominent crossroads inside the vast burial ground. Among the tall royal palms and the thousands of statues burning white under the hot sun, they park their bikes and wait for stragglers to arrive. Then they ride together to the designated mausoleum.

Four dozen of them make their way to the site and listen as Raúl Corrales reads a eulogy. Among the crypts inside is one at floor level with a plaque that reads: *"Pepe Milésima, mecánico de Harley-Davidson, de sus amigos y familiares."* Above the plaque is the familiar shield of Harley-Davidson Motorcycles. After all the bikers have had a chance to pay their respects, they return to their machines, start their engines, and rev them in tribute.

Following the ceremony, they ride together—fifty strong—along the wide Havana avenues. Over the years, this Father's Day event has become the Cuban equivalent of one of the big bike rallies in the United States. People in the streets turn to the devilish sound and the blinding flashes of chrome, and they point, shout, and wave.

The caravan makes its way to the eight-lane highway that loops around the southern outskirts of Havana (known informally as Ocho Vías). The road is perfect for cruising; only occasionally does an automobile appear.

Eventually the riders pull into a *paladar* (a private restaurant), a cabana with a palm-thatched roof and no walls. The Harleys park under the shade of the palm trees as the mild breeze cools their engines. Inside, Nelio and Miriam take charge of ordering food and beer and collecting money, all in U.S. dollars. *Paladares* are only allowed by law to have twelve seats so they join tables together and the women sit while the men hang out in groups, talking motorcycles and drinking beer.

Fried pork steak, *arroz moro*, *yuca*, Hatuey beer. The easy chatter floats in the warm air. The subject is the famed Daytona Beach Bike Week. "*Coño*," someone laughs, "they say Coca-Cola spent $100,000 customizing a Harley just to win the show—$100,000. *¿Tú sabes qué es eso?*"

"It's in that magazine at Sergio's house." "That's how it is there. It's advertising." "You know a new Fat Boy costs more than $20,000?" "I hear in Miami there's a one-year waiting list when you buy a Harley." "*¡Coño!*"

The owner of the *paladar* asks us to leave because he needs the chairs for waiting customers, and once again the Harlistas hit the road like rolling thunder. Ocho Vías is all theirs. They ride helmetless and free.

On Friday nights many of Havana's *Harlistas* gather in the parking lot of the Riviera Hotel near the western end of the oceanfront Malecón. Inevitably a crowd of curious onlookers forms; on this evening they stand in awe of ten shiny bikes. Locals and tourists alike stop and take photographs, ask questions, and wonder at the impressive beauty of these gleaming relics in such a decaying environment. The *Harlistas* proudly show off their wheels.

Sergio's wife Miriam pulls me aside to show me an identification card she has received from the United States. "*Ven acá*," she says. "They spelled my name wrong. How can I get this changed?"

The card is from the Harley Owners Group, and she is the first female H.O.G. in Cuba. A half-dozen *Harlistas* became members last year at about the same time they formed a group called MOCLA (short for Motos Clasicas de Cuba), which they hoped would receive official governmental recognition. Their stated goal is to maintain old and classic motorcycles and to encourage friendship among all bikers. Although membership soon grew to more than 100, state approval is still pending.

I hop on the back of Pedro Vejerano's red-and-white '52 panhead. As we take off, Sergio waves and hollers, "*¡Nos vemos en Sturgis!*"

Pedro gives me a ride down the road to the plush Hotel Nacional. His Harley rumbles and growls its way up the hotel's long driveway. As we pull up at the front entrance, cameras click and heads turn. It's as if a movie star has arrived. Someone asks, "*¿De qué año es?*" Another shouts, "*¡Mira eso!*" And another: "*¿Qué motor es ese, chico?*"

The porter's lips move in a whisper as he says to himself: "Arly Daveeson."

Phillippe Diederich is a writer and photographer who has traveled extensively in Mexico and the Caribbean. His work has appeared in publications such as The New York Times, U.S. News and World Report, Mother Jones, The Atlantic Monthly, *and many other national publications. He lives and works in Houston, Texas.*

★ ★ ★

Ticket to Ride

*The station can be the most compelling
part of a train trip.*

TODAY I TRAVELED BY RAIL FROM SANTIAGO TO HOLGUÍN. THE trains here are old and often run several hours late. They also break down. I purchased my ticket with pesos, the local currency. Tourists pay about forty dollars for the same ride that costs a citizen fifty cents. To get my ticket, I waited in line for several hours last night. I waited with the other passengers even though everyone insisted I move ahead in line and allow the preferential treatment reserved for visitors.

I told them, "No, I will wait like everybody else. I am riding on the same train, in the same section. I am not rich." They listened, and so I continued, "I am a student. Not all foreigners are wealthy, so I'll pay local prices for tickets, and I will wait for them. I'll run for a seat when the train arrives, and I will travel without first-class service. I can not afford to do otherwise."

The people considered this. It sounded right. They withdrew into their hats, resumed their arguments, and continued to wait. A new thing had happened here. The people registered this and they found it good.

I returned to the station this morning to catch my train. There a brother and sister dashed towards the tracks. A mother's scolding gently followed them, urging them back, but not too intensely. The trains were a long time coming. Together we waited. I pressed crushed-ice fruit drinks to my swollen mouth and listened to the same salsa roll over and over on a young man's radio. There was a rumble in the distance.

About the same time, a police captain arrived at the station. He was thick around the middle and impeccably dressed. Confidence dripped out of his person and found a home in the base of his spine and the pits of his arms, staining his uniform beneath the mid-afternoon sun.

The people stepped around him, watching him out of the sides of their eyes. One man whittled his pinky nail with a knife, another fixed his shoe. People seemed very busy all of a sudden, and yet, everybody was watching the captain as he slowly sized things up and squinted at the scene through the sticky haze.

He saw me and leaned over to one of his assistants. The assistant shot off to the ticket window. He returned reluctantly. The train had arrived. The captain moved with imposed urgency, yet calmly walked over to where I stood.

Speaking softly, but wielding a stick of unconfirmed dimensions, he inquired as to why I was not standing inside the specially allocated tourists' waiting area, a hot, enclosed room without any seats. I explained that I had a coach pass and was only able to enjoy the privileges concurrent with the status of such a ticket. The captain was alarmed. "How did you purchase this?"

I assured him that I had waited in line the night before, bought the seat, and fully understood the limitations of such tickets. The captain thought about this. He rubbed his chin, kicked the ground, and stared so intently at a point across the street that everybody looked there too.

The captain coughed and slid his palm along the wet underside of his neck. "Give me the ticket," he stated to the slowly forming crowd. I showed him my sweaty, but official, gray ticket. He took it and held it up to the sun. The people pressed in to see it themselves, all equally curious about the outcome of the issue between the poor tourist and the captain. He shook his head. After a final kick at loose pebbles on the platform, he pushed the official paper back into my hand and declared for all to hear, "You may not use the train without the appropriate tourist-issue ticket."

I was quick to respond. "But the tourist tickets cost so much money. I can't afford the equivalent of seven months rent in this country. I'm not a millionaire. I'm a student. You don't have the right to ask me for more than I can give."

He was not impressed, but the people were aroused. The genetic, electric spirit of revolution was still carried in their breasts, and while I wouldn't have guessed that my activities had been so well observed, the people sprang to life in my defense.

"She waited with us for over three hours last night to get that ticket!" shouted a mother with twin girls.

"She took the bus here and not a tourist car," one old man offered and then disappeared.

"She's been waiting along the tracks for the last four hours." "She is a student!" "Look! She has only what she carries!" "Look! She wears the beads of Yemayá, the God who protects our sailors!" "Look!" They did not stop. I was amazed.

The captain was defeated, but he could not leave the site in shame. The rules were unclear, and it was better to let the poor tourist travel coach. He shook his head and departed with a threat, "My supervisor will be notified."

The people clapped each other on the back and shook hands. I smiled and the children jumped up and down around me. There was no time for thanks. That would come later on the long ride to Holguín. We vied for positions along the tracks, for a ticket did not guarantee a seat. The time for unity had passed.

The train was silent. Its doors were sealed. With a sigh they opened and the people charged aboard. Surprisingly, there were enough seats for everyone. Even though we were all seated and ready to depart, the train was still. It was a part of the landscape, and we were all waiting again. No one was hurried. No one complained. Here the people have as much waiting as revolution in their blood.

*Alisha Berger has lived and studied in Madrid and Paris. She did a clerkship
at* The New York Times, *was a reporter for the* Patriot-Ledger *in
Quincy, Massachusetts, and currently is a writer for the* New York Post. *She
spent several months aboard a sailboat in the Caribbean and explored Cuba
for three months of her journey.*

⋆ ⋆ ⋆

Picture This

Che, we hardly knew ye.

AT THE CHE DAY SALES IN HAVANA, LET ME TELL YOU, BUSINESS IS booming. In the Plaza de Armas, the used book stalls feature enough books by and about Che Guevara to fill a small library. From his motorcycle diary to his guerrilla strategy, it's all there. A few blocks away artisans and folk craft purveyors hawk their wares; every five steps you bump into a table anchored by the image of Guevara on key chains, ashtrays, plates, and paintings. Havana's *artesanía* fair is world headquarters for Tchotchkes de Che.

Over the years I've bought a number of Che keepsakes for my own personal collection. My *checitos* include an ingeniously painted box, eight inches square and a half-inch deep, made of wood discarded from cigar box assembly lines. If you look at it from one side you see Fidel Castro, from the other José Martí, and head on, Che Guevara. My silk-screened Che t-shirt—de rigueur for any foreigner—shows a red Cuban three-peso note with Guevara's face in the middle. Among my favorites is a Che-in-a-bottle; I paid two dollars for it.

My most valuable acquisition stands out for its integrity and durability. It's an original print of the world-famous photograph of Guevara—the one of him gazing intently over the horizon, eyes burning, long hair covered by a beret, acne blemishes that look like battle scars. The photographer was Alberto Díaz Gutiérrez, widely known as Korda, who before the revolution had earned a living snapping fashion and cheesecake shots. At a major speech by Castro in March 1960, Korda was in the grandstand as Guevara, then president of Cuba's National Bank, made his way down the front row.

"To the camera," Henri Cartier-Bresson has written, "Che's eyes glow; they coax, entice, and mesmerize."

That's just what Korda must have thought as Guevara suddenly came into the viewfinder. He saw Guevara's hard and determined visage, his head tilted slightly, the wispy moustache, and his eyes burning just beyond the foreseeable future.

"*Me asustó*," Korda has since said. "I was shook, physically taken aback." Korda called it "The Heroic Guerrilla"; it has become one of the most ubiquitous photographs every taken.

Except for one newspaper appearance, Korda's photograph was tucked away until Guevara was killed in 1967. Magically and majestically, it appeared overnight, ten stories high on the side of a government building in Havana. A shrewd Italian publisher took a print of it back to Europe and turned it into a poster that sold worldwide in the

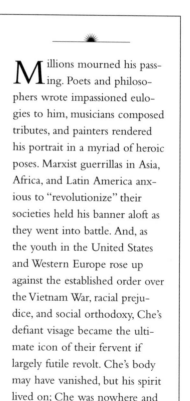

Millions mourned his passing. Poets and philosophers wrote impassioned eulogies to him, musicians composed tributes, and painters rendered his portrait in a myriad of heroic poses. Marxist guerrillas in Asia, Africa, and Latin America anxious to "revolutionize" their societies held his banner aloft as they went into battle. And, as the youth in the United States and Western Europe rose up against the established order over the Vietnam War, racial prejudice, and social orthodoxy, Che's defiant visage became the ultimate icon of their fervent if largely futile revolt. Che's body may have vanished, but his spirit lived on; Che was nowhere and everywhere at once.

—Jon Lee Anderson, *Che Guevara: A Revolutionary Life*

millions. The Cuban government made a documentary about the image called "The Photo that Circles the World."

Korda, then almost forty, didn't claim control of the picture's rights because of ideological obligation and Cuba's withdrawal from international copyright conventions. A colleague from that era says Korda would have been a millionaire "if only he had lived in a different system."

One drizzly Havana evening a few winters ago, my friend Figueroa took me over to Korda's home; I brought enough Havana Club rum for the three of us plus Korda's wife, born after the photograph was taken. Korda and I knew I came with one purpose, but there's a protocol to these things. We chatted and sipped, sipped and chatted, and finally came to a pause.

"Well," he said, "I understand you're interested in looking at some of my work. Let me get my portfolio." He brought out a leather case with scores of prints. I narrowed down the selection to a half dozen. Then to three. Finally, I said, pointing, "I suppose I'm most interested in that one. The famous one."

Korda nodded. He went to a back room and emerged with a print of the photograph.

"How much do you think it's worth?" he asked. I genuinely did not know. I'd never before purchased a famous print personally inscribed by the photographer, a picture that has circled the globe and retained both its historical and symbolic *raison*. Was its worth in Havana the same as its price in New York or Prague or La Paz? Did its value, decades after it was taken, stem from its subject or its notoriety? I didn't want to insult Korda by offering too little, but I didn't want to be taken, either.

"I don't know," I mumbled truthfully. "Fifty dollars? A hundred dollars? I, uh—" Korda cut me off.

"Normally I am paid three hundred dollars for a print. But you are a friend of Figueroa's, and that shows you choose your friends well. Second, you have written about Cuba honorably without resorting to slanderous attacks on our character."

I nodded.

"And finally, you have married a *cubana*, so you are one of us."

Korda leaned back in his chair. "I will let you have it for one hundred dollars."

For all my adult life, in countries throughout the Americas, I have bought items small and large, cheap and pricey, but never have I ever negotiated a purchase in which friendship, literature, and love played so significant a role. For this I am indebted to Korda, and as he inscribed the picture, I poured us a celebratory round of Havana Club.

Tom Miller is the author of Trading with the Enemy: A Yankee Travels Through Castro's Cuba, *and co-founder of the U.S.-Cuba Writers Conference. He is the editor of this volume and a contributor to* Travelers' Tales American Southwest.

CHARLES DEGELMAN

★ ★ ★

Under Havana's Hood

On the roadways of Cuba, a standard
transmission is anything but standard.

CUBANS MAKE THE BEST MECHANICS IN THE WORLD. IF YOU'VE EVER had to keep an old car running, you know what I'm talking about. You don't have the right tools. You work in the street. Your feet stick out in traffic like a couple of ducks. Because of the economic embargo, there have been no new cars or parts coming to Cuba from the United States for forty years. Every piece that breaks has to be manufactured from junk or scabbed onto the machine from other relics. Parts from dead and dying creatures are spirited away to be grafted onto other, more deserving vehicles.

Havana's old cars are parked at the curbs like memories; ancient Fords, Chevys, and an occasional Edsel jockey for space with more recent generations of Russian Ladas and Italian Fiats.

In America, these old cars flash dollars and cents. According to the law of supply and demand, even a derelict version of one of Havana's American cars would command an obscene price from nostalgic collectors. A 1950 Plymouth, its Mayflower hood ornament under full sail, advertises the birth of the Maytag, the Kelvinator, and the single-family home. The tail fins on a '58 Dodge Coronet celebrate America's entry into the space race. A '55 Chevy triggers flashbacks to Ozzie and Harriet, America's favorite '50s television family.

"*Mira, compañeros,*" I shout to my friends as another American dinosaur roars past. "Look at that Chrysler New Yorker!" The smoke from its passage rises to join the cloud of sulfates hanging under Vedado's graceful trees. I don't care about the smog. I breathe it in like perfume and laugh with delight. I can recognize every model, every year, the lines of the bodywork surging up from the archives of my adolescent past like a Marilyn Monroe pinup.

By the simple miracle of their rattling passages through Havana's streets, Cuba's cars confirm that Cuba's revolution is alive, hanging on, making it. Havana's mechanics are thumbing their noses at the American blockade. They have learned how to pick the bones of their vanquished oppressor.

But what about the Cubans? How do they feel about their old cars? Are they inspired by their own ingenuity? Do they celebrate tiny victories over worn-out shock absorbers, disintegrating carburetors, and slipping clutches?

Some *mecánicos* are proud. We drove to a ball game at Havana's *estadio* in a Plymouth that was fifty years old and looked brand-new in the dim light of the Cuban night. The old car rode like a Sherman tank but the tape deck was digital. We listened to Chico O'Farrell play the saxophone while every pothole in the road transmitted itself through the chassis to the steering wheel and the seats.

"*Original?*" I asked.

"*Con seguro,*" the driver replied. "*Puro.*" He laughed and patted the dashboard.

Others were modest about their creativity. After the game, we flagged down a young guy in a Studebaker. It was Saturday night and there wasn't a cab in sight. We asked the driver if he would take us to a restaurant.

"*No problema,*" he replied and glanced in the rearview mirror for the cops. In Cuba as in America, it is against the law for unlicensed drivers to accept fares. We piled in and bumped down the boulevard. The driver shifted the gears with a lever mounted on the transmission hump. From some deep pool, I pulled the recollection that these old Studebakers all had column shifts.

"*Original?*" I asked and pointed to the gearbox.

"*No, no,*" he replied and grinned. "Volga, Russia, *todo*. Motor, *caja*, transmission." My jaw dropped in amazement. This guy had completely replaced the forty-year-old organs of the Studebaker with a twenty-year-old transplant from a Soviet passenger car. It was an impossible task. The cars were different sizes. The engine mounts wouldn't have fit. Did he have to shorten or lengthen the driveshaft? How did he get the shift lever to surface at the right place beneath his hand?

He was a fourth-year engineering student and had done all the work himself. Over and over, I congratulated him on his ingenuity while he laughed and shook his head. "*Insignificante,*" he said. "*Es necesario, simplemente.*"

The next day, I spotted a '48 Buick Special sitting by the curb of a narrow alley. The Buick's grill had long since disintegrated. A bundle of one-inch galvanized pipe sprawled through the broken-out rear window, waiting to be delivered somewhere. The once-skirted and chromed wheel wells had been torched

---

*F*ar from any town, the *botero*, a collective taxi, broke down. The driver tinkered awhile with the motor but returned saying he didn't know what was wrong. The grandfather got out mumbling through his toothless mouth something about *despojo*. He looked around and headed to a bush from which he broke a branch. With it he drew an imaginary circle on the road around the car, then brushed the motor with the leaves. Next he took a white handkerchief from his back pocket, pulled it taut, spit on it, crumpled it, pulled it taut and spit on it again, then spread it carefully over the carburetor. "*Dale,*" he said to the driver who was now sitting dejectedly in the car smoking a cigarette. The driver raised his hand in disdain but obeyed. The car gurgled once, twice, and finally the motor roared. The old man had fixed it without once touching the insides.

—Pablo Medina, *Exiled Memories: A Cuban Childhood*

into ragged half circles to allow for larger wheels to be installed on the axles.

Three men squatted on the ground in front of the Buick. All three were dressed in ragged t-shirts and cutoffs. All three were slathered with grit and oil. Two of them held the knuckle of a universal joint on a paving stone that had been torn up to form an anvil. The third man beat on the joint with a broken ball-peen hammer. The men grimaced while the universal joint jumped and shifted beneath every blow.

"*Original?*" I asked, and laughed.

The hammer stopped in midair. Three strained and grease-stained faces looked up at me. There was no acknowledgment, no reply. Instead the three men turned away and resumed their task. There was no solidarity here, no revolution to celebrate. There was nothing to laugh about.

Charles Degelman lives in Los Angeles, where he writes and edits history books for kids. A longtime performer, Degelman is co-founder and executive director of L.A.'s Indecent Exposure Theater Company. His writing on the arts includes biographies of Mozart and filmmaker John Huston.

⋆ ⋆ ⋆

Sweet Thing

Havana, where flirting is accepted
and sexuality is envied.

THE WORLD MAY MARVEL THAT A HANDFUL OF YOUNG MEN AND women overthrew Fulgencio Batista, a dictator backed by the most powerful nation in the world, but it makes sense to me. After examining scores of grainy museum photographs of Camilo Cienfuegos smoking cigars and Che Guevara flexing his quads, I decided that if I'd seen them and a couple dozen other rugged rebels scaling mountains and reciting poetry with combat boot-clad Castro, I would have picked up my machete and joined them too. Someone ought to put sex appeal in the Top Ten of Most Recommended Revolutionary Traits in Mao's *Little Red Book*.

I'm not the only one who fantasizes about Cuba's bearded heroes. Allen Ginsberg got deported from Cuba in the '60s in part for announcing that Che, the honorary Cuban, was "cute." And I'm convinced that just about every middle-aged *cubana* left on the island has a thing for Fidel. Just ask one to describe her nation's premier revolutionary. Chances are, she'll start with adjectives like charismatic, intelligent, and powerful, and then her voice will drop a lusty octave as she gets to the clincher: "...*y sensual.*" I've gazed upon the bulk of the world's Communist dictators and can vouch that Castro is the sexiest (although, in Lenin and Ho Chi Minh's defense, embalming agents are hard on the complexion). Mao is kind of cuddly in a teddy bear sort of way, but he is no *Comandante*—that's for sure.

And sensuality isn't confined to Cuba's leaders, either. Centuries of mingling Spanish, indigenous, and African blood have created skin colors that range from creamy white to dark chocolate. Noses are aquiline; cheek bones are well-defined. Eyes are almond-shaped and framed with long, black lashes. Smiles are vibrant. Gaits are fluid. Movements are rhythmic. But stunning exteriors are only part of what makes Cubans so exquisite. Theirs is a sensuality that transcends physical appearance. It is an attitude. And it is infectious.

I was feeling anything but sexy when I ventured to the island at the turn of the millennium. My boyfriend of three years had recently dumped me, and I was convinced no man would ever pique my interest again. Until I took a late-afternoon stroll through the barrios, that is. Within five steps, I had unwittingly summoned the attention of every male on the block. Graying men in guayaberas looked up from their domino matches to grin appreciatively. A father and son tinkering beneath the hood of a faded-blue '54 Chrysler wiped their hands on their jeans and waved. Two mulattos sipping Cristal on a second-floor balcony clinked their bottles against the rusty iron railing and called out "*¡Salud!*"

Then came a noise from the shadows of a doorway that sounded like a cross between a hiss and a slurpy kiss. It grated my feminist fibers like fingernails on a chalkboard—until the perpetrator stepped into the sunlight. He was 6'2" and the color of iced coffee. His features were chiseled. His black eyes glittered. He wasn't wearing a shirt. I wrestled my eyes away from his washboard stomach and continued down the dusty street, dazed from the sight of such unanticipated beauty. Two steps farther, another catcall resounded, followed by a lasciviously whispered "*¡Qué guapa!*" Incensed, I whirled around, fists clenched, ready to pounce—and found a tall, dark, and stunning someone grinning at me. The corners of my mouth crept skyward before I forced them down.

Just then, a seventeen-year-old on a Chinese bicycle pedaled over. "Is that a sun you're wearing?" he asked.

I looked down at the sterling silver sun tied around my neck with a velvet ribbon. "*Sí.*"

"And where is your moon?"

Perplexed, I crinkled my brow.

"You don't have a moon?" he asked, concerned. He hopped off his bike and got a little closer. "Well, how about me then?"

I laughed; he persisted. "Do you have a boyfriend?"

"*Sí,*" I lied.

"A Cuban boyfriend?"

"*Sí.*"

"You want to change?"

"No."

"Not even for a little while?"

"No."

"How about just a day?"

"No."

"An hour?"

I stopped walking to peer into the amber eyes of my curly haired suitor. His biceps bulged in a pleasantly pubescent way; a few stray chest hairs peeked through the buttons of his neatly pressed shirt. There was potential. "How about I look you up in a couple of years?" I proposed.

He beamed and whipped out a pen.

Mom always said to ignore catcallers—or, at the very least, not encourage them—but then, she has never been to Cuba. *Cubanos* may whistle at anything lacking a Y chromosome, but somehow, it feels neither predatory nor disrespectful. It is simply an indiscriminate appreciation of the female body. And it did wonders for my tattered self-esteem. There's just something about an island full of gorgeous men calling you *linda*

> Nowhere in the world does a woman get such concentrated, consistent, and flattering attention as on the streets of Havana. There the ogle is raised to the level of a fine art.
> —Helen Lawrenson, "Latins Still Make Lousy Lovers," *Esquire*

that makes you start to believe it. Consider *las cubanas,* the usual target of this unfaltering attention. They are one self-possessed group of women. They wear skintight hot pants and halter tops regardless of body size, unabashedly eat chocolate sundaes for lunch and let their bodies sway like nature intended. Cubans understand that excess flesh is no sin. They celebrate it in all of its jiggly glory.

I saw a phenomenal array of beautiful women on that island, but the sexiest was forty years old and weighed approximately 225 pounds. She swaddled her galactic ass in pink spandex and stuffed her papaya-shaped breasts into polka-dot halter tops. A bouffant of Afro-mermaid hair spilled across her body. When I first noticed this Amazon at a rumba club, the hypnotic beat of the conga drum seemed to have caught her in a temporary trance: she was slumped in a chair, eyes shut, body still. But when the rhythm sped a notch or two, it called her feet to action. Her spiked heels began to pound the beat on the patch of floor beneath her chair. The music worked its way through her tree-trunk thighs toward her massive belly, across her breasts and finally to her head, which started swaying. Suddenly, the music commanded her to stand and, undulating every muscle of her full frame, she gyrated toward the dance floor. And then she began to rumba. Her energy was palpably feminine and undeniably sensual. She was like a Frida Kahlo painting of a fleshy melon bursting with ripeness. She was fertility. She was womanhood.

It had long been a fantasy of mine to learn to rumba, and here was its mistress. I slithered closer for a better view. She peered upon me with charcoal eyes. I smiled hopefully. Winking sassily, she took a step to the side, gyrated, and motioned me to follow. I did, clumsily but obediently. She nodded encouragingly before adding a sensuous hip swivel to the move. When I tried and failed, she seized my hips with her giant hands and swiveled them for me. Before I knew it, I too was doing a rumba. I beamed my gratitude and she winked once more. Then she closed her eyes and absorbed even more of the electrifying rhythms. The deaf could have followed the music's manic beat by watching the rippling of her flesh.

I vowed then and there to return to Cuba with a suitcase full of spandex when I'm flabby and gray to learn the dances of the rumba queens. And to remind myself that sensuality is a state of mind, not body.

Stephanie Elizondo Griest has belly danced with Cuban rumba queens, mingled with the Russian Mafiya, and edited the propaganda of the Chinese Communist Party. These adventures are the subject of her first book: Around the Bloc: My Life in Moscow, Beijing, and Havana. *She has also written for* The New York Times, The Washington Post, Latina *magazine, and several Travelers' Tales books. She once drove 45,000 miles across the nation in a beat-up Honda, documenting U.S. history for a website for kids on a $15 daily budget. Visit her Web site at www.aroundthebloc.com.*

ELISEO ALBERTO

* * *

Havana When It Rains

The sweet pain of nostalgia brings a Cuban
writer to all five of his senses.

IN CUBA, TIME IS MEASURED BY RAINFALL.

"It has rained a lot since we last met," we say; "Four cyclones later," I often heard my grandmother say. The clock counts time shower after shower, as though in our happy little island, stricken by natural catastrophes, political storms and the hurricanes of history, the most characteristic things were the tragicomical sense of life, that slow enjoyment of danger that explains, in my case at least, so many national miracles and absurdities. After all, Cubans are well aware that rain is always followed by calm. And I have started talking about showers because I want to tell you a story. A happy story.

Twenty-five years ago, that is to say, many, many downpours ago, my good friend José Alberto Figueroa and myself traveled all along the Sierra Maestra, going from one end of the range to the other like two young acrobats on a tightrope. Now I can remember a skinny, bearded Figueroa crossing a swollen river in Buey Arriba with his bag of lenses and reels of Chinese film held high above him, shooting blindly so as not to miss the moment at which the waters would swallow him up. I can still hear his laughter. And he makes me laugh too.

At the time we were working for *Cuba Internacional*, a real Gothic

51

cave where chance had gathered together twelve or thirteen madmen who were not afraid of anybody or anything, not even of
daydreaming, perhaps the bravest thing of all in this most extraordinary world designed by God or the Devil where only those who
have their feet solidly set on the ground can triumph.

Everything I know about the godliness of man, about his pho-
bias and stupidity, about the cruelty of hope and the crushing
strength of sadness, everything I love and hate at the end of this
century and millennium, the sensational reveling of poverty and the
immoral luxury of opulence, everything, however little, good and
bad, I learnt from them, the friends of my youth, my brothers, at
that old house on the corner of Reina and Lealtad, in the center of
Havana, where I go back in my sleep with the illusion of sharing
our new nightmares, only to wake up more alone than ever, because
we are not the same as we were then….

In the mountains, the winds of legend were still blowing. While
he dried his clothes in front of a bonfire, Figueroa told me that on
one of his trips through the heart of the mountain he had met a
centenarian weaving straw baskets at the foot of a cliff, in the area
of Buey Arriba if I remember rightly. This craftsman, whose memory had been corroded by the acid of the years, could not remember how to finish off the edges of his basket. Forgetfulness is a rat.
It bites. It gnaws. It swallows, The old man made the frame of his
baskets with the precision of a shipbuilder; he repeated the routine
of his trade, step by step and thread by thread, sure that this time he
would be able to finish it properly, so he wove and wove the reeds
and the palm leaves. Layer after layer, although never finishing off
the edges, so that the unfinished baskets spread out endlessly and
unfinished down the hill, where they sank into the mud.

That man ended up hating himself. He never forgave himself for
forgetting the only thing he had known how to do in this life. It
took Figueroa and me two nights and three days to get to the bottom of the gorge. There was nobody there. We shouted out the
name of the craftsman. The echo sent back our cries, softened by
the hills. The greatest loneliness is the echo shouting in all directions. We rested in the abandoned house. We ate the snacks we had

in our knapsacks. Bread with or without something inside, undoubt-
edly. We had a quick look around. Sunk in the pools left by the
recent downpour, rocky, dilution, green with damp, the worms
and snakes of the wickerwork looked like the roots of an impossible tree.

None of the neighbors
could give us news of the old
man. He was neither alive nor
dead. "Just gone." We went on
our way up the mountain. I
think we were not too concerned about the matter at the
time, or perhaps we were so
concerned about it we preferred to make the effort of
forgetting about it.

The tide of life took
Figueroa and myself in different directions. Every so often
I would walk past the balcony
of his apartment in El Veda, a
magic terrace crowded with
baskets, flowers, and beautiful,
long-limbed women, and I
would say to myself that on
my way back I would knock
on that door that I knew was
always open for old friends,
but in the tropics there is
hardly enough time to kill
time, so I kept putting it off

Vedado is a neighborhood
in Havana. The navel of
the world. The not-to-be-missed
tour of every traveler. I know of
no other neighborhood that is
so beautiful, with its chipped
houses, its stray dogs, its ancestral
narrow streets of rough stones
and that perpendicular sun that
splits the cement of its side-
walks. Vedado is the vortex
around which the country turns.
Now it is invaded by tourists
from the north or by the Olmec
[Mexicans]. No matter. The
vendor of essences keeps piping
among the leaves to make the
hummingbird fall asleep on the
terraces. Vedado is an indescribable feast.

—Miguel Barnet, quoted in
Cuba y Cuba, by René Burri

until later, until tomorrow, not knowing, because I thought then
that I was a poet, that tomorrow never comes or that when it comes
it is too late to say I love you. Life got complicated. Things have got
bad, we whispered. The city got complicated. Havana started to fall
to pieces. Only the girders remained. "Havana cannot take any

more," we sang. Just like that old craftsman in Buey Arriba, none of us knew how to tie up this mad old city that often does not know what it is doing.

Children grew up overnight. Several photographers and reporters from the magazine *Cuba Internacional* went to the lands of the devil: Bogota, Miami, Mexico, Barcelona or Columbus's cemetery. Cruel death took away a couple of members of the old guard without a by your leave, in her usual whimsical manner. I hate her....

The next time I pass Figueroa's house, I will sit for hours and hours on his balcony—"just gone." I am certain it will rain tonight.

Eliseo Alberto, winner of the first International Alfaguara Prize in Fiction, was born in Arroyo Naranjo, Cuba. He received a degree in journalism from the University of Havana, and was editor-in-chief of the literary gazette, El Caiman Barbudo, *and assistant editor of the magazine,* Cine Cubano. *Among his many works he has written three books of poetry,* La Fogata Roja, *a book for young adults that won the Cuban National Critics Prize, and a memoir,* Informe Contra Mi Mismo, *winner of the Gabino Palma Prize in Spain. His recent novel,* Caracol Beach, *was published in English in 2000. He has written screenplays for film and television, and taught at the International Film School in San Antonio de los Baños in Cuba, the Center for Cinemagraphic Training of Mexico, and the Sundance Institute. He lives in Mexico City.*

HENRY SHUKMAN

* * *

Making Music

In Havana, seductive rhythms
are everywhere.

MY FIRST IMPRESSIONS OF HAVANA WILL FOREVER BE INTERWOVEN with the strains of *son*, a wonderful song rhythm upon which salsa is based, that is recognizable as the classic Latin beat. From car radios, from open doorways, from backyard rumbas, music constantly rises up from the city, flowing not so much over the much-vaunted time warp reported by journalists as over what strikes me as typical late-millennium Latin chaos.

The city pulses with all kinds of beaten-up cars—Renaults, Jeeps, the ubiquitous Ladas, the occasional old Mercedes—intermingled with the gleaming Toyotas of the rental-car brigade.

The famous 1950s Cadillacs that still cruise the streets of Havana are not the shark-finned beasts of the Chrome Age that I had always imagined, lovingly buffed and buttressed to growl into their second half centuries, but lumbering beetles, with homespun paint jobs, trundling slowly along the roads. The feat is that they're maintained at all, here in the Land of Shortages, where the only thing there is no shortages of is queues.

From every open window comes the screech of trumpets, the cry of those high-stave, high-octane Latin vocals, I can't picture the city, or a single old Chevy, without hearing that music. There is no Havana, as someone has said, without music.

But there are many Havanas—the tarted-up blocks of the old city, the deluxe hotel quarter; and the Havana of the back streets, tunnel-like alleys that are dark at all times, where even new buildings have semiputrefied to match the old. Backstreets with strands of rhythm and song drifting and throbbing over the heads of passersby no matter the hour. Backstreets where the girls pull out their armchairs into the road and stare at you as you walk by, where the doors of the ground floors stand always open, drawing whatever gasp of air they can into hot little rooms with a sink, a fridge, a bed, a stiff chair, and a woman at a mirror doing her lipstick before the evening begins. In Cuba every evening is, emphatically, a matter of the streets. *¡Nadie a su casa!*—No one at home! Who, after all, would want to be, in heat like this?

Cuba is the land of the night. Take the Salón Rosado. The Salón is part of La Tropical nightclub, a government-owned night emporium with three or four stages and auditoriums, a centralized sound-factory ministering to the music-hungry souls of Havana. The Salón Rosado is a kind of multitiered outdoor party garden, with a stage below and stepped terraces above, where the audience throngs. Tonight it's an anthill of writhing humanity. Way down at the bottom, flanked by gyrating female figures, stands the prince of this house of night, the musician Paulito. Adored by the younger crowd, he waves and screams into his microphone, "*Ina, en la esquina....*" Behind him an arsenal of percussion and saxophones bombards the crowd with hot rounds of ecstasy.

At the edge of the topmost tier, where we are, three young women flex their bodies, grinding their hips, arching their backs, and miming the motions of the love nest to their heroes on stage. After all the queuing to get in, this is how the Cuban cuties celebrate.

Meanwhile Charlie, the Brazilian producer of Los Van Van, pulls a series of mustached faces—Samuel, Miguel, Manuel—through the crowd to meet me. The names and faces keep on coming, all of them famous figures of the Cuban music pantheon. The Salón Rosado's topmost tier is a kind of Olympian playground of the demigods of rhythm. It's possible to talk—at least, to shout—more or less audibly, up here, where we have an eagle's-eye view of the masses below, as well as those bewitching sirens who grace the edge of our aerie.

A lady approaches me for twenty dollars for our drinks. Only after I have paid up and she has disappeared with my change do I discover that she wasn't the waitress at all, just a plucky opportunist doing a little *improvisación*.

People say that in Cuba the operative word is *improvisar*, to improvise—creating spare parts for vehicles, attaching truck cabs to the buses, surviving on $6.60 a month (which, for many, is standard government pay).

Tomás, our driver, improvises by illegally ferrying visitors around. Tomás clutches the wheel of his growling Lada tightly but still drifts alarmingly across the warped highway as he turns his hooded eyes on me. In a grisly French cop movie he'd make a passable villain: a creased face, a laugh so dry it could combust at any moment, and those eyes, never fully open, squinting, probing.

Tomás is taking us to visit a

"Find a place wherever you can," says Athanai, a small-framed twenty-three-year-old with slovenly long hair and a silver hoop in his ear. Athanai's wife, Ileana Wilson, who does backup vocals for the band, and bassist Haruyoshi Mori, known as El Chino, sit on the double bed. The other five band members stand between the bed, bookcases, and a dresser. I squat between guitars, drums, an amplifier, Wilson's teddy bears, Santa Bárbara, and shelves with Lenin's collected works, *The Godfather*, and García Lorca poetry.

As soon as we settle in, Athanai signals to the band to resume playing "Cruz de Oro (Cross of Gold)," a ballad bemoaning the *chiquita* he lost to a rich foreigner. "She chose a material world over my spirit," he mourns, turning to me after finishing the song, one of his most popular numbers.

—Silvana Paternostro, "The Hunger Artists," *Spin*

few of Havana's great musical talents. But he's more than a driver.

"I'm three things," he says, driver, guide, and bodyguard.

We all laugh at this, assuming it's a joke, but for once his parched cackle is quiet. Tomás is, in fact, an ex-police chief and spent fifteen months in the Sierra Maestra fighting alongside Castro and Che back in the late '50s. Now, forty years on, his specialty is light bribery.

"You touch him, he touch you," he says, explaining how people get by on minimal state salaries. He tosses out a few sheets of his sandpaper laugh.

His car decides to have a bad-fuel day. We lurch and die and lurch laboriously toward our first call. Every few yards Tomás hops out, fiddles under the hood, then roars the engine and slips it into gear, whereupon it lurches and dies again.

"No problem," says Sonia Pérez Cassola, who has come along to act as guide. "We're used to it."

As we coast down a long avenue with the engine off, buses and trucks thunder past, horns wailing. Unperturbed, the beguilingly calm Sonia delivers a disquisition on the history of Cuban music: "There are three main types of music—*son*, rumba, and *punto*," she says. "Within *son* you have various rhythms, like *changüí*, *montuno*, and so on. Rumba is basically just percussion instruments, with the people singing, too. And *punto* is another kind of rhythm. Then there are different types of groups, each of which might play any kind of music. If it's a *sexteto*, you have guitar, bass, et cetera, but no trumpet...."

Pedro Luis Ferrer, the bearded Buddha of Cuban *guaracha*, a leisurely song form noted for social commentary and witty lyrics, lives in a mottled and mildewed villa inherited from his mother. When he moved in, the house was dilapidated, with so many boxes piled inside that no one even knew there was a grand piano. He's turned it into an air-conditioned studio, complete with recording equipment, an array of percussion instruments, and a collection of guitars.

A poet, philosopher, and songwriter, Pedro Luis has an Orthodox monk's beard and a frequent smile. When he sings, his face is so expressive that he'd be affecting even if you couldn't hear his rich voice emanating from that barrel chest.

"I'm not interested in what they tell me on the radio or TV," he says, "only in what I see with my own eyes in the street. I live here and work on my songs."

With him all day long is his beautiful teenage daughter, Lena, who sings backup on his albums and has a voice that could break Orpheus's heart. Hers is one of those rare ageless voices, fully acquainted with suffering despite its tender years.

Pedro Luis talks about the conditions under which a *guarachero* writes today: "We're not allowed to talk about politics. All we can do is improvise a little around it." To do anything more explicit is too dangerous.

Lena brings in a tray of tiny cups of delicious Cuban coffee. Within minutes I'm trembling from caffeine. Then after clearing away a few of the cables strung all over the studio to reveal a keyboard, Pedro Luis puts on his specs and sits down to play one of his compositions, a fugue. Like all Cuban musicians, he's marvelously versatile. As he proceeds, all around the room feet tap, hands beat imaginary drum skins. Cubans have rhythm so richly in their blood that even a cerebral fugue comes out danceable. If Bach had lived in Havana, the fugue we're listening to is what he'd have written.

Then we're heading back to the *escuela*, chugging along streets gold-leafed with late sun to hear Adalberto Alvarez, a famous *son*-leader (and a Santería priest), stage an impromptu concert on the school grounds. Students mill around the stage, while Adalberto, resplendent in white linen and gold chains, conducts his band through the set from behind his gleaming kettledrums.

It is another long Havana night. Hours after sundown we're all standing around the marble-floored sitting room of Sonia and Barbarito's house, while Barbarito, looking stern as he concentrates on his fingering, plucks and strums his way through a *son-changüí*. He's accompanied by his sixteen-year-old daughter at the piano and his twelve-year-old son on the *cajón* drum, while Sonia sings in a vibrant contralto. Between numbers, Barbarito makes the rounds with a bottle of Havana Club. This is a family quartet that knows just how to express its harmonies.

It's midnight on the terrace of the Hotel Nacional, the Art Deco extravagance where gangster Meyer Lansky once ran the casino. In the corner a small band roams through a bolero. Reclining on a sofa under a huge colonnade, I think to myself: *What do the Cubans have?*

The dark sea, the huge sky, the clothes they stand up in. And their music. Music is the gold, oil, minerals of Cuba. They have the best architecture, the best climate, the best education (my chambermaid has a Ph.D.), the most beautiful people....

What don't they have?

Money. They're trained in everything: how to pour beer, how to rouse a crowd of 5,000 at midnight, how to play lead guitar in a smoochy number at three A.M. Here, professionalism achieves its peak—in a land where it finds no recompense.

Where does their love of

music come from? Where is the source of this soul? I won't find the answer without heading east, to the Oriente, the Sierra Maestra, the source of *son* and revolution.

The *jilguero*, a noted Caribbean songbird, is not found on Cuba. Except, that is, in the little terminal of the Baracoa airport in Cuba's far Oriente, where Jilguero Pinareño, wearing a porkpie hat and gray mustache, is singing his way through a *son* improvised then and there on his equally improvised guitar, a curious nine-stringed hybrid.

His band, the Cuarteto AeroCaribe, is desperately but impressively improvising too, in hope of tips. The maraca player, a thickly mustached young man, floats his instruments on the beat, perfectly placing nicks in the music like an adze tapping at a tree trunk. It's only now, with this impromptu performance by a traditional *sonero*, that I realize *son* is actually alive and not just a fossil in the archaeology of salsa.

I had heard that the *son* houses of Santiago, big city of the east, had become touristy, but that Baracoa, still farther east, near the tip of Cuba, remained a bastion of traditional music.

The town was founded by the Spaniards in 1512, just twenty years after Columbus himself nosed into the Bay of Portosanto here and raved about its loveliness, or tried to: "I was so astonished at the sight of so much beauty that I can find no words to describe it."

Today Baracoa is a rotting flower of colonialism, dense with ancient houses with enormously high doors and windows, adorned with tremendous arcades and sagging roofs. Some of its buses are mule carts, and in one square, on top of a pillar in a little hut, is the town TV, unlocked every evening by a policeman while a crowd gathers on concrete benches to watch.

Once a week for as long as anyone can remember, sleepy Baracoa has woken up sharply for its infamous Noche de Baracoa, a ritual that turns everyone out into the streets on Saturday night—and turns the town into a maze of heaving music that lasts far into the small hours.

*

Baracoa is very poor, very hot. After several alternate drenchings and dryings my shirt has acquired a tie-dye effect. Everyone is praying for the tardy rainy season. It's a relief when an explosively beautiful sunset smolders over the town.

Of that day my memory produces only a few images: an MZ motorbike without a seat; a shop window with kids toys of, to Western eyes, almost unbelievable crudeness: plastic sticks meant to resemble rifles; triangles of murky-colored plastic supposed to be racing cars. An old man sits at the roadside while a mechanic repairs his upended wheelchair. And all around, outside fabulously dilapidated wooden houses, men, women, and children sit on creaking iron chairs.

As darkness falls, makeshift barbecues appear on the streets, salsa tapes start to play, and fashions from every decade of the century emerge—evening dresses with slits to here, nip-waisted little '40s numbers, Audrey Hepburn suits, skin-tight tiger-striped flares á la Mick Jagger circa '72, and hemless micros that would have Jane Fonda (circa '68) blushing. Cuba, immune from fashion fascism, can pick and choose what it likes. Meanwhile, musicians arrive on bicycles, carrying instruments on their backs, and in the space of fifteen minutes—as long as it takes night to fall—the town turns into a music buffet.

First there's the brass band under the laurel trees of the Parque Central, screeching and honking its way through "El Bodeguero," the ancient horns buttressed by a bank of African percussion. Then the rumba gets going in the colonnade outside the *casa de cultura*, led

I drifted over as they played a medley of Broadway show tunes, movie themes, and marching songs. I was envious of the oboe player, disarmed by his station in life as nothing more than an afternoon musician for a small-town Caribbean ensemble. I could think of no more noble calling than playing oboe in the Baracoa municipal band.

—Tom Miller, *Trading with the Enemy*

by a team of five drummers and singers and two mesmeric dancers whose feet perform miracles of high-speed intricacy. But the most sought-after action, once you have pushed through the throngs of black mini-dressed *señoritas* dancing to street sound systems, is in the *casa de la trova*.

Every Cuban town has one of these, a kind of village hall cum concert hall with a busy rum bar. On a little stage adorned with rudimentary murals, before several rows of dutiful listeners, the town troubadours vaunt their wares. *Soneros* of all ages, from teen to teetering, test their ability to rouse a crowd. A backing band of bass, guitar, and shaker-scraper-bangers, grinning and dancing in formation, provide a springboard to launch the maestros.

As night wears on and the rum kicks in, the rows of chairs are abandoned in favor of dancing that would shame any Miami salsa slicker. All is well until a cat fight breaks out. A svelte lynx sitting out a song is set upon by a rabid bobcat with a big bunch of black hair. Up goes a chair, down comes the guitarist—the bone of contention, it turns out—and in come the men in blue, who in Cuba are never far away.

Two minutes later we're all out in the street wondering what to do next. Which, this being a Noche de Baracoa, is easily settled: it's up to the 485 Club, where El Ruso is swinging his own *son* band through its routine, spurring on a young lady performing the *pilón* dance. This is really something to see. The girl spins like a top, flexes like a yogi, and in between mimes a pestle-and-mortar grind. Her pirouettes would do fine at the Ballet Rambert, but in addition she has that rhythm, that foot-tapping something for which Cuban DNA holds the key.

This is a night without end, the kind Cubans live for. At some point it dissolves into moonlight on the seafront, rum under a palm tree, a new friend called Lazaro plucking a guitar, cigarettes glowing like stars in the dark. But it never really ends. All that happens is that I wake up and find it is the next day and Baracoa has another week to get through. But somehow it seems it will be easier than the last. That is the *soneros'* everlasting promise.

ROBERT STONE

_* * _*

Havana Then and Now

The more things change, the more things change.

Late one sad Thursday night in October, two Americans
retired to the bar of the old Hotel Inglaterra in Havana. We had
spent the evening in a suburban apartment, watching a speech of
Fidel Castro's on television. At the Inglaterra, among the tiles and
potted palms, an orchestra in Cuban costumes from a forties MGM
musical, faded and shiny with too much dry cleaning, was playing
"Siboney." Three young Germans were cuddling with some local
lovelies in spangles and mascara. A lone, gaunt Irishman sat taking
pictures of the band. The light was yellow and smoky, the streets outside unlit and sinister. A man in dark glasses sat by the entrance door.

One day there may be a market for Soviet bloc nostalgia; movies
will delight audiences by reproducing the hotel lobbies of the late
twentieth-century Communist capitals. At the Inglaterra that night
everything was in place—the bored tourists, the hookers, the hokey
native orchestra, the watcher at the door. Also the hustlers and
black-marketeers in the blacked-out adjoining streets. All that was
missing were the official Gypsies and the Arab thugs chain-smok-
ing under fringed lampshades.

In terms of the big picture, of course, a lot was missing: namely,
the Communist bloc, of which the Inglaterra lobby had become a

melancholy souvenir. It was a rather obvious irony. While Eastern Europe whirled between the future and Bram Stoker's Baedeker, Havana, Cuba, of all places, was imperfectly replicating Warsaw or Bucharest in the age of Brezhnev.

There were a few local touches. *Granma*, the Communist Party daily, was the only newspaper available at the hotel kiosk that evening....

If the walls of the Inglaterra could bear witness, they would attest to countless journalistic misrepresentations, slight liberties with the facts, colorful invocations of reality. During the 1890s, when the American yellow press was hounding the Spanish rulers of Cuba into an unequal war, Hearst's and Pulitzer's star reporters pioneered the Ramos gin fizz at the Inglaterra while calling on heaven to witness Spain's supposed atrocities. And from the hotel the Hearst artist Frederic Remington, lacking the verbal resources of his colleagues, sent the famous complaint to his boss: everything was quiet, Remington told Hearst, and there would be no war. More American schoolboys today probably know Hearst's celebrated reply—that if Remington furnished the pictures, he would furnish the war—than know who said, "Don't give up the ship."

"No man's life, no man's property is safe," wrote the *New York World's* James Creelman, a frequent Inglaterra guest at that time. "American citizens are imprisoned and slain without cause. ...Blood on the roadsides, blood in the fields, blood on the doorsteps, blood, blood, blood!" In the face of these conditions, American reporters could be seen daily on the hotel's terrace, composing their dispatches, having their shoes shined.

The Inglaterra was always the stuff of dreams, celebrated for its formal elegance and its misunderstandings. Insults in the lobby led to duels, wars were conceived, American misconceptions and gaucheries gave way to more exotic ones, Russian or Chinese.

From my own room at the Inglaterra later that night, I could look out on the spires of the Teatro Nacional next door. It took me back, I had been in Havana once before, more than thirty-five years earlier, in another world. The theater's preposterously heroic mass still towered over the old city. There are no white skyscrapers in Havana. That Havana rose elsewhere, in exile across the Straits of Florida. Seeing all that stone heraldry of the theater in the tropical moonlight, Castro's Victor Hugo-like cadences still sounding in my brain, I felt absurdly complicit in Cuba's fortunes.

Havana was my first liberty port, my first foreign city. It was 1955 and I was seventeen, a radio operator with an amphibious assault force in the U.S. Navy....

One of my mentors in those days was our chief radioman, Schultz. I asked him what Havana was like.

"In Havana," Schultz told me, "you can get an around-the-world for a dollar."...

I remember that as we steamed past the ramparts of El Morro Castle, into Havana Bay, an elderly Cuban couple stood applauding on the opposite shore of the narrows, in the park around the Castillo de San Salvador. I reported the incident to Schulz.

"They must own a whorehouse," he said.

They hadn't looked to me like the sort of people who owned a whorehouse. Neither then nor since could I altogether reason out a political position that would lead citizens of Havana to applaud the visit of a U.S. Navy transport. It seemed to auger well, though.

The USS *Chilton* was not an attractive vessel, and the Navy did not offer it for display. We tied up at one of the docks at the south end of Havana Vieja, Old Havana, not far from the railroad station and the old city walls. Walking out of the shadows of the covered wharf and into the bright sunlight of the street, I took my first step

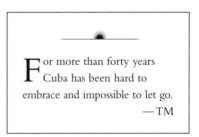

For more than forty years Cuba has been hard to embrace and impossible to let go.
—TM

into that problematic otherness that would so tax our country's moral speculation: the un-American world.

Touts were everywhere and the streets smelled weird. Led by the old hands, a bunch of us made our way to the Two Brothers bar. The Two Brothers was an old-time waterfront saloon with a big square bar, a jukebox, and a fat Central European bartender whom I later liked to imagine was actually B. Traven. It had everything but women. After a great many Cuba libres, it was decided to go to the Barrio Chino, Chinatown, for more serious action....

I still recall the name of the cabdriver who took us to the brothel in the Barrio Chino; it was Rudy Bradshaw, and he was a Jamaican immigrant and spoke English like us. The place was called the Blue Moon. It had a curving wall of translucent glass bricks and a bar with a travel-poster photo of the Havana skyline. Young women came out to be bought drinks and taken upstairs. One of them approached me. I have many recollections of that day, but I can recall neither the woman's face nor her name nor the details of our encounter. I do recall there was a certain amount of laughing it up and pretending affection and also that there was paying. The bill came to quite a lot of money. I presume I was cheated in some way, but everyone was nice.

Afterward we went out into the streets of the Barrio Chino. The Barrio Chino in those days was large, and thousands of Chinese must have lived there....

Many had settled in Havana after working as plantation laborers, and some of them no doubt hoped to slip into the United States, smuggled over by characters like Hemingway's Harry Morgan. There were many good Chinese-Cuban restaurants and curio shops and Chinese markets, but what the world knew best about Havana's Barrio Chino was the Teatro Shanghai. The Shanghai was a blue-movie parlor and burlesque house that was home to the Superman Show, the hemisphere's paramount *exhibición*.

Viewers of *Godfather II* will have some idea of what the staging of the Superman show was like, since part of the act is briefly reproduced in that film. One of the performers was always a nearly naked blonde whose deportment was meant to suggest wholesomeness, refinement, and alarm, as though she had just been spirited unawares from a harp recital at the public library. What on earth, she seemed to be asking the heartless, brutal crowd, am I doing onstage in a Havana pork palace? Another performer was always a large muscular black man who astonished the crowd and sent the blonde into a trembling swoon by revealing the dimensions of his endowment. There were other performers as well, principally a dog and a burro. Suffice it to say that the show at the Teatro Shanghai was a melancholy demonstration of sexism, racism, and speciesism thriving in prerevolutionary Havana. I hasten to add that during much of the time this vileness unfolded I was blessedly asleep, having drunk myself into a state of what might be described as American Innocence....

When I woke up the next day my mood was penitential. At the commencement of liberty, I joined forces with my best buddy, a bookish electronics technician who had the kind of reverence for Ray Bradbury that I had for Hemingway. Abandoning our role as boozing, wenching buccaneers, we resumed existence as high-school dropout teenage savants. Instead of carrying on in the red-light district and having our pictures taken with parrots, we were determined to behave like proper expatriates. We would go and do some of the cool foreign-type things experienced world travelers did, like drinking black coffee very slowly from very small cups. At dusk we set out for the Paseo del Prado, the grand boulevard that runs between the seafront and the Parque Central.

In memory it is probably too good to be true—the crowds ragged, elegant, ebullient, restrained; the graceful women variously haughty or laughingly un-self-conscious; the men in guayaberas and straw hats, gesturing with cigars, greeting one another and parting with quick handshakes and *abrazos*. The coffee in small cups was fine, the air was sensuous and fragrant. The park was full of almond trees and poincianas. There was music everywhere; conga bands filled the street with metal syncopation and the flatted wail of African flutes. There were fortune-telling parakeets. A delicious breeze rustled through the foliage from the seafront. At the time I noted also the beggars blind with untended cataracts or crippled by polio, squatting in doorways. (Unless something unforgettably bad happens, better memories always prevail.)

For me, in 1955, this Havana served as an introduction to the older, unreformed world. In fact, things were changing ruthlessly in the mid-fifties. A line of towering new hotels stood in the Vedado section of the city, a couple of miles west along the seafront from the end of the Paseo del Prado. An extension of the Florida Gold Coast, the Vedado casinos went a long way toward financing the mob's expansion of the mainland. In 1955 they represented someone's bright dream of the future. Reflected in the silver surf, they twinkled at night like the Playboy Philosophy itself. George Raft actually ran the casino at the Capri. Howard Hughes would have been at home atop any one of them.

For the most part, sailors stayed out of Vedado, where their troublesome, penniless presence was unwelcome. At the time, I was struck less by the frivolity of Havana than by its unashamed seriousness. It was then that I first saw the facade of the Hotel Inglaterra. Its formal elegance and polite luxury embodied something I had never quite experienced outside of books. Beside the Inglaterra stood the overdone but monumental Teatro Nacional, a structure besotted with its own aspirations toward high culture, fearlessly risking absurdity, all trumpets, angels, and muses. It was a setting whose pleasure required a dark side—dramas, heroism, sacrifice. All this Spanish tragedy, leavened with Creole sensuality, made Havana irresistible. Whether or not I got it right, I have used the film of its memory ever since in turning real cities into imaginary ones....

Returning to Havana late in 1991, I'd felt by the end of my first day in the city like a petty harbinger, a terminal gringo whose marginal appearance argued the ungood. Standing on the Malecón at dusk, looking toward the lights of Vedado, it was incredible to think that so much time was lost to me, or at least had gone by.... The Vedado lights were fewer and dimmer than the ones I remembered, sacrificed, like so much else, to shortages. It seemed I would miss out on the good times again.

A rush hour of sorts was under way. In the evening's strange storm light, the promiscuous whirl of odd contraptions rattling past the proud street's crumbling arcades had the aspect of a dream. There were Plymouths with Looney Toons curves and fanged, finned De Sotos, not to mention Soviet-made Ladas and the largest number of motorcycle sidecar combos assembled since the blitzkrieg. The defiant posters in front of the old American embassy were exercises in socialist realism, but magical realism seemed more appropriate to the frame. Everything in the early evening's landscape appeared fantastic. The painted slogans above the crumbling buildings were like artifacts from the past. Havana was an exercise in willpower, a dream state being grimly and desperately prolonged....

I spent a week, often accompanied by an American supporter of Fidel who lives part of every year in Cuba, listening to the residents of Havana. In a Vedado apartment an old Spanish Loyalist refugee expressed determined devotion to Castro and the regime. A writer's wife reverently showed us a photograph she owned of Che Guevara, taken while he was ill in the mountains, looking Christ-like and sacrificial. Another woman, the wife of an official, showed me a picture she had taken of Fidel at rest, displaying it with moving motherly affection. Many of those I spoke with were artists and professionals whose attachment to the government ranged from enthusiasm to sympathy to resigned acceptance. In a comfortable farmhouse outside the city I talked with members of a family whose large landholding had been taken over by the state and who had seen numerous relatives flee to the United States. It was clear they felt that the revolution had given them more than it had taken away. The same seemed true of another family I was introduced to in the old slum of the Barrio Chino. Many of the enthusiasts were people of principle who resembled not at all the cynical apparatchiks I used to encounter on visits to Eastern Europe.

Still the mood of the city seemed forlorn and surly. In the downtown streets youths hassled tourists for dollars. Prostitutes were out in numbers near the Vedado hotels, and there were endless lines in front of the ubiquitous "pizzerias" in which scorched cheese concoctions were dispensed, uninteresting but filling meals to augment the rationed goods available in state groceries. In one of those consumer crises that bedevil socialist economies there was an absence of soap in the city, eroding morale among the fastidious *habaneros*, forcing people to wash their clothes, their dishes, and themselves in

Chinese toothpaste. A surprising number of young people, encountered casually on the street, denounced the government in bitter and obscene terms. Many of these youths were poor and of color—the very people who, in theory, benefited most from the revolution....

One aspect of the situation in Havana was brought home about the middle of the week, after I had dinner with two other Americans in town, a man and woman about my age, at Hemingway's old haunt in Habana Vieja, the Floridita. Lobster was on the menu at $35 a claw. There were daiquiris. Musicians played "Guantanamera." Outside, we started walking the streets of Habana Vieja, as romantic a collection of Spanish colonial buildings as the hemisphere affords but, in present circumstances, crumbling and run-down. About two blocks from the Floridita, on the picturesque Calle Obispo, we were jumped and knocked to the pavement by four or five youths who grabbed the woman's bag and disappeared down the cobblestone streets.

The *habanero* tries by all means to be a beautiful, agile animal, a quick creature. The streets of Havana are filled with that agility. The house then is the place where the eyes recover quiet.

So Havana buildings matter for their cracks, for what they leave open to indiscretion, for how much of an entry they allow. They matter for their holes. To say "stroller" in Havana is to say "voyeur."

There's much of the voyeur in those gazers in the street. In Havana one is used to looking at faces, bodies, the way a tourist examines a monument, sometimes even more brazenly. The *habanero* looks at faces with his whole heart and soul.

—Antonio José Ponte, "Eyes of Havana," *Aperture,* Issue 141

It was a fairly noisy business, with shouts and curses and laughter from the kids who had the bag. Police state or not, no cops were forthcoming. If Calle Obispo had a branch of the feared Committee for the Defense of the Revolution, the committee was either in recess or had decided to exclude yanqui visitors from its protection. The few cautious citizens who appeared were curious but fearful. They conveyed a sense of not really requiring our presence and expecting the same. Back at the Floridita, a bartender poured free drinks. Someone called the police who eventually arrived.

Walking into the old Spanish fortress that serves as headquarters for the city police in Habana Vieja, it occurred to me that no tour of the twentieth century could be complete with out a visit to a Communist police station. This one was the traditional precinct green. Behind the desk was a sergeant who looked for all the world like a New York Irish cop, complete with jug ears and an attitude. He was smoking a cigarette under a sign that said NO FUMAR. A few locals were standing against the walls, looking as though they foresaw some unhappy outcome.

One of us pointed out to the sarge that his smoking was a violation. He grinned at this piquant demonstration of North American political correctness and explained that the sign was for people in front of the desk, not for him. There was a second sign behind him that read PROHIBIDO ENFADARSE, "It is forbidden to get mad."

Presumably this was also directed to the public....

Downstairs at the Inglaterra the band played "Siboney," the old stones of the city were bathed in moonlight, the scented air was full of tragedy, heroism, intransigence, sacrifice. The terminal gringos at the Inglaterra were getting it all wrong. "Literature, espionage, revolution, and sex." "Blood, blood, blood!"...

Among the ghosts of the Inglaterra, it is not hard to sympathize with Cuba's refusal of her assigned role in the American Century. A hundred years ago, in the fullness of our gilded age, we came weeping at our own propaganda, the particularly American variation on crocodile tears, reflecting the pity of the eagle for the forsaken lamb. (During the Vietnam era, I heard somebody remark that you could always tell the objects of American benevolence by the hunted look in their eyes.) Fair-haired Protestant heroes, descendants of Drake, we dashed the whip from the cruel Spaniard's hand, banished the sneering inquisitor. We announced the imminence of order, commerce, and light. But, of course, Cuba as the chaotic and materially backward country was useful to us in a variety of ways.

Descendants of Drake, it turned out, and equally of Blackbeard and Henry Morgan. What happened next is well known, and even if we were not at the root of Cuba's problems our proximity and involvement never represented a solution to them. At best we offered Cubans an opportunity to emulate our own pragmatism, optimism, and common sense. At the same time, we offered our worst, a prolonged insult, a dehumanizing, sometimes racist, condescension. Such attitudes are hard to forgive. People take them personally.

We ought not to be surprised that, led by embittered middle-class Spanish-Cubans such as Castro, Cuba took an opportunity to decline our half-hearted offer of middle-class progress. In doing so she was being true to the aesthetic and aristocratic foundations of her culture, embracing faith and heroism, declining mediocrity....

Neither Cubans nor Americans much love irony, but the ironies of the Hotel Inglaterra abound. It is unlikely that Castro, in spite of what he has since said, set out to make Cuba a formal member of the Soviet bloc. He was, as he claimed, a follower of José Martí and thus an opponent of American domination. A great dreamer, he saw himself as a hemispheric figure, a successor to Bolívar. He came to power in the post-Bandung world of Sukarno, Nkrumah, Nasser, Tito. No doubt he entertained the notion that in some Siberian vault a college of wise Marxist gnomes had it all figured out, economically speaking. He himself was a soldier, a knight of faith. He may have been the only Marxist head of state on earth who actually believed in the doctrine. For that he probably deserves to be left holding the bag.

> To the traveler who sets out for the first time to make a tour of the island of Cuba there is seemingly no end of curious things to be seen in city and country.
>
> — *Harper's Weekly*,
> March 6, 1880

★

At the end of my stay, I got tired of the bar at the Inglaterra so I walked down the Prado to the Wonder Bar for a final daiquiri. As Graham Greene reported in *Our Man in Havana*, all the appetites of the Antilles are catered to there. You can get anything, nothing is changed. Errol Flynn is the bartender. Remember him? He claims Hemingway still comes in. And George Raft, too, he says. The music's great, and Havana's just the way I remember.

It's a very romantic place, the Wonder Bar, though louche as can be. It's where Cubans and North Americans meet. Everybody gets what they like, but nobody gets what they deserve. The Cubans are always talking about the United States, and the Americans talk about Cuba. Everyone's an expert and gets everything right. People's eyes are bright with dreams. Everybody's beautiful.

Some people say the Wonder Bar doesn't exist, but don't believe it.

Brooklyn-born Robert Stone is one of America's sturdiest authors. His service in the Navy, which began at age seventeen, followed by involvement in the Beat scene and with Ken Kesey's Merry Pranksters, then observations gleaned from covering Vietnam as a journalist, have given him the background to such works as A Hall of Mirrors *(winner of a William Faulkner Foundation Award),* Dog Soldiers *(winner of the National Book Award),* A Flag for Sunrise, Outerbridge Reach, *and* Damascus Gate, *among other novels. He lives in Westport, Connecticut, and Key West, Florida.*

PART TWO

SOME THINGS TO DO

✦ ✦ ✦

Viva Los Diplomats

The national pastime was never so international.

As Fidel Castro's motorcade passed us on the highway west of Havana, the five black limos seemed to leach the light out of our bus, creating a momentary panic. Our Cuban guide, Rey, riding shotgun, sat straighter in his seat, whispering, "*Madre de Dios.*" Lazaro, our driver, ripped the red-white-and-blue glasses off his face and hurled them into the aisle.

Traffic on Cuba's highways is sparse, so it is not unlikely that el Presidente noticed our bus driver at a time when he was still wearing 3-D glasses, steering with one hand, and holding a Hooters calendar in the other. Nor is it unlikely that Fidel suffered the subliminal impression of several gringos dancing with bottles of *aguardiente* and toasting a sacred figurine—a papier-mâché infielder in a red Cuban uniform—on the dashboard. Fidel rode on. Being ballplayers, we all instinctively lunged to catch Lazaro's glasses in midair. Being slightly drunk, we all missed. Rum was spilled. So was a box of cigars.

In the commotion, someone cried, "Dear God, not the Cohibas!" Another warned, "Keep your hands off the floor, gentlemen, unless you want to get spiked."

Rey, who works for the Cuban government's Department of

Tourism, turned and made a shushing motion. "Don't you understand? That was Him, the Maximum Leader! Or maybe his brother,
Raúl. We never know where they are, or where they will be."

Our winning pitcher studied the motorcade. "Classic defensive
diamond pattern," he observed. "Fidel's probably in the middle car.
Midafternoon, security people are at the peak of their game. Too
late to be hungover, too early to be drunk." Having run for the U.S.
presidency in 1988 on the Rhinoceros ticket along with Hunter S.
Thompson, Bill Lee, the former Red Sox great, was more likely
than the rest of us to know about this kind of thing.

Through the rear window, we all watched as one of the motorcade limos braked briefly. It was as if someone had turned to take a
second look—someone in the middle car.

Lee nodded. "Rey, you think he knows we're here? Or that
we won?"

Rey was handing the 3-D glasses, but not the calendar, back to
Lazaro. "Fidel? Fidel knows everything that happens on this island.
He is a very great man!" Rey flipped to Miss December before he
began to smile. "Believe me, if el Presidente doesn't know you yanquis are here, he soon will."

We didn't go to Cuba expecting to win two out of three baseball games, or to see Fidel's motorcade, or to be blessed and given
sacred beads by a Santería priestess, yet those things and more occurred. We went out of a pure love of the game—though, altruism
being a favorite disguise of the truly selfish, we had hunted around
for a good cause until we found one. We were going to supply baseball gear to a Cuban youth team. But not just any Cuban youth
team. The previous year in Key West, I had met Danilo Arrate
Hernández, director of Cuba's Museo Ernest Hemingway. He told
me that back in the 1950s, Hemingway, who was living in the
Havana suburb of San Francisco de Paula, founded the Gigi Stars, a
youth-baseball team nicknamed after his son Gregory.

"One day, Ernest caught local boys throwing rocks at his mango
trees," Danilo said. "When he told them they should be throwing
balls instead, the boys explained that they had no money for base-

balls. That was true, though it was also true that the boys liked to eat mangos." Hemingway bought enough uniforms and equipment to outfit a team, and he sometimes drove players to games in his Cadillac convertible.

"Sadly," Danilo added, "the community of San Francisco de Paula is very poor. When Ernest died, so did his team."

That story gave us our inspired excuse. Why not collect equipment for the kids, fly to Cuba, and restart Hemingway's ball club?

Granddaughter Mina Hemingway, who lives in Florida, seconded our charitable mission statement with an official letter of introduction and congratulations. Danilo was delighted by the proposal—"I am answering your communication full of happiness," his letter started—and he got in touch with Tom Robertson of Associated Travel Consultants in Courtenay, British Columbia, which packages baseball tours of Cuba for amateur players. Perhaps Robertson could arrange for transportation and a guide, and schedule a few games for us? Robertson immediately went to work setting the itinerary. "We're not just discussing a destination," Bill Lee told me last March when I called to invite him. "I think we're tapping into a very powerful karmic dynamic: literature, baseball, Communism—plus I hear the island distillers make excellent rum. My fantasy has always been to get Castro out on a few slow curves, then bodysurf the Bay of Pigs. Cuba's made for left-handers. We've got to go."

Lee had taken a team to play in Cuba once before, and it was his pledge to join us in our current venture that motivated the guys on my Roy Hobbs League team to rally to the point of obsession. Actually, anyone who plays in a league founded for aging wannabes and named for the fictional hero of *The Natural* is obsessed to begin with. But our goals did become loftier. Instead of collecting gloves, balls, and bats for one youth team, we wondered, why not make a few more calls to round up enough for four teams? And certainly we should take at least one set of catcher's equipment. And spikes—the kids would need proper shoes.

"Know what would be nice?" one of us mused. "To have simple

t-shirts made, with a team name on the front. Nothing fancy, but not cheap—that would be an insult to the game."

Three months later, we would leave for Cuba with sixty new major-league-style uniforms.

Of course, our financial requirements grew with our acquisition list, and we decided we would need a sponsor. But where could we find a business run by people big-hearted enough to make this kind of donation without any expectation of a tax break or benefiting from improved community relations?

Hooters came immediately to mind. The chain of hugely successful sports bars was founded in Florida by quirky friends of mine who are, in fact, from Iowa, a state not known for sharp edges or hard questions.

"What do we get out of this?" Hooters executives Champ Regnier and Dave Lageschulte asked after I requested a few thousand dollars.

I thought for a moment. "We'll take your chicken wings with us and be the first to eat them in Havana. I'll get a cooler, carry them on the plane, and document the whole event. We'll give you a photo for your wall."

Regnier and Lageschulte, excited about the deal, wrote us a check.

Prior to boarding Cubana Aviación out of Nassau, we took inventory. Most of the equipment came from Bartley's Sporting

> When the government abolished all professional sports on the island in 1960, viewing them as counter to the principles of the Revolution, more than eighty years of Cuban professional baseball came to a halt. Selling baseball players, Fidel believed, was a crude manifestation of the worst elements of capitalism, akin to slavery, and he referred to professional baseball as *la pelota esclava*. For Fidel, the first Serie Nacional in 1961–1962 was *el triunfo de la pelota libre sobre la pelota esclava* (the triumph of free baseball over slave baseball).
>
> —Milton H. Jamail, *Full Count: Inside Cuban Baseball*

Goods, in Florida; the rest we collected from Little Leagues and our own garages and rec rooms. In cardboard boxes, we'd packed the new uniforms, eight sets of catcher's gear, three hundred baseballs, seventy-five pairs of spikes, two dozen aluminum bats, a mess of fielder's gloves and batting gloves, six cartons of new hats, a crate of Hooters calendars, dozens of Hooters t-shirts and caps—plus a hundred orders of chicken wings with blue cheese and two dozen orders of Buffalo shrimp with hot sauce on the side. And curly fries.

"This is a metaphor for free enterprise and the entire American system," Bill said when he saw all the goods. "Wholesale capitalism, gross excess, and exploitation of the masses. The calendars alone could cause fighting in the streets. We're not just starting a baseball league, we're ideological-plague carriers. We may be the final nail in the coffin of Communism."

I said to our teammates, "Didn't I tell you this was going to be fun?"

The customs officer at José Martí International surveyed the stack of boxes and said something in Spanish, which we interpreted as "Your luggage smells delicious. May I take a look?"

Of course he could. On Fidel's island, people in uniform can look at anything they want, anytime they want. I knew this because this was my sixth trip to Cuba in the last twenty years. Not that I'm an expert; my visits had always been lazy-gringo samplers, though one did include twelve days in Mariel Harbor during the refugee boatlift of 1980. Mariel was a dangerous place, it was a dangerous time, and the pissed-off attitude of the uniforms more than reflected the combat-ready footing of two ideologies in conflict. The brutal poverty of the country post-Soviet Union—Cuba's "special period" in Castro-speak—has softened some but remains pronounced.

This time, there was nothing at all sinister about the Cuban officials. They met us upon our arrival, seemed pleased to see Americans, and kept only a peripheral eye on us, as if they expected us to do something amusing. We obliged by juggling baseballs and giving away small gifts, but not the chicken wings. Several officials asked for a taste, but we had promises to keep.

Outside the terminal, Reynaldo "Rey" Sarenzo, forty-three, and Lazaro Peña, thirty-two, were waiting in the nearly new fifteen-seat Toyota that, for the next week, would serve as our rolling home. Its most compelling amenity was a massive cooler full of shaved ice, bottles of Cuban beer and cola, and a case of seven-year-old Havana Club rum. Once we'd taken seats, Rey, whose English was excellent enough to convey his likable, smart-ass sense of humor, opened a bottle to toast us and "the greatest game in the world!" But first he dumped an ounce or more of rum directly on the floor.

"For the old and dead ones," he explained.

It was the first of many rum offerings made on that little bus.

I'd done enough reading to understand his ceremony. The island's most widely practiced religion is Santería, an Afro-Cuban belief, similar to Haiti's voudou, in which it's common to make gifts of alcohol and tobacco to deities and dead ancestors. The religion is so widely accepted that predictions of Santería priests, the *babalawos*, are reported in Cuba's state newspaper. Many believe that Santería plays a prominent part in Castro's political decisions and that he could not remain in power if not for the backing of the *babalawos*.

The first chance I got, I took Rey aside and asked if he could introduce us to a Santería holy person. The entire flight down, I'd listened to Bill rave about the quality of Cuban baseball, and I'd understood that we were about to have our asses served to us on a variety of platters. The simple fact that the better team does not always win, however, is one of the game's great charms. It also suggests to me that baseball has far more in common with alchemy than it does with chemistry. With its strange tertiary multiples and mirrored pyramidal shapes, baseball inspires religious considerations that nonplayers might call superstitious. I figured that any blessing couldn't hurt us. I wasn't being flippant or disrespectful in asking; I was serious.

Even so, Rey's response was chilly. "A Santería person? I wouldn't even know where to find one."

The chill didn't last, though. As Lazaro drove us toward Havana, we spotted kids playing baseball in an open field. They were using a carved limb as a bat and a stone wrapped in tape for a ball. Day after day, as we toured the country, we would witness variations on the same scene. The absence of equipment does not make the game impossible for those who love it, and no one loves baseball like a Cuban.

"Rey, pull over!"

He was slow to understand. Why would we want to watch children playing?

But that was exactly what we wanted to do. A familiar point of discussion among my teammates is that in the States it's rare to see kids playing baseball just for fun. Either games are organized by adults or the fields lie empty. Games chosen by kids tend to rely on indoor joysticks.

At the side of the road, we sat for a minute or two before we cracked a box and selected a bat, some balls, and a few caps. The game stopped as we got off the bus; the kids froze as we approached. They found their feet, though, when we lobbed a ball toward them, and then they swarmed us.

We handed out the gear without explanation and drove away. It became our favorite thing to do in Cuba, giving us a Lone Ranger-esque feeling of pure devotion to baseball. But no one was af-

On Calle 292, a block from Matanzas Communist Party headquarters, a photo of a familiar baseball player on a bedroom wall evokes one of my favorite *cha-cha-chas* from childhood. Written by Enrique Jorrín, "*Miñoso al bate*" (Miñoso at Bat) is about the stellar Cuban player of the Chicago White Sox. The refrain of the song goes like this: "*Cuando Miñoso batea de verdad/la bola baila hasta cha-cha-cha*" (When Miñoso really swings true, even the ball dances *cha-cha-cha*).

—Alan West-Durán, "Lilting Long Ball"

fected as deeply by the first stop as Rey and Lazaro. Both had tears in their eyes as Rey gushed, "We are men, but we also have hearts!

Clearly, you are men with hearts, too. You must drink this bottle of rum to celebrate your generosity!"

Perhaps Rey and Lazaro had nothing to do with it, but the next day, outside the Ambos Mundos, our hotel in Old Havana, we encountered a middle-aged woman in white robes, whom we would later learn was a highly respected Santería priestess. She gave us each a strand of red-and-black beads, and then led us to an outdoor market where we found our papier-mâché baseball player. The woman refused money, but rummaged through our wares until she found what she desired in trade: three Hooters t-shirts.

In Viñales, in the mountains of western Cuba, we could look down from our hotel's pool bar onto the red-tile roofs and dirt streets of the farm village where we were to play our first game. It lay in a long valley bounded by rain forest bluffs and copper-colored fields. The ball diamond was across the river, hidden by mango trees and a grove of coconut palms.

Bill was sitting beneath the thatched chickee, holding the papier-mâché ballplayer we were already calling Changó. In the other hand, he held a red chili pepper. We'd stopped along the way and picked a bagful from a farmer's garden, surprised that Cuban restaurants, unlike Hooters, did not offer hot sauce. He took a bite of the chili, chased it with half a beer, then used his hand as a fan, saying, "You know why Puerto Rico and Southern California produce so many pitchers? All the spicy food. It puts a fire in your belly and protects your elbow from harm. You ever hear of Pancho Villa having a sore arm? Nope. He could have pitched to a hundred if he'd dodged that bullet. By the way…" he swallowed the rest of the chili and took another gulp of beer, "does anyone here really give a shit about winning?"

Of course we didn't. Why else would we be sunning ourselves, drinking *mojitos*, and soaking in the pool with only an hour to go before game time? He nodded. "We need to pick up at least four more players to field a team. I've got this theory that every healthy Cuban male can play baseball, so it really doesn't matter who we pick. Plus, I kind of go by names. You know how certain guys have a baseball name and you just know they're going to be great? Like Cesar Geronimo or Bernie Carbó—those kind of names. The manager of our hotel, guess what his name is: Angel Cordero. He's got to be a shortstop, right?"

Viñales Stadium is a horseshoe of pink cement and rusting fence posts that frames a field on which burlap sacks serve as bases. When our bus pulled up, there were so many people milling around that we thought our game must have fallen on the same day as the local fair.

But no, they'd come to see us play the Viñales Veterans. There had to be three hundred people, many of them schoolkids released from class to watch the big game. There were lots of cops and soldiers, too, which lent an officious, nervous air.

The Viñales players wore piecemeal uniforms from several teams and many eras, but they could play. They could all play. On that day, though, we played pretty well ourselves. Terwilliger set the tone with his first at-bat, hitting a 420-foot cannon shot over the center-field wall. Everyone in the stands stood and clapped as he rounded the bases. That quickly, we had bona fide fans.

Then Bill took the mound and set the first three batters down in order, throwing mostly fastballs but also two monstrous curves. If you doubt that there is a quantum talent gap between anyone who has ever played in the major leagues and the rest of us, it's probably because you've never caught for or hit against one of them. Behind me, the umpire kept count of strikes and balls by using five stones as a kind of abacus.

We all hit, and continued to hit and score runs throughout the game, while Bill dominated from the mound. We were having fun, and the Cubans seemed to be, too. There was only one uneasy moment: The Viñales pitcher was a big guy with good velocity, a Castro beard, and a quick temper. When he finally got a hit off of Bill, he called our pitcher a particularly unattractive name from second base: *maricón*.

None of us spoke much Spanish, but you can't play baseball in Florida without knowing the meaning of *maricón*.

"It's Señor Maricón to you, asshole!" first baseman Stu retorted.

Perhaps Stu's insistence on proper forms of address opened things up for the spirit of civility and fun that took over. We won, 11–4, which didn't seem to be a big deal until Rey pointed out that no American amateur team had won in Cuba since Batista heard the tanks rolling into Havana. Our local ringers had accounted for two of the runs, but we'd have taken credit for the victory even if they had scored them all. A team's a team; plus, for old ballplayers, any excuse to have a party is good enough. We weren't going to allow impulsive thoughts of fairness or maturity to spoil it. We sat around the field sharing beer with the Viñales players, who seemed genuinely pleased for us, even the Castro clone. When we stripped off our jerseys during the cooldown, they immediately noticed the beads we wore and pointed, nodding as if it all suddenly made sense. *"Sí! Santería! Santería!"*

Their reverence lent our little Changó additional credence. We placed him on the dashboard altar of the bus and made many offerings. Seeing Fidel's motorcade seemed a stunning affirmation of the war god's power, and symbolic, too: two diverse cultures, traveling in opposite directions, meet in unexpected apogee, then separate at speed. As one of us said, "Hello, Hooters wings; goodbye, revolution."

We took the party up the mountain to our hotel.

Capitán San Luis Stadium was home to one of the island's finest teams, Pinar del Río. Yet its condition seemed to reflect a strange indifference or vacancy of pride that didn't mesh with the passionate people we'd met in a nation that idolizes baseball.

The neglect of the stadium could have had nothing to do with economics. With Cuba's state-controlled workforce, it doesn't take money to cut the grass, rake a field, or mop feces off the floor. The decay was not recent; it seemed elemental, like the odor of an unhappy home. In the entire stadium, only the outfield billboards were in top condition: THE REVOLUTION LIVES IN OUR HEARTS! EXERCISE, NOT OBESITY! YOUR CHILDREN MUST ATTEND SCHOOL!

Our opposing team, a much better squad than the one from Viñales, was unaffected by the sloppy conditions. There were several former national-team players on its roster, including Porfinio

Pérez. Pérez has pitched in eight national championships and is known as the Man with a Hundred Moves for his many different windups. At fifty-three he still throws in the mid–eighties, but people come to see his theatrics. In one windup, he double-pumped, held the ball behind his right shoe as he squared himself to the plate, and then made the ball magically reappear a microsecond before he threw. In another, he tossed the ball up under his left leg as he drove homeward, caught the ball with his right hand, and delivered.

I flied out to center my first time up and decided I didn't care to bat against Señor Hundred Moves again. So I walked over to the Pinar del Río dugout and asked if our teams could switch catchers.

Of course. They would be honored.

Catching for Pérez was one of the highlights, not of just the trip, but of my undistinguished ballplaying career. We never discussed signs; we didn't have to. He knew exactly what I wanted and where I wanted it. If I set up outside, he'd drill my glove an inch or two off the black every time. If I set up inside, he'd put the ball right on the hitter's hands or just below the knees. He had four pitches, including a big curve that rivaled Bill's. I stayed behind the plate, a catcher for the Cubans, for eight innings. We beat the gringos, 7–2.

The next day, with me back catching for my countrymen against the same team, we were humiliated for five brutal innings. Every batter they sent to the plate crushed the ball. We couldn't get an out.

In the stands were hundreds of people who, embarrassed and rooting for us, took up the chant "*Ca-na-da!...Ca-na-da!*" They were operating under the mistaken assumption that anyone who played as badly as we did had to be from sled-dog country.

Down 7–0 in the sixth inning, Rey and Lazaro came to our rescue. They went to the bus and returned with Changó and the entire cooler of beer and rum. Rey filled a shot glass for Changó, saying, "You are not beaten, my friends, you're just thirsty!"

He was right. On the mound, Stu's anti-inflammatories apparently kicked in, and he found his fastball. Then we began to hit, each and every one of us. In the field we could suddenly do no wrong. If someone were to tell me that scientists had developed a supersensitized voltage meter that registers changes in baseball momentum, I would believe it. No one who plays the game can doubt its galvanic shifts. The score changed gradually—7–2, then 7–5—and finally we had a huge rally in the top of the last inning. The final score was 12-7, us.

Our fans continued to chant, "*Ca-na-da!...Ca-na-da!*" until Matt stood on the dugout and admitted what we would not admit before: "*We're Americans! U-S-A! U-S-A!*"

Being unsophisticated by nature and ballplayers by choice, we were unprepared for the diplomacy required of us the next day at the Museo Hemingway. We knew we were expected to deliver our boxes of equipment for the children of San Francisco de Paula. We didn't know we were expected to be at a formal ceremony attended by members of the Communist Party and the region's department of sports.

Danilo had arranged the whole affair, demonstrating a faith in us that we did not deserve. The morning got off to a shaky start. We'd been up very late, squiring Changó around Havana and making the usual offerings.

Some of us felt unwell.

Worse, we'd gone eight days without doing laundry. Even if we had brought appropriate clothing, that clothing would no longer have been appropriate.

Danilo wasn't available when we arrived, so we proceeded to open our boxes and spread out so much gear that the steps of Hemingway's house looked like the residue of a sports-warehouse explosion.

Which is when Danilo showed up. "We've not yet completed the documents," he said, and ushered us into an air-conditioned room where a half dozen very somber Cuban officials sat waiting. They did not seem reassured by our appearance. Two of them made un-emotional speeches, which Danilo translated. I made a stumbling declaration, which I hope Danilo edited. We sat sweating in the silence while forms and pens were circulated.

"A toast to children," Danilo said, after we'd signed papers to transfer the equipment. We all drank.

After drinking more and signing more—the papers to officially found the Hemingway Baseball League—one of us proposed "a toast to baseball, the only game worth a damn!"

The mood began to lighten.

One of the officials was about our age and had played on the Gigi Stars. "Next year," he told us, "I'll have all the Gigi Stars back together. We'll play a game, and then we'll watch the children play a game." He smiled and warned, "You'd better bring a very good team!"

Half an hour later, some of us were playing catch beneath Hemingway's mango trees. The rest of us were showing party members the proper way to use 3-D glasses while viewing Hooters calendars.

They caught on quickly.

Randy Wayne White is author of the best-selling Doc Ford novels, and a contributing editor to Men's Journal *and* Outside *magazines. He was a skiff guide on Sanibel Island, Florida, for many years and now lives on Pine Island where he has given up fishing to play men's baseball.*

CRISTINA GARCÍA

✦ ✦ ✦

Slow-Motion Island

*The author leads us through an innocent and lovely land,
where grapefruit has the power of romance and the native
dance is named for the sound of shuffling feet.*

THE MOUNTAINS ARE WHAT DEFINE THE PLACE. THEY ARE VISIBLE
in almost every direction, black and humpbacked, darkly polished at
dusk. They are modest-looking mountains, and no one but a ge-
ologist would know by their appearance that they are mostly marble. After you realize that the mountains are made of marble, you
start to notice that almost everything else is, too—that there is a
quiet luster to the island.

The roads of the Isle of Youth, the largest of Cuba's many off-
shore islands, glitter with marble gravel. The floors of even the most
unassuming offices and restaurants gleam with the polished stone.
Solid marble tables, tables requiring a pair of burly men to move
them, tables you might see in the boardroom of a Fortune 500 company, are a fairly common sight here. In the employee cafeteria of a
local marble quarry, even the lighting fixtures—glossy, foot-long
cylinders suspended from the ceiling—are made of marble.

This casual cohabitation with luxury gives this island a charm-
ingly modest air, like that of a privileged, yet unspoiled child.
Visiting the island, in fact, is like going back in time to a more
innocent Cuba, slower-paced and neighborly, immune to the daily
pressures of survival and the quest for the almighty dollar.

I'd been to Cuba twice before, to visit relatives in Havana and to the bustling seaside town of Guanabo. If the tempo of life in these locales is akin, say, to cruising in a '57 Chevy, imagine the Isle of Youth as something of a leisurely ride on a sleepy donkey. I had expected slow, maybe even slower. What I found was *slowest*. Here the sight of someone in a hurry would be cause enough to make you stop whatever you're doing.

I remembered a story my mother once told me. She said that when she first came to New York City, after a relatively quiet life on a provincial cattle ranch in Cuba, and saw people running up the stairs of the subway, she anxiously assumed that a massive underground fire was sweeping the city. On the Isle of Youth, the atmosphere and pace were so seductive that I took for granted such lilting tranquility went hand-in-hand with incurable happiness.

Along the streets of the main city of Nueva Gerona, horse-drawn carts ambled shoulder-to-shoulder with vintage cars and squeaking bicycles. Everyone, it seemed, was eating ice cream. I stopped at a gas station that doubled as a convenience store and picked up the day's flavor: a strawberry so sweet it made my teeth ache. Children were everywhere, many in bright school uniforms. The parks were clean and neatly tended. Only the hibiscus assaulted the visual harmony with riotously clashing reds and pinks.

Part of an archipelago of mostly tiny islands, the Isle of Youth lies about thirty miles off the southwestern coast of Cuba. In the last five hundred years the island has been known by at least a dozen names: Camarcó (as it was once called by its original Indian inhabitants), La Evangelista (*gracias a* Christopher Columbus), and Treasure Island (for pirate treasures reputedly buried there). A century later more ominous names were in usage: Isla de los Deportados and La Siberia de Cuba, because of the infamous penitentiary built to house the country's hardest criminals and political prisoners, including a young Fidel Castro. For many years it was know as Isla de Pinos. But in 1978 it was renamed Isla de la Juventud, or Isle of Youth, at least in part because of the many international schools Castro built on the island.

The island, by whatever name, is shaped like a right-handed mitten woven in tropical greens, the solemn gray-black of its mountains, and the rusty-brown shade of its rich, citrus-producing soil. Most of its 90,000 inhabitants live in the northern part of the island; the southern part is largely swamp-land, home to crocodiles, more than a hundred species of birds, and myriad other wildlife.

While the island is undeniably beautiful, its beaches are not the most resplendent, the nightlife is barely existent (unless you consider as entertainment the highly interpretive Far Eastern music at the local Chinese restaurant), and its cultural amenities are few. Yet the islanders seem to feel no compulsion to measure up against other places. This wasn't complacency, I realized, merely an easy confidence. After all, the islanders here were born with marble spoons in their mouths.

Even the island's native music, the *sucu-sucu*, is a slower, countrified version of salsa. One afternoon, as I sat poolside at a hotel, a local trio started up its carefree rhythms. I asked the singer about the origins of the name.

"Watch my feet," he retorted.

The *sucu-suco* was created here on the Isle by native *pineros, orientales, gallegos,* and maybe African slaves had something to do with it, too. So all these people together, with their idiosyncrasies and their isolation, created a new rhythm that wasn't a *son montuno* or a *guaracha* but something different. It began evolving in the last century, because my great-grandmother told my father how they did it then, when they called it rumba or *rumbita.* Then around 1910, people here began calling it *cotunto,* but, by the twenties, all those names had disappeared in favor of *sucu-suco.* Because, at the at time, lots of Americans were coming to Cuba and especially to the Isle—their project was to grab the Isle—and they heard this music they called *suc-suc* from the sound the dancers made. Pretty soon it became *sucu-suco.*

—Mongo Rives, quoted in *Cuba's Island of Dreams,* by Jane McManus

I thought it an odd response, but just as I was beginning to feel extremely foolish, the revelation hit me with the force of a punch-line belatedly understood. *Sucu-sucu. Sucu-sucu.* It as a shuffling sound his sandals made as he danced. *Sucu-sucu. Sucu-sucu.* All the dancing islanders made the same shuffling sound.

There is much to boast about on the Isle of Youth even if the islanders themselves practice some self-promotional restraint. The one exception may be their monument to a renowned Holstein, which, with remarkable revolutionary fervor, produced a record 240 pounds of milk on a single day in 1982. The statue is massive, the cow's expression sublimely benign. It is an unabashedly favorite island landmark and a popular destination for school trips.

These days even the former prison is a pleasant diversion. When I visited El Presidio Modelo, goats and lambs were grazing peacefully on the grounds, and the bars of the cells had been pried off. The setting was so serene, a picnickers' paradise, that it was difficult for me to imagine its violent past. Built in the 1930s during the brutal dictatorship of Gerardo Machado, the circular prison was patterned on a maximum security penitentiary in Joliet, Illinois. After the revolution, authorities tried to convert it into a polytechnical school, but the transformation didn't take. "Too many ghosts," a toothless groundskeeper matter-of-factly informed me. "The students complained they couldn't concentrate on their studies."

It is ironic, perhaps, that many of the schools and dormitories dotting the countryside are considerable more depressing-looking than the prison.

A few thousand foreigners study on the island, down from a peak of nearly twenty thousand almost two decades ago. Students used to come here from all over the world, particularly from countries where Cuba had special interests, such as Angola, Mozambique, and Nicaragua. Since the dismantling of the former Soviet Union, and Cuba's subsequent economic hardships, the island can no longer afford so many mouths to feed. As a result, the nightclubs, sports fields, and subsidized restaurants on the island are considerably quieter than they used to be.

One night at a Chinese restaurant (where the average meal costs two dollars), an Angolan student asked me for a light for his cigar. He told me—in perfectly accented Cuban Spanish—that it was his fifth and last year studying agronomy in Cuba.

"What are you going to do after you graduate?" I asked, finishing my chow mein.

"Going home to plant yams." He didn't seem particularly pleased with the idea.

It was never a problem for me to decide what to drink on the Isle of Youth. At breakfast my first morning, I ordered grapefruit juice. It was absolutely delicious, sweet, and thirst quenching, nothing at all like the grapefruit juice I remember accompanying my high school cottage cheese diets. I complimented the waitress and asked her for another. From then on, grapefruit juice was automatically served to me everywhere I went on the island. I began to get a little paranoid. Had word gotten around? There were other beverage options. How could everyone assume I loved grapefruit juice?

I never did find out, but after awhile I stopped fighting it. And so grapefruit juice it was—for breakfast, lunch, dinner. Snacks, too. Gallons of the stuff. A veritable river of grapefruit juice. I began to think I must have enough vitamin C stored in my body to carry me well into the new millennium.

Need I say that grapefruit is the most widely cultivated crop on the island? It comes in white, red, or pink, with or without seeds. In addition to the ubiquitous juice, local industries produce grapefruit wine, grapefruit vinegar, and grapefruit whiskey, as well as a native brand of grapefruit *aguardiente*, a liquor so potent it made my scalp prickle for a solid hour. There are groves of mangoes and bananas and coconut trees, too, and fields of *boniato*, a sweet potato-like tuber, all of which scent the air with a heady redolence.

At the turn of the last century, following the Spanish-American War, many Americans settled on the island, believing it would soon be annexed by the United States. A number of these immigrants set up grapefruit plantations, and one of these citrus growers was the maternal grandfather of American poet Hart Crane. Crane himself first visited the island in 1916 as a teenager and wrote numerous poems about his impressions of the tropics. (Sixteen years later, as he left the island on a ship after another visit, he jumped overboard to his death.)

I found no trace of the Crane family at the American cemetery on the outskirts of Nueva Gerona, now a weed-choked grove of humble Yankee headstones and quiet epitaphs. Nothing at all like the Cuban cemetery on the other side of town, with its elaborate marble tombstones, marble mausoleums, and florid marble pledges of eternal love. On the Isle of Youth, even the poorest of the poor can afford a sumptuous headstone.

On the road to the west coast I stopped off in La Victoria, the island's first planned community. The simple homes looked clean and freshly painted, each with its own porch for after-dinner rocking and chatting. Revolutionary slogans were painted on many of the walls. My personal favorite: *Coño, se pudo*, which roughly means, *Dammit, we did it*. Regardless of one's personal point of view about the Cuban revolution and its aftermath, you do have to admire a certain pride.

The farther west on the island I went, the more people assumed I was there for the scuba diving near Siguanea Bay. I'm not a diver, barely a snorkeler, but for the first time in my life I regretted not being able to venture deeper. To hear scuba divers talk about the spectacular coral reef is to suffer wet suit envy.

"It's like a miniature Great Barrier Reef," a German diver told me. "The colors are from another planet."

I felt condemned to the diluted spectrum of the terrestrial. The young lady on the German diver's lap, a good-looking *mulata* wearing a neon-green bikini and a marble medallion around her neck, seemed bored by our conversations. She obviously took the island's natural riches for granted.

The next day I decided to brave La Ciénaga de Lanier in the south. A dismal, potholed road cut its way through the mosquito-infested swamp. My driver told me there was only a slim chance of spotting a crocodile or a *jutía* (a sizable, tree-climbing rodent) since they mostly come out at dawn. Nevertheless, lathering on the insect repellent, I kept my eyes peeled.

I had no luck on the crocodile front, but I did see, in order of impressiveness: a wild boar, a palpitating iguana, several oxen recalcitrantly blocking our path, a fleeing deer, scurrying tangerine-colored crabs, and always, the heavy gliding presence of the *tiñosas*, the black vultures permanently overhead. I was mesmerized, too, by what my driver called *amaziles*, slender swamp trees with a reflective, coppery bark, that set the landscape aflame with shimmering light.

My driver had promised to escort me to the Punta del Este caves deep in the southern swampland. There are no markers on the road that tell you where to park, no admission charges, no warnings not to touch ancient pictographs. The caves were so primitive and pristine, in fact, that it was easy for me to imagine that I'd discovered them myself. Small bats flapped by, disturbed by my presence. An enormous beehive, humming indifferently, was firmly embedded in the ceiling of the front cave.

Once my eyes grew accustomed to the darkness, a series of extraordinary paintings came into focus. Concentric circles in red and black, serpentine lines, arrows, and triangles covered the walls and ceilings of the cave's many chambers. Interspersed with human and animal figures, the pictographs are believed to be a rendering of an advanced celestial calendar designed more than three thousand years ago by the Ciboney Indians.

A few more miles down the swamp road, a gradual curve of beach materialized, picture-perfect against the aquamarine ocean— a setting complete with an old dock, a decaying rowboat, and a cluster of coconut palms, I pulled off my shoes and waded hip-deep into the sea. It was January. The water was cold by local standards, but to me it was bath water warm rippling with the softest of breezes like certain memories. I wanted to stay, to float there forever.

Reluctantly, I got back in the car and made my way toward Cocodrilo, a fishing village on the southwest coast settled by Cayman islanders in the early 1900s. The cliffs were black and volcanic-looking on this side of the island, the sea a deeper shade of blue-green. Piglets rested in the shade beneath the thatch-roofed houses, precarious on short stilts.

One of the blue-eyed descendants of the remaining dozen or so Cayman islander families ran a turtle-hatching station on a promontory overlooking the sea. His name was Jackson, and he was sixty-five years old, although his tanned, weatherworn face looked appreciably older.

"I still speak English with my mother," Jackson said, his whole face crinkling as he smiled. But the language, he added, is dying out, succumbing to the rapid-fire Spanish of the Cubans.

Then he reached elbow-deep into one of the shallow, open-air tanks and pulled out a green turtle for my inspection. He remembered the days before the sea turtles needed government protection.

"These have the best meat," he said. "We used to make a good soup from them."

Back at my hotel outside Nueva Gerona, the pool beckoned. There was a live band, and many locals stopped by for a beer and a *sucu-sucu* or two. The rhythm was infectious. It was virtually impossible not to shuffle my feet beneath my seat.

I ate lobster, a local specialty—cheap and plentiful—and the ubiquitous side dish: fried plantains, the ripe, sweet ones known as *maduros* or the crispy green ones called *tostones*. For dessert, what else? Candied grapefruit.

One evening, I took a walk along the Río las Casas and watched the fishermen return after a long day at sea. It felt good to watch people and greet them—and have them watch and greet me in return. More than anywhere I've visited, the Isle of Youth slowed down time, opened my eyes, and permitted me to see again without preconceptions.

Near the end of my stay I bought a small, marble ashtray on the island. I don't smoke, but now at home I like to run my fingers along its edges, rub its smooth shallow dish. The ashtray sits on my nightstand, a bit of casual island splendor, a reminder of everything I'm missing.

Cristina García travels almost exclusively with her daugther, Pilar. Together they've ridden elephants in Vietnam, sailed Lake Titicaca, and rumba'd in Cuba. She also contributed "Simple Life" in Part One.

STEPHEN SMITH

✦ ✦ ✦

The House of Tango

In Cuba, learning to dance can be as
furtive and elusive as life itself.

I CAN'T REMEMBER HOW MANY TIMES I WALKED PAST THE EMPTY Roseland supermarket between Calle Aguila and Calle Galiano before the House of Tango materialized on the opposite side of the street. It wasn't the sort of place you would think you could miss, with its pictures of brilliantined men, and the cry of a balladeer hanging in the air. Yet I had never seen it before, and could find no reference to *la casa del tango* in four guidebooks. In the parlor of the House of Tango, a small elderly man was sitting on a stool beside a gramophone player. He was resting his head on a speckled hand. Two highly made-up old ladies were sharing a couch with a younger, bearded man who was reading *Granma*. The four of them were listening companionably to a tango tune as though they were sitting out a number at a *thé dansant*. They were surrounded by images of glamorous women and matinee idols. Publicity stills and record sleeves decorated all four walls and the ceiling. There was a portrait of a diva, Libertad Lamarque. Her diamanté necklace, earrings and hairband were all real, or at least 3-D: her jewelry included solid nuggets of paste and her hair band was whiskery with feathers. But the star who had the best showing was a man with slick-backed hair and a horsy mouth—a swarthy George Formby.

101

He was Carlos Gardel, the elderly man told me. He was an Argentinean singer, the master of the tango. Everywhere you looked, you saw his face. There was even a likeness of Gardel behind the dial in the middle of the telephone. "He was born in France and raised in Buenos Aires," said the man. "That is his scarf and that is his hat." A length of white silk and what looked like a shiny chimney pot were composed on top of an upright piano. The old man was a musician himself, he said. His name was Edmundo—like Edmundo Ross, the bandleader, you thought. You pictured him on stage in younger days, dapperly captured in a single spotlight, the music stands behind him hung with tabards on which his monogram was picked out in lamé.

I had always thought of tango as an Argentinean invention, but Borges called Havana "the mother of tango." The Cuban writer Guillermo Cabrera Infante claimed that a faithful biography of the dance would document spells in Cádiz and Montevideo; but its birthplace had been Cuba, he said. I asked Edmundo about tango. "It's poetry, it's kindness, it's tragedy," he said all at once. "It is the Bible of life. In turn, Gardel is the God, he's my God. He's also *Cristo*." Edmundo lifted his eyes to the glossy ceiling.

There was one particular picture of Gardel, said Edmundo. It was a large, damp-eyed study which Edmundo had had framed. It hung above chests of drawers which were full of mug shots and biographical details of famous tango artists, arranged in alphabetical order. Edmundo often spoke to this picture of Gardel, he confided. The twenty-fourth of the month would be the anniversary of the singer's death. He had perished in an air crash in Colombia in 1935, on his way to concert dates in Cuba. I thought of Glenn Miller, Buddy Holly—the faint-making Gardel had been the original rock 'n' roll air fatality.

"*¡El tango es Gardel!*" declared Edmundo with sudden heat. The Argentinean singer sang to women, to love. In a quavering voice, Edmundo started to sing. "The day you love me…" He was seventy years old. He had spent fifty years in show business, a humble servant of the tango, but also a comedian. He had been collecting tango records and memorabilia for fifty years, and had founded The

House of Tango thirty years ago. His life was made up of these formidable round numbers. Edmundo told me that he had been married for fifty years. Proudly, he indicated one of the painted grandmothers on the couch. "Claribelle," he said. "She is my sweetheart. *¡Mi novia! ¡Mi novia eternal!*" The woman simpered demurely.

I asked Edmundo if there was anything unique about the Cuban way of love.

"*¿El secreto del amor aquí?* It has been somewhat misunderstood." He looked out at the street, at the Roseland supermarket with its bare, unvisited aisles. I tried again: "I've heard that there is something special about the bottoms of Cuban women." I smiled self-consciously at the ladies on the couch.

Edmundo said, "One of the characteristics of the Cuban women is to have a great development in the bottom but it doesn't have anything to do with the tango. The tango has rhythm, it has cadency, it is a sexy dance. It is erotic, sensual. It is also very romantic. If you want to understand *el secreto del amor aquí*, you should know the tango."

Perhaps he was right. After all, the tango was a euphemistic coinage for romantic entanglements where I came from. "It takes two to tango," we said, when what we really meant was that one person wasn't likely to have got another into bed unless that other had been willing. "Could you teach me?" I asked Edmundo.

"Ha! I'm too old. Anyway, it is better for you to learn from a woman." He got to his feet and fell into a little shuffle. It was as if he was determined to disprove his own claim about his age. He soft-shoed the distance to his chests of drawers and looked through his files for the address of Purita. I should go and see her, he said. She was the best dancer in Cuba. She was young, she danced on television. "When Purita has turned you into a tango dancer, come back here, and you can be a member of *la casa del tango*."

Purita lived on St. Rafael in central Havana. A tense-looking young man in a moustache was waiting for me in the lobby of her *edificio*. He led me up three flights of steps in the half-light. There was a grille in front of an open doorway, and a smiling woman in her late twenties in a halter-neck top and shorts: Purita herself. Her apartment was as dim as the stairwell. Light filtered thinly through a dusty window in Purita's kitchenette, and just about crossed the yard or two to her sitting room before it failed altogether. Pushed up against the walls of the sitting room was her furniture—a green sofa, two armchairs with black and red cushions, a dining table with four chairs, a rocking chair, two old, upright refrigerators, and a push-bike. The walls were covered by pictures of Purita: Purita on her wedding day, testing the strength of a courting-grille—a professional photographer's set-piece in Cuba; Purita seen in medal-clinching attitudes on the dance floors and tango oches of Latin America. Several of the pictures had been mounted on crushed paper got up to look like velvet. Purita's mother came into the room, a white-haired woman with a businesslike handshake. I suspected that she was the curator of the Purita museum. There were also several images of a younger version of the mother. In one, a formal but glamorous head-and-shoulders, the straps of her evening gown had been substituted for brightly colored feathers, like Libertad Lamarque's plumed headdress at the House of Tango.

The music roars over our voices and beautiful bodies young and old sway alive with fever. A baby sleeps on his mother's chest as she dances in the circle where the musicians jam. He is absorbing the rhythm through his purrs, taking it in and dancing in his dreams. Salvador González, the muralist, whispers in my ear. "I tell you in all humility, if there is one place where you can find rumba in its pure form, it is here. This is a pure gift." The crowd closes in, the smell of Cohiba cigars wafts around me, a bottle of Cuban Cristal beer is in my hand and I'm dancing.

—Wickham Boyle,
"Rumba Alley"

From the start, I sensed that the tango was the dance for me. "You must be like a block of wood," Purita said, little knowing that my entire ballroom career thus far had been based upon mimicking timber. We began with "the basic step." I had to crook my left arm at the elbow, and brace my right arm in order to hold my partner around the waist. "Tighter, tighter," said Purita. I was to stamp my right foot, and lead off with it, sliding the left up to meet it. "Not too far," said Purita. "Imagine you're painting the floor." With these moves under my belt, I was allowed an early breather. I had to hold myself perfectly still, all except for my right forearm. This was called upon to give Purita a pretty blatant goosing in the small of her back, in the name of guiding and propelling her. She sold dummies this way and that, like a rugby three-quarter. She was a foot shorter than I, but very quick on her toes. She reminded me of Mick Jagger. It wasn't just the way she made her lower lip stick out sometimes, or a kind of ugly-beautiful look about her, but her toned ruthlessness—though, of course, she was, at twenty-eight, young enough to be a Rolling Stones granddaughter, or date.

I had to wait until she had completed five shimmies before striking out again. This time, it was with the left foot, in a flat-footed action recalling an ice-hockey stick. I swung my right shoe into the same neighborhood as the left, though leaving a distance of a country yard between the two. I brought my feet together, at the same time turning at my right heel so that I was at right angles to the direction from which I had come, ready to repeat the sequence.

Purita said I was lunging too far with my initial step. At least, I consoled myself, I was punctuating my movements with just the right amount of arrogant Latin heel. But no: "You must slide," she corrected me. "You are painting the floor." I had been trying to think what this expression reminded me of; of course—it was "wiping the floor." Nor was Purita satisfied with my deportment. I was insufficiently wooden, something my previous dancing partners would have found difficult to credit. "What about his shoulders, Braulio?" she asked her husband. "They are not square, no?" Braulio agreed with his wife about the roundness of my shoulders: he brightened just to have been asked. Purita said to me, "You must be like a blockie."

She showed me more moves: "the eight steps," she called them. I had suspected that I was having it too easy while Purita was selling her dummies. Now it emerged that I was expected to match her virtually swerve for swerve. First, I swiveled forty-five degrees on my right foot, dragging my left round to join it; then vice versa. One more time, the same as the first; and I was supposed to finish with both toecaps pointing at Purita. This exercise also proved ticklish. She told me to think of my feet as snakes, but I couldn't make them wriggle over her tiles in a convincingly serpentine manner.

I wanted to know when Purita was going to teach me how to hurl her away from me, and save her in the nick of time from dashing her brains out against a refrigerator with a languid and yet utterly masculine catch. "Ah, the *tombe*," said Purita. "Not yet." First I had to learn a gesture which might have come from a Tudor court. From the upright position, I had to slide my left leg behind my right, in a flat-footed style, while at the same time pointing a pretty ankle with the right. This was the *quebrada*. Looking over my shoulder, Purita watched a reflection of my feet in her television screen.

Purita told her husband to play "Jealousy." It seemed the right choice for that temperamental dance, in that hot, cramped room, with Purita's husband watching unhappily from the dining table. If he was jealous, it wasn't of me, I felt, but of all the men who had held his wife so tightly and intimately, and above all of Amado, Purita's long-time partner. Amado appeared in many of the pictures on the walls, haughty and ponytailed. Purita had been dancing with him since they had met at a party when she was a girl of thirteen. They were spotted by a professor of dance who got them their break on Cuban television—"Purita y Amado" was now a fixture of the winter schedules. They had recently made their third movie; they had performed in Brazil and Venezuela; they had appeared before Fidel himself—he had asked them how long they had been practicing, and told them how much he had enjoyed their routine. Purita and Amado were stopped in the street and rung up on radio phone-in programs by people who told them that they loved their dancing. They were the Fred and Ginger, the Torville and Dean, of Cuba. When I had told Julietta about my classes with Purita, she said that she thought Amado might be gay—it was the way he talked, she said, the pitch of his voice. Be that as it may, Amado was once married to Purita for seven years.

And so we went on in Calle St. Rafael: the throbbing chords of "Jealousy;" me storking or craning between the chairs; Purita saying "Be careful!" when she meant that I shouldn't overreach myself, and "Be a block!" when she meant that I shouldn't let my shoulders drop; and my fingertips sliding in and out of her shorts.

Purita's husband put on a smart shirt. He was going to work. Braulio was in charge of lighting at the Nacional, the grandest hotel in Havana. He was cheered by the rather deliberate kiss that Purita fed him at the door—it might have been from her repertoire of dance moves. She asked me at the end if I had enjoyed the lesson, and I answered truthfully that I had. I had felt the effects of the heat and humidity, that was all. I thought of footballers buckled by cramp in South American World Cup ties, and wondered if I shouldn't be calling for salts: the sweat was cold-compressing out of me.

One day, Purita and I had a little audience: Braulio, of course, but also Purita's mother, who stayed for the whole session (instead of retreating in a somewhat martyred way, as was her custom) and a genial old boy who was an admirer of the mother. I had arrived early. Purita and the others were talking in the gloom—it had turned five o'clock, and though the sun wasn't setting in Havana until around eight then, the apartment didn't admit much light at the best of times. They didn't seem fazed that I was early, though in general the Cuban trend was towards lateness. (When I called at the Press Center one morning and asked to see Almeida, I was told that he'd be appearing soon. "A Cuban soon," the receptionist advised me drolly.)

When I finally encountered Amado at Calle St. Rafael, he was wearing what appeared to be a knitted singlet, and a pair of footballer's shorts in make-believe satin. He had let his ponytail down. It fell into the type of long, would-be feminine cut favored by men who appear on daytime television saying they are really women trapped in male bodies. He was just leaving, Purita said, and I sparringly suggested that he was afraid of the competition from me. At this, the great Amado snorted and pulled up a chair, insofar as the cramped dance floor would allow. I could feel his disdainful eye on me as Purita and I went through our paces. "No, no, no," he said. He got up. "You must push her—excuse me." I stood aside and Amado took Purita's arms as though he was gripping a longbow. He nodded in the direction of her husband, her second husband; his successor. Braulio put "Jealousy" on again.

Amado strong-armed Purita between the sofa and the refrigerators with a look that suggested he was deliberating whether to ravish her on the rocking chair or set her to work down a nickel mine. "Do you see?" he asked me. He cast Purita aside and turned his attention to me. "Hold me," commanded Amado, "I will be the woman." He was one of the hairiest men I had ever seen, never mind danced with. We executed "the eight steps," my size elevens threatening to overwhelm his unexpectedly petite pumps. "Your shoulders must be square," he said. Grimly, he reached under my armpits and tickled me.

"It's so that your shoulders will be level," said Purita.

Amado and I danced on. We went into a *quebrada*. He grunted that my *ganchos* were "O.K.," and I knew a moment of hot-making pride.

Purita taught me how to turn through 360 degrees while making *quebradas*. She taught me the *tombe*, and I learnt to catch her on my knee. She showed me the *mariposa en círculo*, the butterfly in a circle. Braulio chalked a circle out on the tiles, but the step eluded me. It was as though I had a faulty gyroscope. After half a revolution, I became a Frankenstein's creature of shorting ganglia. Stalling for time, I told Purita the winsome story of the domino-marked butterfly which had alighted on my bare heel as I was riding a bus in the countryside. Maybe this was a sign, I said, that given time, and sympathy on the part of my professor, I would one day master the—but Purita was cross with me. "You are not practicing enough," she interrupted me. "The *mariposa en círculo* is your special task for the next class." She could be critical, especially of my shoulder action, which she said spoilt otherwise encouraging work by my legs. But in what turned out to be our last class, as we were tacking up and down the sitting room with less than the usual amount of drag and resistance from me, she exclaimed, "You're a dancer of tango!"

I didn't believe her. On the other hand, I have a card in my wallet from the Asociación Cubana Amigos del Tango which has my name on it, and "*Asociado de honor*" written in Edmundo's hand.

Born the same year as the Bay of Pigs invasion of Cuba, Britain's Channel 4 News reporter Stephen Smith has been fascinated by the island since he first heard the hijackers' slogan "Fly me to Havana!" He is a regular contributor to the London Review of Books *and author of* Cocaine Train: Tracing my Bloodline in Colombia, Underground London: Travelers Beneath the City's Streets, *and* The Land of Miracles, *from which this story was excerpted. He lives in London.*

* * *

Fishing for Bone

A good fish is hard to find.

"BEFORE YOU HOOK A BONEFISH," SUGGESTED COMPANION ED Rice, "it would be a good idea to get an EKG."

The reason, I would learn, is that hooking a bonefish is like standing on a highway overpass with your fly rod, then letting your line down and snagging a Ferrari.

We boarded a skiff from our floating hotel, *Tortuga*, and our Cuban guide, Yonger Morales, fired up the 60-horse outboard before we could sit down. He grinned and said, "We go for bone."

Bonefish, a slim, silvery fish, may first appear small compared to many other fish prized around the world by sport anglers. Some may even say, "What's the big deal?" All it takes to find out is a few seconds with one on the end of your fishing line: big bonefish have burst speeds where they are capable of streaking 100 yards in a few seconds.

My mouth felt dry from excitement. For months, I had envisioned this day, fishing for bonefish in the virgin waters off Cuba and sharing a boat with the master himself, Ed Rice of Vancouver, Washington. And now it was happening.

Yonger pushed the throttle forward, and we were off, zigzagging through cuts in the island mangroves, streaking through narrow channels, whipping across cays and flats lined with eel grass. As the boat raced, the heavy air felt cooler, and I thought of Rice's remarkable array of experiences. He has fished in forty countries, six continents, all of North America including eighty different weeks in Alaska. In the process, he has caught 200 species of fish on the fly rod, more than anybody in the world.

It took nearly an hour to reach our destination, never seeing another boat or person. While we breezed along, Rice turned and said, "You know, fishing Cuba is like entering a time machine and fishing the Florida Keys fifty years ago."

He rated it in a class with other "world-class virgin waters," such as the Kamchatka Peninsula in Russia for steelhead, the waters of New Guinea for barrimundi, and the Gulf of Carpenteria off Australia, and Africa "for nearly everything."

We were in the heart of this paradise, Jardines de la Reina, a string of tropical islands with white sand beaches and coral reefs, fifty miles off the south coast of Cuba. It is under the control of the Cuban government, which limits access, over an area covering 3,000 square miles.

Ahead was a tidal flat that stretched for nearly two miles, the water just a foot or two deep with perfect clarity, tinted emerald from a sea bottom coated with eel grass, turquoise inshore along the white-sand beach shallows. The surrounding tropical islands were filled with mangroves, their roots exposed during low tide.

Rice was first to take the casting platform at the bow of the boat, while Yonger climbed aboard what is called a "poling perch" set at the stern, where with a long pole, he could propel the boat slowly across the flats. We constantly scanned the surface, both near and far, searching for any sign of bonefish. It can be a swirl on the surface or a mere gray shadow, but the classic sighting is an inch of tail fin sticking into air, complete with a trailing streak in the water behind it.

"I never cast to a bonefish I can't see," Rice announced, his nerves a bit frayed from the anticipation.

The quiet was broken only by the sound of water dripping from Yonger's pole as he pushed the boat along slowly.

Then, suddenly, he simply said, "Bone."

"There," Rice immediately countered, pointing 125 yards ahead. I looked closer. It turned out there wasn't just one, but maybe a dozen, all tailing.

In silence, Rice prepared his cast, first with a series of false casts to generate distance and load his rod, then shooting the line ninety feet, complete with gentle landing, five feet in front of the bonefish. He didn't wait. He stripped three quick yanks on the line, making his fly, a Clowser minnow, appear as if it were a small, live fish.

"Eat it," Rice begged to the fish, his voice a whisper.

A moment later, there was a swirl on the surface, Rice set the hook—a bonefish was on—and in the next three seconds that fish sizzled sixty yards off to the right, streaking for the mangroves. The line cut through the water, following the fish like a vapor trail.

Rice, a bear of a man, leaned back with his ten-foot rod, plying heavy pressure, trying to keep the fish from getting into the mangrove roots.

And then, just like that, the fish was gone, throwing the hook.

Rice laughed. "Now you can see why we love them," he said, "because they can drive you crazy."

Later, in a quiet moment, he added, "It's the closest thing to catch-and-release hunting there is. Spot and stalk, then turn them loose and start all over again."

When fishing is at its best here, you can get twenty "shots" a day, that is, twenty times where you have spotted bonefish and then get a chance to cast to them. At its worst, when the wind is blowing hard, you still get five to ten shots, though highly developed casting skills are needed.

This abundance has as much to do with habitat as the region being a marine refuge, where all fish are released (and commercial fishing is banned). The flooded mangrove islands are a nursery area for smaller fish, which provide the nearby flats and reefs with huge schools of bait fish. During low tide, the bait fish are flushed out to the flats, and in turn, the bonefish, tarpon, and permit are provided with an unlimited supply of food. There are also abundant numbers of jack crevalle, mutton snapper, and dozens of other species.

"That's why there is no better place for a chance at the grand slam of fly-fishing," Rice said. The grand slam is where in a single day, an angler catches a bonefish, the fastest of all fish in the world, the tarpon, the most acrobatic, and the permit, the most elusive.

In one period here, Rice caught (and released at the boat) the grand slam twice in three days, which in the world of fly-fishing, is similar to taking the space shuttle to the moon.

While the bonefish has the fastest burst speed, it is the tarpon that is most spectacular and the permit that is the most difficult to hook and land. Tarpon are sought for their gill-rattling jumps, often clearing five feet, and average thirty pounds here, often bigger. Permit, which average twenty to thirty-five pounds, are extremely shy and require perfect technique to hook, then the power to handle their bulldog runs with a fly rod. Rice prizes the permit as "the most challenging fly rod fish in the world."

"You can hunt permit for days," Rice said. "There are not a whole lot of them, and so when you finally see one it's really something.

"When you make the cast, to make it eat, it takes certain technique, and often a permit simply chooses not to eat. The secret is knowing when they eat, because they do not pull the line. You need a sixth sense, knowing when to set the hook.

"If you do hook up, they are incredibly strong. They are smart, strong, powerful, and just plain tough."

To complete his first grand slam, it took Rice—who can beat a 100-pound tarpon in 15 minutes—25 minutes to bring a 28-pound permit to the boat, where after a personal photograph, it was released.

I kept repeating this scene like a film loop in my mind for days, as we stalked bonefish, tarpon, and permit across the Jardines flats.

The miles of flats provide a seeming infinity of places where you can find fish that have never been cast to. Aboard our skiff, we explored the mangrove islands, white-sand beaches, and miles of flats and coral reefs covered with emerald, blue-green, and turquoise waters.

The world record for bonefish is nineteen pounds, and one day, in another boat, Charlie Meyers from Denver spotted one in that class, perhaps four feet long and fifteen pounds, he estimated, maybe more. "But I couldn't get him to take."

Another day, in three hours, I had a sequence of five "shots," where bonefish were hooked on three, landing two, lost one, missed one—and had a sharp-toothed barracuda sever my line instantly with the other. By midweek, I was trying to hone the art, zeroing in on my casts, trying to develop a sharper eye to spot the fish. And looking for a big one.

At one spot, shallow and wind-protected by mangroves, even the lightest breeze had died and the sea glassed out, when the streaks across the surface from tailing bonefish could be spotted from a quarter mile.

My guide, Pedro Marín, stared across the flats. The water was only a foot deep, acres of it.

"Big bone," Pedro suddenly said. "Big bone."

With polarized glasses to eliminate the glare, I looked ahead and saw it: eighty feet ahead of the boat, a bonefish had just come to the surface, cruising slowly no faster than a slow walk, its giant tail cutting the surface like a sail. It appeared alone, a solo runner.

This is what I had come for.

As we approached, I considered that I had done every-

As virgin as the day Columbus named them for the Queen of Spain on his 1494 voyage to the Americas, Los Jardines de la Reina flaunt their verdant beauty in a myriad of coralline islets that stretch for some 130 miles through the Gulf of Ana María off the southern coast of central Cuba. Bonefish abound in the surrounding waters, crustaceans and exotic coral formations populate extensive reefs, giant turtles lumber ashore to lay their eggs, and pink flamingos flutter in shallow lagoons. Otherwise uninhabited and virtually unblemished, Los Jardines de la Reina lie far beyond the explosion of tourist development filling north shore keys. On Cayo Anclitas (Little Anchors), fishermen and divers—limited to twenty a week—are accommodated in a floating hotel fifty miles out to sea from the mainland departure and supply port of Jucaro, in Ciego de Avila Province.

—Jane McManus, "Los Jardines de la Reina"

thing possible to prepare for this moment: The best Sage 8-weight rod, a 10-footer for casting distance, the highest-quality Abel saltwater fly reel, loaded with floating line and backed with 300 yards of 30-pound Spectra, a fresh 10-pound leader and 100 percent-strength knots.

As I prepared my cast, adding line with a series of false casts, I was almost hyperventilating from excitement. Gently, gently, I said to myself—if you slap the water with your fly, you might as well drop a bowling ball from a helicopter, either way, the fish will be spooked and run off.

This is sight fishing at its best, like a big-game hunter sneaking up on a cheetah, and the Clowser minnow was delivered eight feet ahead of this giant bonefish. There was no further wait: it grabbed instantly, the hook was set with a yank on the line, and the battle was on.

For the first few seconds, the bonefish swam one way for about fifteen feet, then turned and swam the other for fifteen more, taking little line. Then in the next five seconds, it just milled around, nothing special at all. But I could see the fish, and it was a big one, an eight-pounder perhaps, maybe even a ten-pounder. But it was fighting like a carp.

"So this is the great bonefish?" I remember thinking, questioning myself, questioning my dreams.

Well, it was just fifty feet away, so I decided to reel it in, let it go, and maybe go looking for a big permit, a fish that could really test me, not like this sluggish fellow.

But when I leaned back hard on the rod, applying full pressure for the first time, to impose my will on the fish and bring it in, a funny thing happened.

It woke up.

In the next six seconds, that big bonefish scorched through the water, first searing straight off for sixty yards, then turning and bursting in a mad dash for the mangroves, adding another forty yards. I put all the pressure I could muster on the fish, trying to turn it away from the mangroves, trying to stop the run.

It just kept on going. The fish sailed into the mangroves, and you could hear the water splashing as it surged through the roots and trunks. Five seconds later, it emerged on the other side of the thicket, in an open flat, and just kept sailing off, and an instant later, was gone, the knot breaking at the hook.

I looked down at my reel. In no more than ten seconds, it had taken 200 yards of line.

Later that night, I was telling the tale, and the others at the camp merely nodded. Turned out just about everybody who has hooked a bonefish has experienced a similar fate.

After a sumptuous lobster dinner, I went out on the deck of the *Tortuga*, and drew on a smooth Cohiba cigar, and thought of the wonders and mysteries of this extraordinary tropical wonderland, and how few people even know of its existence.

Tom Stienstra is an outdoors writer for the San Francisco Chronicle *whose reporting has taken him in search of Bigfoot, on white-water canoe trips, and in search of big fish and wilderness experiences from Central America to the Arctic.*

ANTONIO LÓPEZ

✦ ✦ ✦

Museum Piece

The revolution lives in 3-D!

JUST DAYS AFTER THE CUBAN MILITARY SHOT DOWN A BROTHERS
to the Rescue plane, I find myself a grenade's throw from the
Malecón, standing in the shadow of a SAU 100 Stalin Tank. It was
a monument marking another era when Cubans picked off exiles,
during the CIA-sponsored invasion at the Bay of Pigs. Supposedly
Fidel fired this tank at an enemy jeep, so I am somewhat confused
when a hobbling man with a week's worth of gray whiskers tells me
its barrel is like the cross that bears Jesus.

Initially he thinks I'm Spanish, but upon learning I'm *norteamericano*, the soft-spoken *habanero* declares Jesse Helms is the world's
greatest friend of democracy.

"He's no friend of democracy, believe me, you've got the wrong
guy," I cough. "He hates democracy and hates Communism because he's a politician...and he's a fundamentalist...."

The Christian part pleases him. Within the covers of a coveted,
wrinkled *Time*, he reveals a flier for evangelicals. He asks if I have
any American magazines. I shake my head, then whisk away to the
nearby entrance of the Museo de la Revolución, a monument
dedicated to the "natural rebellion of the Cuban people." I peek
back at the *viejo* and wonder if this guy's rebellion is also natural.

117

It is my last day in La Habana before heading back to the Yucatán. A Congolese youth, Abebe, who had become my de facto guide through the city's underbelly, soured my experience through his constant anti-Communist rants and superior mastery of Humphrey Bogart trivia. Today he is no longer beside me bumming the clothes off my back, cigarettes and beer, nor hocking bootleg Cohibas. It is time to get the *fidelista* version of things, and this museum, one of Cuba's many politically oriented exhibition spaces, provides a magnificent study of his official worldview. Formally the presidential palace which housed the notorious dictator, Fulgencio Batista, the Museo's Spanish revival exterior is not unlike an elaborate éclair, with an ornate interior designed back in 1913 by Tiffany & Co. of New York. Inside, opulent gold-trimmed molding frames a magnificent cupola, with a Social Realist mural depicting an angel-like nymph waving the Cuban flag in Chiaroscuro light. This is one of the few cathedrals I've entered in Cuba, a church to the Communist Party.

I'm led up a marble staircase which ascends to the third floor where the exhibits begin. This same stairway was the scene of a botched assassination attempt in 1957 when student militants were ambushed by Batista security guards and slaughtered on the spot. I snake through a maze of rooms outlining a carefully scripted plotline.

Museums, which evolved out of the European *cabinet des curiosités*, initially were designed to show off the spoils of colonialism. Here I'm confronted with a cabinet of curiosities that's practically Fidel's closet: a vast collection of Revolutionary ephemera ranging from Che's asthma inhaler and beard fragments to bloodied vestments from martyred guerrillas. There's also a shirt from Fidel's wartime lover, Cecilia Sánchez. Each room and display is choked with Fidel quotes, as if his word is the Lord Himself, validating each carefully selected remnant of the struggle as justification for the current political reality.

I wend from the evils of colonialism, slavery, and Native American genocide to Independence; from José Martí to yanqui imperialism, highlighted by a photo of a Marine urinating on a statue of José Martí. Then I'm confronted by something so surreal it could only have been hijacked from a parallel reality occupied by a socialist-run curio museum in Niagara Falls. In a life-size diorama emulating a jungle scene from the Sierra Maestra, wax dummies of Che and Camilo Cienfuegos burst over a rock outcropping, rifles in hand, with the grit of revolutionary fervor, oozing godlike invincibility and polyurethane sweat. Even stranger, accompanying the effigies are stuffed steeds that were their actual horses!

Descending floors, as I get closer to the moment of revolutionary triumph, 3-D models of key battles and gruesome photos, sensational like the tabloid press, build up the argument for the rise to arms. And are there weapons! A virtual armory of pistols and rifles of every sort in glass cases far outnumber more peaceable items, but an old typesetting machine attracts my attention, and wood-cased radios satisfy an antiquated electronics fetish. At some point I encounter Che's Bolivian body bag—an old U.S. postal sack.

Suddenly I find myself in a room alone with a uniformed museum guide outfitted in a well-pressed sky-blue skirt and pinstripe blouse not unlike an old-fashioned stewardess, with

Herbert L. Matthews, reporter for *The New York Times*, published an interview with Fidel Castro. To prove his statements he produced an unclear photograph of Castro. The military chiefs of the province told the General Staff so emphatically that no such interview had taken place that the Minister of Defense publicly denied it had occurred. And even I, influenced by the reports of the General Staff, doubted it. The interview had, in fact, taken place and its publication was of considerable propaganda value to the rebels.

— Fulgencio Batista,
Cuba Betrayed

a red bow tying oak-colored hair back into a meticulous ponytail. As she diligently minds the exhibits, I'm finding myself madly attracted to her. She holds herself very properly, this socialist stand-in for Judy Garland, politely guiding me display by display, describing in perfect detail every event leading to the seizing of the capital in 1959 by the beatnik-looking guerrillas. With a perfect, articulate grasp of official Party history, she's very sweet, reminding me of my studious high school classmates who made honor role and never smoked cigarettes. I spend nearly an hour with her, but because of my difficulty with Cubanese, I'm enraptured not by tales of military heroism, but by her glowing sapphire eyes.

Knowing that my plane leaves at dawn the next morning, I see this relationship going nowhere except into the floor's final exhibit. I thank her for her excellent work, offer a tip, but she refuses. I consider it a faux pas, remembering that Communists don't take tips, but she's gracious. My last glimpse is of her squeezing her palms together, standing perfectly straight, her red bow glistening in golden afternoon sun now beaming past chalky-white shutters.

On the ground floor final exhibits provide a Revolutionary postmortem. Clippings from international solidarity presses, demonstrations of the state's proactive programs, and acerbic anti-U.S. propaganda close out the show. In one corridor three hand-painted cutouts of counterrevolutionary figures occupy a "*Rincón de los cretinos*"—Corner of the Cretins. One representing a jackbooted Batista reads, "Thank you, cretin, for MAKING the Revolution"; under Ronald Reagan a quip remarks, "Thank you, cretin, for STRENGTHENING the Revolution"; and finally, George Bush, dressed like a Roman emperor, is captioned, "Thank you, cretin, for CONSOLIDATING the Revolution." The viciousness of the display is somehow charming. Like a good lefty tourist, I snap a few photos for the anarchists back home.

A small shop with the requisite Che t-shirts is my last stop. I browse and purchase some revolutionary memorabilia with red Che-emblazoned tourist dollars, one of the few opportunities I had to actually buy something in Havana.

The museum's crown jewel floats outside in a crystal pavilion: the leaky boat that carried Fidel and eighty-two men to Cuba from Mexico in 1956. Named *Granma*, it's also the moniker of the Communist Party's daily paper which is used as toilet paper where I'm staying. Other revolutionary artifacts abound: a bullet-ridden

"Fast Delivery" armored car, B-26 fragments from the Bay of Pigs, pieces of a U-2 spy plane. It's the low-tech, anti-imperialist anti-thesis of the Smithsonian's Air and Space Museum.

As I exit, I'm stricken with the morbidity of it all. Not only is the Party betting heavily on dead men and deeds of the past, when I re-enter the street, Fidel's ubiquitous "Socialism or Death" sentence monopolizes the cityscape. It is often accompanied by Che, a pop icon in replace of the Coke logo, whose far-off gaze manages to haunt the city like the ghost of socialism's past. Bicycles clink by, sunlight slowly dissolves. My stomach grumbles, and I wonder what the cute docent will eat for dinner tonight, if her parents would like me. If I have it right, the city should be bustling with revolutionary fun, yet I feel utterly alone. I head to my apartment to commune with the frog who lives in the shower.

Antonio López is a self-educated journalist who learned the ropes editing and writing for an early-'80s punk fanzine, Ink Disease. *In addition to travel writing, he covers art, culture, and music for Buddhist, lefty, and punk rock magazines. He lives in New Mexico.*

$\ast \overset{\ast}{} \ast$

Bring on the Cubans!

A musical and erotic night on the town leaves
fans delirious and exhausted.

BY TEN O'CLOCK THE MIGRATION HAS BEGUN. THOUSANDS MOVE slowly on foot through the humid night streets. They squeeze into buses or haggle lifts from cab drivers cruising in their compact Ladas and battleship fifties Chevrolets. At the outdoor dance hall La Tropical, a line forms around the block. Some patched and polished rustbuckets, a few new Japanese cars, and one Mercedes share the parking lot; hundreds of bicycles fill a smaller fenced-in area guarded by an attendant. A vendor sells rum from a wooden cart, serving it with a squeeze of lemon in disposable cups or pouring whole quarts into empty plastic water bottles. Young police officers mill about, keeping their eye on the complacent crowd. At the door people pay the equivalent of about fifty American cents for admission. Foreigners fork over ten dollars U.S. to enter the VIP lounge, a balcony bar that overlooks the action, where between sets musicians and their guests sit at the best tables.

About six thousand people have crowded onto a dance floor the size of a small ice rink. Most are black and in their twenties. The men wear athletic jerseys, baggy jeans, and big sneakers; the women midriff tops and shorts, or sleeveless dresses. Some have on souvenir t-shirts from a past Calle Ocho Carnival or a Jon Secada concert. A few sport baseball caps or shirts printed with the stars and stripes of the American flag.

At least a hundred more spectators climb onto the stage itself, a sauna where the air feels twenty degrees hotter than out on the street. Five hours will pass before this Monday evening's headliner, Manolín, El Médico de la Salsa (The Salsa Doctor), goes on with his dozen-piece orchestra. During their nearly three-hour set, the band members will douse the crowd with buckets of cold water. But everyone is already wet with sweat after dancing to Elio Revé y Su Charangón, the venerable big band whose director, a crusty sixty-seven-year-old who wears his gray hair in a fade and sports a huge gold pendant, has seen some three hundred musicians pass through his ranks in almost forty years. The club's emcee, Juan Cruz, a Cuban Dick Clark who favors guayaberas and a straw porkpie, has been hosting shows since the days of the legendary vocalist Benny Moré.

About midnight he announces that the orchestra fronted by smooth-voiced

W e started to dance. Almost immediately, I relaxed into the sound and let it overtake my crowded mind. I looked out at the faces that surrounded me and felt myself moving in time with this mass of people squeezed into a hidden salsa club far outside the heart of the city. Next to me, an elderly couple danced in each other's arms with the ease of longtime partners. She added a quick kick to her back step; he always gave her a little push to twirl just one more time. A young man behind them caught me staring and smiled good-naturedly, and I didn't blink away with dread that I would be approached and hassled. Instead, I smiled back. This club wasn't a pickup scene; it was a huge meeting place to release energy and celebrate. People rarely changed partners. Susan and I danced alone, side by side, but it felt as if I danced with everyone in the room.

—Michelle Snider, "Pligrimage to Somewhere-Outside-Havana"

singer Issac Delgado won't go on because of technical problems. The next two hours go by without a sound from the stage, but everyone stays put, laughing and talking, their loud banter peppered with a street slang that most Spanish speakers would need a translator to understand. No one seems peeved or impatient. This is Havana, after all, and if a band doesn't play tonight, there's always tomorrow.

"The only country where you can go out and dance to live music Monday, Tuesday, Wednesday, Thursday, Friday, Saturday, Sunday is Cuba," says David Calzado, a bandleader who has come to see the show. "It doesn't matter if people have to work the next day; they go out and dance, and they ride home all packed together on the bus, and everyone is smiling."

Finally Manolín, tall and handsome with large hooded eyes and close-cropped hair, takes the stage. Typical of current Cuban dance groups, his is a big band that features three singers, two pianists, a horn section, and Afro-Cuban percussionists, as well as a bassist and drummer. Dressed in matching plaid flannel shirts, long-sleeve white t-shirts, and low-slung jeans, the musicians look sharp, but they're already slick with sweat in the late-spring tropical heat.

The crowd dances side by side or in tight pairs, putting on a spontaneous, erotic display. Women swivel their hips in a maneuver appropriately referred to as *la batidora* (the blender) or do *el tembleque* (the shake), punching the air and rippling their torsos as if they've just received electroshock. The men bob with a cool side-stepping motion accented with a pelvic thrust, holding their partners from behind. One couple at the singer's feet seems intent on demonstrating every position of the Kama Sutra with clothes on.

Hands wave above heads as Manolín launches into the chorus, the essence of Cuban dance music, improvised call-and-response lyrics over a rolling piano chord progression and clave percussion. The ritual goes on for half an hour, the singers prancing and rhyming, spinning metaphors that have sexual, social, and sometimes political meanings, and the euphoric crowd shouting back their words.

By the time the music stops and people straggle to the door, it's nearly five in the morning. As he departs, one fan leaps up as if to take a lay-up shot. He's giddy, on top of the world, ready to take on anything. To prove it he shouts, "*¡Que vengan los americanos!*"

Bring on the Americans!

Judy Cantor is a Miami-based journalist, Latin music critic, and content producer. She travels frequently to Havana to worship the son.

WIL S. HYLTON

✦ ✦ ✦

From Tip to Tail

*Two cyclists cross the country, and set
the record for unpreparedness.*

I AM LOST. OR RATHER, *WE* ARE LOST. MY BUDDY LOU AND I, TWO skinny yanquis in the middle of Cuba, drenched with sweat, doubled over our bicycles, gasping for breath, exhausted. It's late and dark and hot and sticky. We've come sixty miles today, lugging two hundred pounds of equipment, and despite our best efforts to stay on the main road, we ended up here, inside a field of sugarcane. Yes, *inside* it, buried in it, wedged between twelve-foot stalks, which arc over us like a canopy, painting the navy sky in narrow black streaks. We'd happily get on our bikes and cycle out of here if only we knew where "here" was, if only we knew which way was out.

I'm holding our map under Lou's dim headlamp, searching for a clue to our whereabouts, when I hear a sound in the distance. A low, rattling sound. Lou and I exchange relieved glances as we wait, listening to the noise approach; then a young cyclist in cotton pants and boots emerges from the stalks.

"What's the problem?" he asks, smiling.

"Lost," I say. "We're trying to get to Jagüey Grande."

He shrugs. "I'm going that way. You can follow me."

We pedal behind him, and after a few miles, he stops at an intersection. "I have to go straight. You should turn left," he announces, looking expectant. But just as I'm reaching into my bag for a tip, his hand snakes out, grabbing something from my handlebar pouch. And then he's gone, disappeared into the night, leaving behind only a slight suction sound, a whispered *whooph* that nearly evaporates into the breeze. For a second, I'm dazed, not even sure what he stole. Then I realize: It was just a plastic baggie. But it happened to be an important baggie. It was the baggie with my camera, my glasses, my driver's license, my passport, and almost all our money.

"What was that sound?" asks Lou, straining his eyes in the darkness.

"He took my shit," I mumble, dumbfounded.

"What shit?"

"Everything."

Lou's quiet for a minute, then straps on his helmet. "Let's go after him." We mount our bikes and take off as fast as we can, but it's soupy with blackness and we're fatigued, and after only a few minutes, our pace falters. It's hopeless. We'll never find him. Not here. Not now. So we just cycle along slowly, hoping we'll come upon a town. Darkness whirls by, warm breeze, sugarcane. In the hazy recesses of my imagination, I picture the guy's shit-eating grin as he opens my bag and discovers $4,000 cash, a U.S. passport, a New York driver's license, and a palm-sized digital video camera. He's probably wondering when the next flight leaves for Miami. Me, I can't even think about America. With no money and no passport—no identification whatsoever—I won't be going home anytime soon.

It seemed like a good idea at the time. Really, it did. *Bicycle across Cuba.* Sounds so...dramatic. So stouthearted. So manly. And we were pretty sure that nobody had done it before. Not all of it, anyway. Not from tip to tail, not every painful latitudinal inch.

After all, the western tip of the island is a military zone. You need special permission just to enter. Even with permission, you'd have a brutal ride: thirty-five miles over loose sand. After that, there are 1,100 miles to go, through rain-forested mountains, across dry savannas, over winding dirt roads and diesel-dusted highways, knocking on doors for shelter, trading pens and lighters for food, and filling your water bottles from rusty public tanks. Cuba is bigger than Haiti, the Dominican Republic, Puerto Rico, Jamaica, the Bahamas, and all the U.S. Virgin Islands combined—no small feat to cycle. We doubted that anyone had ever tried.

Of course, like so many big ideas, ours seemed gradually dumber as we looked into the details. For one thing, and we realized this would be important, neither of us knew anything about bicycles. I hadn't even owned a bike in more than a decade. Lou estimated that he'd cycled about two hundred miles in his life. Neither of us could tune brakes, adjust a derailer, or even change a tire. We were what you might call, in bicycling lingo, *idiots*. Still, we began planning our route.

We decided to start at the western tip of the island, in the military zone, for a variety of questionable reasons. For one, we thought it would be nice if our route began on the left side of the map and progressed to the right, just like a sentence. For another we knew that the western end was flat, whereas the eastern end was mountainous, and we preferred to start with the flat part. Finally, we chose to start at the western tip because it's closer to Havana, so if we ran into early trouble, it would be easier to pack up our gear and bail out.

We estimated that the trip would take two full months, not because it would take that long to cycle across the island but because it would take *us* that long to cycle across the island.

We chose October and November, in order to return home for Christmas with a tan. Then we got two Stump-jumpers and considered ourselves ready. We didn't bother to look at the precipitation maps or the temperature indexes. We didn't bother to consult any experts. We simply cleared our calendars for those two months, and when the first week of October arrived, we packed our stuff into Lou's car and drove up to Toronto, where we caught a direct flight to Cuba.

Right in the middle of hurricane season.

We're just getting comfortable, lounging around a thatch-roofed bar in María la Gorda, on the western tip of the island, when the hurricane strikes. It doesn't look the way you'd expect: terrifying, tormented, raging with electricity. Instead, it looks merely like a hard morning rain, and as we amble back to our room to prepare for the day's ride, we think it'll pass.

We're overconfident. Yesterday, we covered the first thirty-five miles, the military zone, and it went more smoothly than we'd expected. I took several falls when my bike hit the sandy patches, but it didn't matter because nobody was looking. We cruised along the southern shore, the nearly transparent water lapping at the white sand, and somehow we did the distance in less than four hours. Then last night, the military guards and some of the hotel staff toasted us at the outdoor beach bar, saying we'd made history, that nobody had ever cycled the peninsula before.

So today we're all ego, tuning our bikes in the rain, filling our water bottles from a public tank, unintimidated by the storm. But when noon rolls around with no break in the cloud cover, I start to worry. All around the hotel, employees are rushing around frantically, reinforcing windows with masking tape. It occurs to me that there's probably a reason for this odd behavior, so I ask somebody, who breaks the news. It's gonna be blasting at a hundred miles per hour. It's gonna be here soon.

When I tell Lou, he looks alarmed.

"What're we gonna do?" he asks.

"Start riding?" I suggest.

And sure enough, in half an hour, we're on the road, hydroplaning wildly over potholes, trying to break through the hurricane's wall. I'm shrink-wrapped into my rain jacket, which is stretched so tightly over my backpack that I can barely move my arms. In the saddlebags attached to my wheels, I've got all my luggage wrapped in plastic, but I know that everything is going to be soaked. The plastic was supposed to protect my things from rain. But this isn't rain. This is a hurricane.

Riding against a thirty-five-miles-per-hour head wind is a Sisyphean affair, and it's no use trying to enjoy the landscape, no use trying to make out the contours of the horizon. All we can see are gray streaks of rain growing dim as night falls. It's five hours before we get to our destination.

Ciudad Sandino is all but invisible at night, a little huddle of cinderblock houses along the road, with about ten electric lights among them. Lou and I knock on doors, asking for a place to crash, and find an obliging family with two spare bedrooms, which we rent for $35. We hang our clothes on the furniture to dry, then lie down to sleep. Outside, the wind is howling, the rain is bucketing, and trees are falling down. I dream about motorcycles.

Come morning, when we stumble into the living room, we get our first glimpse of Fidel. He's on TV, telling reporters not to worry about the hurricane, that it always rains in October and everybody ought to know that. He looks old but strong in military fatigues. His manner with the reporters is very personal, very informal, standing in a big crowd of them, leaning close to each questioner, smiling as if they share a secret. He reminds me of Bill Clinton, the way he affects a rural sort of warmth.

> By the mid-1890s, the Havana weekly *La Gimnástica* could write of Cuban youths enjoying "la high life habanera." Cycling—excursions and organized competitions—became popular during the 1890s, particularly among women. By 1894 at least four cycling clubs had been organized: El Sports Club, El Club Velocipédico, El Club de Biciclistas de La Habana, and El Club de Ciclistas de Matanzas.
>
> —Louis A. Pérez Jr.,
> *On Becoming Cuban*

After breakfast, we hit the road. Against the head wind, we go slowly, pulling into the next town at dusk. Sumidero looks a lot like Sandino, except the electricity is out, so it's darker. We spot an old man standing on his porch, eyeing us in our spandex and our bulbous helmets. He waves us over, inviting us out of the rain, and we ask if he know where we could spend the night. Sure, he says, hold on, and he disappears down a muddy alley. A few minutes later, he comes back with a younger friend, who smiles under a straw hat and shakes our hands furiously, saying, Welcome, welcome, my name is Antonio, welcome.

The electricity is still out when we pull our bikes around to Antonio's place, so we stand in the kitchen with his wife, Xiomara, who's cooking beans and rice by candlelight. Xiomara has her straight brown hair cut to her shoulders. She has high cheekbones and a flirtatious smile, and she's given her good looks to their daughter, Angelica, a nine-year-old with deep, black eyes and rose-colored skin.

When the lights finally come on, Antonio fixes a bath for Lou. First, he takes a bucket of water and drops a bundle of exposed wires in it, with two of the wires sticking out over the side of the bucket. Then he sticks the two stray wires into a wall socket, and the underwater bundle makes a loud popping sound, hissing and steaming. In about five minutes the water is scalding. As Lou washes up, I sit with Angelica, who tells me about her schoolwork. She's studying Cuban history, she says proudly. They're focusing on the early colonial years, and she beams as she recounts the tale of Diego Velázquez, who sailed across the Atlantic in 1511 to stake his claim on Cuba.

"For what country?" I ask.

She frowns, confused.

"Do you know what country he was from?" I ask again.

Pursing her lips, tentative, she says, "The United States?"…

By the time Lou and I pedal into Havana, we can see just how different the capital is from the rest of the country. We've come two hundred miles in two weeks, battling our way across the Pinar del Río province, a tumbling landscape of tobacco and sugarcane, of box-shaped mountains and vine-draped porches. Where hunchbacked old men till the soil with oxen and children rush to the road when we pass, shouting, "*¡Olé!*"

Havana, by contrast, is another planet, a modern metropolis, a place with hotels and fancy restaurants, fresh-baked bread and discotheques. We dig in and enjoy, but after three days of luxury, we begin to feel guilty, so we remount our bicycles and head east, back into the real Cuba, rural Cuba, the other 44,000 square miles.

It's a relief to be back on the bikes, and although we'll miss the soft mattresses and air conditioning, we're glad to be rid of the hus-

tlers, or *jineteros*, who circle the streets of Old Havana selling illicit
everything. In fact, we're so happy to be away from them that we let
down our guard. In the town of Matanzas, we ignore people who
warn us to lock our bikes. In the town of Cárdenas, we let a crowd
of strangers mill about our equipment while we eat lunch. And by
the time we get to the savanna near Jagüey Grande, we feel relaxed,
even safe.

Then it happens. Nightfall, the sugar field. Two skinny yanquis
lost in the middle of Cuba. That's when we get robbed. It takes a
full thirty minutes of cycling through night soup before we find a
town. Another twenty minutes, and we're telling our story to three
cops. One of them wears a uniform. A second wears a white sweat
suit. The third wears green fatigues.

They walk us to the police station. The floor is littered with
car parts and cigarette butts. I'm put in a tiny office with three
new cops. Two of them glare at me while the third spits out a
series of rapid-fire questions: Name and address? Married? Parents'
names? It occurs to me that these are strange things to ask a robbery victim.

How did I get to Cuba? What airline? How big was the plane?
How much did my ticket cost? Did the plane make any other stops?
Then he asks for my address again. Again about the price of my
ticket. Again about my parents. At first, I'm confused. I can't figure
out where he's going with this. But when he asks my address for the
third time, it hits me: He isn't trying to help me; he's trying to trip
me up. He thinks I'm lying.

And as soon as I realize that I'm being tested by this cop, I can
feel my heart rate quicken. It's two A.M. One of the plainclothes is
asleep, snoring. Then the guy in fatigues comes into the room with
a fifty-pound sack of oranges. In another room, Lou is answering
the same questions. I realize that this isn't likely to be over soon.

It takes two hours to convince the cops that we're not spies, but
they're not done with us yet. They still have to hammer out a report
on a manual typewriter, get a sketch artist to draw a picture of the
thief, and send out an alert to the Cuban National Police detailing
our description of the suspect. By the time they're done, it's morn-

ing. Outside, roosters are bleating freedom cries. Inside, Lou and I are imploding with exhaustion.

At nine A.M., they throw us into an unpainted, unupholstered patrol car, which sputters and stalls and stinks of gasoline as it hurdles over potholes, heading back to the scene of the crime. We're in the custody of about thirty officials, mostly out of uniform. They stand in the middle of the sugar field, arguing among themselves, waving their hands wildly, trying to guess where the thief might have gone. Lou and I fall asleep in the car.

In midafternoon, they take us to another precinct for a lineup. Along the way, we are assured that the whole thing will be anonymous, that we'll be looking through a one-way window. When we get there, two fat guys take us to the "one-way" window, which is actually just a square hole in the wall covered by venetian blinds. There's no windowpane, and as soon as they've lined up the suspects, they flip open the blinds, leaving me and Lou face-to-face with eight guys who can see us just as clearly as we can see them. None of them looks remotely like the thief—our guy was young, light-skinned, clean-shaven, muscular, and fairly short. We're looking at tall guys with dark skin, skinny old dudes, even one guy with a full-grown goatee.

After explaining this to the cops, they finally give up and take us to a private home where we can spend the night. It's about five P.M. We huddle in our room, trying to figure out what to do. Two things seem clear:

The police have no idea what they're doing.

They're wasting our time.

We decide to leave town quickly, but we aren't sure where to go. We know that we'll have to go back to Havana if we want to get more money. But we also know that if we can't get money, we'll have to go home. After three weeks and three hundred miles, we're not ready to give up so easily. There are two things we want to see: the crocodile-infested Zapata National Park and the Bay of Pigs. Then we'll talk about giving up....

To Americans, the Bay of Pigs is a battle. To Cubans, la Bahía de Cochinos is a place. And the Bay of Pigs *is* quite a place, surrounded on three sides by a marshland known as Zapata National Park. By the time Lou and I arrive, we're more than ready for the soothing splendor of wilderness, and we spend a full day in the company of a bald, burly park employee named Francisco, who takes us out in a flimsy sedan, raising German binoculars to his eyes and pointing out dozens of species of birds—flamingos, herons, ibis, wrens, and the smallest bird in the world, the bee hummingbird, which hovers above a quarter-sized nest holding two tiny eggs. Francisco flashes delicate smiles, pauses at a watchtower, smells the air, and predicts rain. And at the end of the day, we invite him out for a drink in the dining area of a crocodile farm, where we sip beers surrounded by reptiles lashing at the walls of their cages.

The next morning, Lou and I cycle farther south to Playa Girón, the landing site of the Bay of Pigs invasion. As we pass through town, a tiny middle-aged woman with cropped hair and dark, glittering eyes rides up beside us on a blue Chinese bicycle, asking if we need a place to stay. When we say yes, she offers a room in her home, and we accept, following her to a colorless, six-story apartment building, then lugging our bikes up three long flights of stairs.

Her name is Maritza and her apartment is an oasis of hue: blue walls, a yellow tablecloth, pink bedsheets. There's a photo of Che Guevara on one wall and a collection of glass figurines on a small wooden bureau. We're surprised to find a hot shower in the bathroom, and we both bathe, changing into our cleanest dirty clothes.

With some coaxing, Maritza sits with us for dinner, but she doesn't eat, saying she's not hungry. She notices that I'm sniffling from a slight cold and offers me medicine, a difficult item to obtain in Cuba. I accept, and she looks pleased, and somehow, as the evening progresses, we open up to her, tell our story, how we've been robbed and have very little money. How we must return to Havana to see if we can get more. Maritza frowns, says that crime is very uncommon in Cuba. She apologizes in the name of all Cuban people, saying it's terrible when one person makes the whole country look bad. She tells us that Cuba is a wonderful place and that she hopes we don't get a bad impression, that she has a friend who can drive us to Havana, that she can keep our things at her house, can do our laundry for free, can guard our bikes, and that we can pay for our room and board when we return with more money. We're stunned. This poor, single woman offering to help a pair of Americans—here, of all places, in the Bay of Pigs.

When Maritza's friend arrives the next day in his 1957 Chevy, we kiss our hostess on both cheeks, then make the drive back to Havana in less than four hours.

Once in the city, I suddenly feel alone, scared. We have less than $300. We can't use American credit cards, because they aren't accepted by Cuban banks. We can't withdraw money from our accounts. We can't write checks. Nothing. The Western Union office will make transfers only to Cuban citizens, and even then there's a maximum of $300.

On three hundred bucks, I could probably make it a month in, say, Guatemala. But in Cuba, fat chance. The Cuban economy doesn't adhere to market principles; you pay whatever the Cuban government feels like charging, which is usually more than you'd like to pay. As far as Castro is concerned, the main reason you're allowed in the country in the first place is that you've got the cash to help save his foundering economy. Knowing this, we figure we'll need at least three grand to finish our trip, and even that's cutting it close. We check into a hotel and spend a restless night, wondering what sucker will be willing to send us so much cash....

I call my editor, heart pounding....

By the time the money arrives, I'm sick and tired. We've been in the country for more than five weeks, have cycled only four hundred miles, and during that time, we've taken no more than four hot showers, eaten approximately seven decent meals. I'm ready to give up, go home, leave the bikes with Maritza, and never come back. But I can't. We can't. We came here to discover Cuba, and now, for the first time, frustrated and exhausted, anxious and irked, with barely enough money to survive, I feel like we've finally found it.

Back at Maritza's place, our spirits brighten considerably, and not only because she has done our laundry, has a hot shower, and prepares a steaming plate of fried bananas with fresh fish, but also because she's such a cheerful soul, chatting excitedly about her week and saying that she's called several friends along our route who will be expecting us....

Most Americans in Cuba don't have trouble with the immigration department. Castro wants you there. After all, as an American,... you're a potential ally. If you have a good time in Cuba, you might speak out against the embargo. For Castro, that's invaluable. The embargo is every bit as crippling as it was intended to be, prohibiting any foreign company from doing business with both Cuba and the United States. If, for example, a British fast-food chain wanted to open a franchise in Havana, the company would promptly be banished from the United States. Needless to say, that's a loss few companies are willing to take, and those that do take the risk generally prefer to ship top-dollar tourist items, like soda and cigarettes, not the low-revenue products that Cuban citizens need. As such, tourists rarely lack for amenities, while in the general population, scarcity is customary, dearth routine.

There is one place where food and medicine enter Cuba from the United States without difficulty: the U.S. naval base in Guantánamo Bay. Located in the far eastern portion of Cuba, a landscape of sandy plateaus and cascading rocky cliffs, Guantánamo is hardly the "hot zone" that it's made out to be in movies like *A Few Good Men*. Though the perimeter is surrounded by Cuban guards, forty years of stalemate have tempered the hostility on both sides, reducing confrontations to an occasional middle finger or mooning. The American side of Guantánamo resembles nothing so much as a suburban subdivision, freckled with shrubbery and culs-de-sacs, movie theaters, Laundromats, even a golf course. The Cuban side is indistinct from any other small Cuban village, with disheveled buildings, tattered roads, stray dogs, and beggars, including one little girl in a ripped dress who keeps trying to steal money from Lou's pocket.

We check into a hotel on the edge of town, and we're just starting to settle in when Lou and I are accosted on the back patio by a group of five men who tell us to follow them into an unused room.

At first, I'm skeptical, but when one of the guys produces a card that says INMIGRACIÓN, we go along without argument.

Inside the room, the windows are boarded shut and there's no bed, just a telephone and a few plastic chairs that are difficult to see in the darkness. Right off the bat, the immigration guy starts thinking of reasons we should stop our trip. First, he instructs us to return to Jagüey Grande and help the robbery investigation. Then he warns us that the roads ahead are poorly paved, that the mountains are too steep, that there's a hurricane. But when we tell him that we don't *care* about catching the thief, that *all* of the roads have been poorly paved, and that we've *been* through a hurricane, he gets firm. You can't finish your trip, he says finally, because you don't have a permission slip from Havana.

"Well," I say, suddenly smiling, "we'd really appreciate your help getting permission. You know so much more about the system here than we do."

It seems to work. By the time we walk out of the room, he's promised to call us by 5 P.M. with an answer from Havana. But when five rolls by, then six, then seven, we realize we're being jerked around. Lou and I have a conference. Two things seem clear:

The immigration guy has no idea what he's doing.

He's wasting our time.

We decide to slip out early in the morning. We're only 120 miles from the finish line. With a little luck, we'll get there without getting caught.

And the next morning, we're off, heaving over mountains, spinning our pedals wildly on the uphills, then barreling down at forty miles per hour, then huffing it back up. By evening, we're within fifty miles of the tip. All we want is to collapse on a bed—even a lumpy Cuban bed—but we know we can't. If we go to a hotel, we'll probably be apprehended. So at dusk, we swerve off the road, stash our bikes in some bushes, and spend a night tossing and turning on the hard ground.

Sunrise, we hit the road again. Same thing: five thousand foot peaks, blistering sun, salt crystals on every skin surface. Only this time, we're operating on about two hours of sleep, and when we ar-

rive at a ten-mile dirt road leading down to a lighthouse, we wonder if it's an optical illusion. Our trip is supposed to end at a lighthouse on the eastern tip. Could this really be it?

We power down the road, bouncing around on rutted mud and
rocks, wobbling and groaning as we jump bumps and skid through
slicks. And after half an hour, almost unbelievably, we're there, staring over the windward passage toward Haiti, the first people ever
to cycle across Cuba.

There's a small staff working at the lighthouse—the operators,
the cooks, a security guard, and a medic who's wearing a Red Cross
t-shirt and drinking moonshine out of a plastic cup. He offers me a
shot, then another, and pretty soon I'm getting tipsy as we stare out
over the vast water, the sun dropping behind us.

"I'm drunk," he mumbles, and at first I just nod, like, "Yeah,
well…" But then he gets more serious. "I'm drunk, but I'm proud."
He juts out his jaw. "I'm Cuban!" With a flourish, aware that everyone is watching him now, he walks over and grabs a nearby statue
of José Martí, a hero from the War of Independence. "Cuban!" he
shouts, hugging the statue. "We're with Castro until we die!"

And somewhere in the back of my mind, something clicks. All
this time I've been agitated about not having a good time in Cuba.
Because I like the *idea* of the place. I like the history, the people,
and I like that it's a social experiment, a grand, sweeping vision that
reconstructed an entire country from the bottom up. The whole
thing sounds great on paper, this share-and-share-alike bit, but
being here, I've been disappointed. I've felt that the place is full of
filth and squalor, that by my standards, it's as free as a prison. I'm
sure, in fact, that I'd be miserable here, where I couldn't leave my
province for Havana without special permission, where the electricity goes out for half an hour a day, where information is controlled by the government.

All this time, I've been trying to like the reality as much as I like
the idea, but I haven't been able to. And yet, sitting next to this
medic, this effusive, proud medic, I realize that I've been disappointed precisely *because* I don't live here. The people of rural Cuba,

the people outside of Havana, the majority of Cubans, aren't comparing their nation to ours. They're comparing their nation to what it used to be. And looking at it that way, a lot of Cubans *are* satisfied. Many of them not only like Cuba, they love it. Francisco loves Cuba. Maritza loves Cuba. This drunk, happy medic loves Cuba.

I don't need to love Cuba.

They do

And they do.

Prior to cycling across Cuba, Wil S. Hylton had climbed Cotopaxi, the tallest active volcano in the world, had trekked forty-two miles in a single day, and had lived in the wild for three grueling months. He had not, however, owned a bicycle in more than ten years, and hadn't a clue how to change a flat tire. A writer-at-large for GQ, *he has also written about his adventures for* Rolling Stone, Outside, *and* Details.

CHRISTOPHER P. BAKER

* * *

We All Scream for Ice Cream

The ice cream parlor games are so much more interesting in Cuba.

COPPELIA HAD BECOME PART OF MY DAILY ROUTINE. I WAS A CREA-
ture of habit, always choosing a seat downstairs at the counter, but
one Saturday for a change I joined the *cola* for an outdoor section
where the late-afternoon sunlight filtered down subaqueously
through the trees. The line curled out of the park and along Calle
21. I had become inured to the *colas'* interminably slow progress,
but that day I was still in the spot where I started after twenty minutes. What on Earth was going on? I strolled to the head of the
line. The section was empty, but the neighboring sections were full
of happy customers spooning ice cream with gusto. I asked the couple at the head of the line if this section was closed.

"*Sí*," the woman replied.

"All day long?"

"*Sí, compañero.*"

Then why was she standing in line? "Is it closed every Saturday?"
I inquired.

"Only on Mondays," she replied.

Five waitresses were seated at one of the tables, gossiping, oblivi-
ous to our welfare. I leaned over the gate.

"Excuse me. I'm sorry to bother you. Is this section open?"

140

"Yes," one of the quintet answered.

"Then how come there's no one sitting down? All the other sections are open."

"*Horita mismo*," she replied, looking away. ¿*Horita mismo?* literally, "any moment now" is the Cuban equivalent of Mexico's *mañana*. Cubans have learned to shrug and put up with bureaucratic indifference. I hadn't been in Cuba long enough.

"How long is *horita mismo*?" I might as well have asked her when she expected Fidel to retire.

"¡*Horita mismo!*" she replied, as if I were the village idiot.

"How many minutes?"

"¡*Pronto!*"

The other patrons gawked, mixing astonishment with their amusement.

I persisted. "Yes, but how many minutes exactly?"

"Ten minutes!" she shot back.

"Thank you!" I looked at my watch and walked back to my place in line. Ten minutes came and went. The *cola* didn't move. We stood in line like torpid reptiles warming their blood in the sun. I thought about joining another line, but then? Surely, any minute now! I breathed deeply and tried patience. The inertia tired me out.

Another ten minutes passed. The waitresses were still gabbing merrily. I pushed open the gate and entered the hallowed sanctum.

"Excuse me, but there are two hundred people waiting in line." The uninterested quintet looked up and said nothing.

"Do you have ice cream?"

"¡*Sí!*"

"Then what's the problem?"

"*El helado está demasiado duro.*" I couldn't believe my ears. How could the ice cream be too hard? I'd been waiting in line for forty minutes. I swept my arms over the other sections. "What are the other patrons eating?" The waitresses shrugged and turned away.

"What did they say?" Cubans asked as I rejoined the line.

"The ice cream is too hard!"

They raised their eyebrows in disgust, too afraid to take on the lie. Making sense of this island was an exercise in madness. At times I thought I was posing in front of a fun-house mirror.

"Where are you from?" someone asked.

"Could this happen in England?" asked another.

"It's better not to fight the system," said a third.

"You're a foreigner," added a fourth. "For you to protest isn't a problem, but we have no rights. If I'd made the same scene and protested this disgrace, I might spend six months in jail."

Interminable minutes passed. Some of the other patrons wandered off and returned with snacks. I grew increasingly agitated. After ten more minutes, I could contain my frustration no longer. I stormed into the serving station. Six large tubs of vanilla ice cream were set on the counter, so I marched up to them and plunged my forefinger into one of the tubs. Soft! I knew it!

"Who is in charge here?" I demanded. The staff glowered. No one spoke. "Doesn't anyone here have responsibility?" One of the girls pointed out a man in a navy-blue shirt. I called him over. He consulted the waitresses, then repeated what they had told me.

"The ice cream is too hard."

"That's ridiculous," I replied. "It's soft. Look!" I showed him the

---

We talked about what the Doc had said on the subject of the blockade. It was easy to buy tires if you had dollars, and, yes, the tires were American, blockade or no blockade. "We have our own blockade," he added. I heard this cryptic phrase more than once. Cubans' fondness for puns and double meanings, together with a more recently acquired wariness, meant that discretion, or obfuscation, sometimes got the better of candor. The expression appeared to refer to the intransigence of the government. Julietta said the surly gateman was an example of Cuba's own blockade: he was kept in his job by the rigid shibboleth of full employment.

—Stephen Smith,
The Land of Miracles

incriminating hole I had made. He sighed and walked away. Disgruntled Cubans were now pressing at the gate and voicing their disgust. Patrons in other sections looked up from their bowls. Then a uniformed *custodio* ushered us all back into line. The line stayed frozen in place.

I began to hatch a plot for a charge up the hill. We would seat ourselves and start banging our spoons: "*¡Helado! ¡Helado!*" I was preparing to do just that when the line magically began to move.

As I reached the gate, the *custodio* put his palm up to my face: "Full!"

I saw vacant seats. I pushed past him.

The waitresses ignored me until finally one asked if I had pesos. I replied that I did.

"You're a tourist?"

"Not exactly."

"*¿Un residente?*"

"Yes, I'm a resident."

She wanted proof.

I came clean: "O.K., I'm a tourist."

"In that case I can't serve you," she replied, "You have to buy your ice cream over there, at the hotel, in dollars." She pointed to the Hotel Habana Libre.

"But I eat here every day. Over there." I pointed at the counter. "I've been coming for almost a month and have never been refused before."

She rolled her eyes and asked the others at my table for their orders, so I tried being nice. Turned humble. Told her that I'd been standing in line almost an hour. She said nothing and merely pointed at the hotel. Ubiquitous and elusive forces opposed my every step, making a Pilgrim's Progress out of a weirdly illogical sequence of simple events. Steamed, I began scribbling notes. That seemed to unnerve her. She rushed off to consult with the manager and returned. "*No problema, señor,*" she said contemptuously, and took my order.

I devoured the ice cream almost as soon as she brought it and asked for a second bowl.

"That's not possible."

"Why not?" I always had two bowls, which was not unusual. Most Cubans ate two or three bowlfuls at a sitting.

She struggled for a moment, the silence pregnant as she sifted through her mind for an answer. "The ice cream is too hard," she replied, whisking away my bowl while the last scoopful was still cold in my mouth.

Christopher P. Baker is a writer and photographer who grew up in Yorkshire, England, surrounded by rain, snow, sheep, and coal slag heaps. After earning degrees in geography, Latin American studies, and education, he settled in California. He misses the sheep, though not as much as he does Cuba, his first love. He is the author of several books, including the Moon Handbooks to Havana and Cuba, *Cuban Classics: A Celebration of Vintage American Automobile, and* Mi Moto Fidel: Motorcycling Through Castro's Cuba, *from which this piece was excerpted.*

BOB SHACOCHIS

* ✦ *

An Ernest Land

*The fun of the Hemingway trail
is in the detours.*

WE WERE ON OUR WAY TO OBSERVE THE FORTY-FIRST ERNEST
Hemingway International Classic Billfish Tournament—one of the
oldest billfishing competitions in the world. North American anglers,
for the first time in years, had found a way to participate in this most
prestigious event, dropping bait into the socialist sea. We figured to
wet a line, then travel the length of the island from Havana eastward
to the beaches and freshly painted facades of the *turista* archipelago
of the north coast, then to the mountains, the Sierra Maestra, where
it all had started, where a young university student/gang mem-
ber/lawyer/baseball pitcher had decided that it was time to take
paradise off the market, choosing instead a course of ultimate adventure, the Everest of political endeavor, revolution....

   In the beginning was the word, and the word was Ernesto himself, the progenitor of the marlin tournament, and an honorary god
in the Cuban pantheon of machismo. Off and on throughout the
1930s, Hemingway leased Room 511 at the Hotel Ambos Mundos,
conveniently around the corner from La Bodeguita del Medio—a
bar crazy enough to let writers drink on credit—and a ten-minute
wobble from a more sophisticated watering hole, El Floridita. Papa

found Cuba a resourceful environment in which to pursue his three addictions, writing, billfishing, and boozing, and he immortalized each pursuit. His alcohol-infused wisdom still adorns the wall above the bar in La B del M—MY MOJITO IN LA BODEGUITA, MY DAIQUIRI IN EL FLORIDITA.

In 1934 Hemingway commissioned a Brooklyn boatyard to build the *Pilar*, his legendary thirty-eight-foot marlin hunter. Five years later, a fifteen-acre farm south of Havana caught the eye of Hemingway's third wife; they rented Finca Vigía, and Hemingway spent much of the next two decades there, purchasing the place in 1940 with his first royalty check from *For Whom the Bell Tolls*. By 1950 Hemingway's own ascent to fame paralleled Havana's burgeoning notoriety as the New World's most decadent amusement park, a saturnalia orchestrated by Cuba's corrupt military dictator, Fulgencio Batista. Batista's Babylon offered a standard buffet of sin—prostitutes, drugs, gambling at Mafia-owned casinos, live sex shows at the seedier nightclubs, and a more restrained extravaganza of tits and ass at the dazzling Tropicana—and well-heeled tourists poured onto the island

Not long after Ernest Hemingway died, Fernando Campoamor, a writer, mixologist, and longtime Hemingway drinking buddy, was shooting the breeze with the owner of La Bodeguita del Medio and some others, and together they invented the line MY MOJITO IN LA BODEGUITA, MY DAIQUIRI IN EL FLORIDITA. It sounded like Hemingway, it reflected his drinking habits, and it would surely be a hit with foreigners.

With the encouragement of tourism officials, they hired a calligrapher to write it out and forge Hemingway's signature, then they hung it above the bar in La Bodeguita. "The little joke grew into a big lie," Campoamor confessed to me with a sly grin years later. The big lie now appears as gospel in dozens of Cuba travel guide and magazine pieces.

—TM

to be thrilled by the wicked ambiance. Down at the Finca Vigía, Hemingway finally figured out what to do with all his wealthy friends, the celebrities and playboys, the hunting buddies and would-be heroes who kept circling through Havana. He herded them into a bona fide fishing tournament.

There's a fascinating photograph, shot from the bridge of a sport-fishing boat on the event's tenth anniversary in May 1960. A young Fidel Castro is hunkered over Che Guevara, who sits in the fighting chair; two lines are in the water, but Che's legs are stretched out, his booted feet rest on the transom, and he's reading a book. As judge and sponsor of the competition, Hemingway had invited Castro as his guest of honor, hoping to convince the charismatic warrior, who seemed permanently attired in olive fatigues and combat boots, to present the winner's trophy. But Castro himself, the luckiest man in Cuban history, won the tournament, hooking and boating the largest marlin.

There's a second photograph: Hemingway and Fidel, *macho a macho*, beaming, Papa surrendering the trophy: the two men who helped define their times. They had never met before and never would again. That day Hemingway rode the *Pilar* out into the Gulf Stream for the last time; soon he would leave Cuba for good and go to Spain, then Idaho, where a year later he would commit suicide. That same year, 1961, his tournament disappeared behind an iron curtain of ill will manufactured by uncompromising ideologies. There were far worse casualties, to be sure, but once Hemingway came ashore off the *Pilar*, no other North American boat would participate in his tournament for three decades. Not until a good-natured, tenacious, fish-crazed egomaniacal heart surgeon from New Jersey chutzpahed his way onto the scene.

"The Americans are in a position to win this tournament," Dr. David Bregman proclaims as we breakfast with him on Saturday, the final day of the competition. The Cubans at the table suppress laughter. The U.S. team—three boats from New Jersey, two from Florida, one from Baltimore—have managed a paltry two fish between them even though the action has been hot thus far.

Naturally, since the Cubans know the fishing grounds, a Cuban boat is in first place, and two Mexican boats are not far behind. But in the end the Hemingway tournament is no more Cuban than an international banker's convention in Miami Beach. The theme is Cuban, the stage set is neo-Floridian, and far below the surface creak the worn-down gears of everyday Cuban life. But the tournament unravels somewhere else.

Over eggs, the Professor, Caputo, and I receive our sailing orders. The three of us will ride out with Doc aboard his forty-eight-foot Viking, the *Heart Mender*. We will observe to our hearts' content, but Doc will attend to any fishing—after all, he reminds us, it's his boat. As the last Cubans drift out of the dining room, Doc snatches a platter of sliced pineapple off the serving table and foists it upon the Professor.

"Quick," Doc urges, "don't let them see you." He requisitions two more platters—cold cuts and watermelon—and, chuckling, he and the Professor make a mad dash for the rental car. Clearly, Doc and his crew are having a splendid time.

"My Spanish is great," explains Doc as we rocket past the police checkpoint at the land-ward entrance to the marina, barreling toward a gas pump at the back of a gravel lot. We slide to a halt just before we hit the attendant. "I took a couple of years in school and—it's amazing—it's all coming back to me. "*Donde es el gasoline?*" he queries the pump jockey, who shrugs his shoulders, and off we speed at an alarming velocity toward the *Heart Mender*, the first U.S. registered vessel to enter Cuban waters legally (except for the Mariel boatlift, which doesn't count) since the early years of the revolution. It's almost nine A.M.—starting time—and Doc is in the mood for battle....

I retire with our host and the Professor into the boat's swank, air-conditioned salon, and without much prodding Doc launches into a soliloquy on the two subjects he finds most praiseworthy: himself and fishing. It so happens that after he coinvented the intra-aortic balloon pump in 1969, he became a brain in demand, addressing international medical conferences and training surgeons in the Soviet Union and China. In 1989 the Cuban government wanted to enroll his expertise and asked him to be one of the head-liners at a national medical conference. Doc said he would if he could bring his boat from Key West and fish. The Cubans thought about it and said, why not? The U.S. State Department said no. But Doc had once operated on Armand Hammer's brother, and....

"Doc!" both mates holler simultaneously—the divine interruption. Doc bolts from his seat. It's 9:15, and the *Heart Mender* is hooked up, the unlikely champion Dr. Bregman on center stage, a fighting belt strapped around his sizable waist.

The first mate spikes the rod into the holder above Doc's groin, creating a literal connection between the fisherman's masculinity and the furious instinct of the unseen beast. "Tip up," coaches the captain from the bridge. "Let him dive." This is a kill tournament; there'll be no cavalier tag and release. Sweat pours down Doc's torso as he bows forward and reels back, bows and reels. After five or six minutes the beast rises, blasting through the indigo surface, its bill parrying the lethal air. It's a marlin, a stand-up blue big enough to take the trophy, and it dances with magnificent rage for fifty feet or more, the iron-black sword of its bill slashing the Havana skyline.

After twenty minutes, the fish is just off the transom, ready to boat, panting as it lies twisted on its side in the transparent seas, one fierce eye condemning the world above. The mate extends the gaff over the side, maneuvering for the right mark, the perfect moment. Then the marlin spits the hook. With cool contempt he throws the line into Doc's face and is gone, leaving us a silenced, awestruck crew. Doc hands the rod to the mate, accepting the loss with grace.

"A brave fish," he declares in fluent Hemingwayese. He unbuckles the plastic belt, tosses his baseball cap aside, and retreats to the comfort of the chilly salon, dismissing his crew's efforts to console him. He plops down on the couch, the good sport, reflective, storing away the memory....

From the beginning, the Professor offers a dissenting viewpoint to our initial impression of Havana. "No, no, no, señor," he says, which is the extent of his involvement with the Spanish language. What he sees from the balcony is not the city's imminent disassem-

blage but something on the order of an exotic passion permanently
flaunting the edges of self-destruction, semiferal but with a hip
intensity, sidling up to disaster and then fluttering away, a city like a Latin woman, beautiful but exhausted, dancing through the perfumed night with a gun in her hand.

We mobilize for an assault on the city's ambiguous appearances, walking first to the Plaza de la Revolución, a vast open space resembling The Mall in D.C. but dropped into the middle of a massive empty parking lot in a tropical Newark. To one side sits a reviewing stand made of white stone, with a marble podium facing out on a macadam lot, its field of telephone poles wired with spotlight and loudspeakers. Here Fidel enacted, in the early days of the revolution, his "democracy of the people," tutoring the masses for hours on end, haranguing them like a fire-and-brimstone preacher, making them laugh like a stand-up comic, building them up to whatever emotional pitch the day's challenges required, until—and this is the vital and democratic part of the ritual—they shouted back to the Maximum Leader in unison: O.K., have it your way, *jefe*, we want to go home.

> Every bartender has his own style of mixing *mojitos*, but each uses a teaspoon of white sugar, $\frac{1}{2}$ ounce of lime juice, a sprig of mint, and an ounce of sparkling water. Then we crush the mint on the sides of the glass while mixing all the ingredients, and add three cubes of ice, another ounce of sparkling water, and finally $1\frac{1}{2}$ ounces of silver, dry Havana Club rum. We'd usually put the rum in last because often there wasn't room for the full amount. When you put the rum in last, it's the first thing the customer tastes.
>
> Sometimes we'd recycle the mint in the *mojitos*. When a truckload of *yerba buena* was a few hours late or never arrived from the *campo*, we'd clean the dirty glasses, put the old mint to one side, wash it, and put it in fresh glasses.
>
> —J. C., former bartender, La Bodeguita del Medio

If you've seen televangelists browbeating an audience, you won't be shocked to learn that this system works, more or less, nor will you be thunderstruck to hear that all domiciles throughout Cuba's cities and countryside, even the humblest shacks—especially the humblest shacks—have antennas on their roofs and, down below, old black-and-whites burning blue through the evening hours.

We stroll into Old Havana down narrow cobbled alleys eerily Neapolitan, though Havana's streets are by far the most tranquil and nonthreatening of any I have walked in the Latin diaspora. Urchins flutter around us hoping for Chiclets, but by Monday they'll be uniformed and back in school. In the stone-paved Plaza de la Catedral, a man approaches me, asking for a cigarette. He is white-haired and constitutionally thin, dressed in immaculate khaki work clothes. He wants a light, then the lighter, and though I give it to him I take it back, since I have no other and Cuba is out of matches. He gasps when I tell him we are from the States. North Americans,... he loves them, hates Castro.

"Life is very bad in Cuba."

"If you say so," I say, but in truth he looks no worse off than his blue-collar counterpart in Miami. If he had been in Mexico City, or Port-au-Prince, or Lima, or Kingston, if he had a context in which to place his misery, perhaps he wouldn't be so quick to claim it. What is absent in his denunciation, what is absent throughout Havana, is the dead tone that marks deep suffering and despair.

Like so many others, my new friend wants to change money, my dollars for his useless pesos....

He suggests we walk down Empedrado, a street as old as the New World, to La Bodeguita del Medio. The Bodeguita is just opening its doors, but already a crowd has assembled outside the establishment, a joint instantly recognizable as one of the solar system's last repositories of cool, a neighborhood hangout with global traffic, a place where dialectics and rum fuse into a collective, joyous, cacophonous blur. Behind the counter two bartenders manufacture endless *mojitos*, twenty at a time, for the relentless tide of thirsty *turistas* that churn through, sweeping in and sweeping out, glancing cross-eyed at the ubiquitous graffiti and taking deep dizzying whiffs of the proletarian smells of bohemian Cuba. Across the street, three plain-clothes police officers stand like statuary, arms folded, glowering at the escalating euphoria.

My new friend displays a tremendous appreciation for both rum and drama. "Let's get cigars," he stage-whispers repeatedly, peering anxiously toward the door. The bartender has adopted Caputo, channeling him free *mojitos* in exchange for baseball updates. The Professor sponsors English lessons for two saucy dreamettes who are instructing him in a language of their own: cognac, they say; champagne. "The cigars, let's go," my friend mumbles. I nod and we're out the door, he walking a half block in front, broadcasting guilt, cringing in posture, the worst black marketeer I've ever encountered. I feel like arresting him myself.

Down Old Havana's strange and marvelous streets I follow him until he ducks into a made-to-order shadowy portal, the arched entrance to a decrepit palace divided long ago into apartments. We ascend a marble staircase, right-angling up through medieval space, musty, and decomposing. Sensing our arrival, an old woman, his mother, opens the door. Only a television set places the apartment in any world I know, otherwise, the precise honey-colored shafts of light, the glassless windows, the crumbling textures and bare furniture, the provisional quality of its humanity are, in their extremeness, too unfamiliar for me to recognize except as Hollywood augury.

The deal takes less than a minute. The seller needs dollars; as a skilled tradesman he earns 200 pesos a month—the price of shoes on the black market. The buyer—well, the buyer doesn't need, doesn't even like cigars. The buyer is simply seduced. The buyer finds official Cuba enigmatic, the image formulaic, but how easily and swiftly the rhetorical veneer is scratched and another secret revealed. Bedding Cuba: the historical precedents are countless, large scale and small; it's a North American tradition. Scruples barely make it as a footnote, a tiresome annotation. I zip the wooden box of cigars into my knapsack and, warned by the dealer's mother to be careful, we return to La Bodeguita, where silence and fear are obsolete....

As we head east out of Havana I ask the driver to sidetrack off the main highway to the fishing village of Cojímar, home port of Gregorio Fuentes, the now-ancient captain of Hemingway's *Pilar*. As we draw close, the land begins to roll a bit, its soft hills lined with cottages not unlike the conch houses and art-deco bungalows of the Florida Keys. We stop at the turquoise cove where once the *Pilar* was the undisputed queen of the fleet. A small, austere park pays tribute to Cojímar's most illustrious friend and patron. After the village heard of Hemingway's death, every fisherman donated a brass fitting off his boat, and the collection was melted down to create a bust of the writer that stands watch over the quay.

We locate Gregorio's modest house, and he invites us to crowd into his living room. Throughout the last thirty years, he has been harassed by curiosity seekers and schemers, but now it seems everyone believes he is dead, and he lives in the isolation he has always sought. Still, he appears pleased for the chance to unscroll the past once more, remarking that it might be his last opportunity, and he talks for hours in firm and measured speech. The incarnation of Hemingway's protagonist in *The Old Man and the Sea*, though the writer couldn't have had any idea back in 1951 that one day his true subject would be Gregorio himself, stepping transcendently into the portrait:

> The old man was thin and gaunt with deep wrinkles in the back of his neck. The brown blotches of the benevolent skin cancer the sun brings from its reflection on the tropic sea were on his cheeks.... Everything about him was old except his eyes and they were the same color as the sea and were cheerful and undefeated.

From 1935 to 1960 the two men were in many ways inseparable. During World War II they patrolled the coast for German U-boats; during the struggle against Batista, Gregorio tells us, he and Hemingway kept an eye on the local waters to assist Castro and his rebel armies. Hemingway even took Gregorio to Africa to hunt lions.

"Hemingway is the only North American in the world for me," Gregorio says, sitting erect in his chair. He wears a wristwatch with a marlin on its face, though he hasn't fished since saying goodbye to the man he still refers to as Papa.

"Before he died," says Gregorio, "he made his last will and left me a document to hand to Fidel Castro. I was called by Fidel to read the testament, and everything, all Hemingway's property, was for the revolution, but the yacht and the fishing equipment were for me. Fidel said to me, 'When you get tired of the yacht, bring it to me.' And I answered, 'I'll never be tired of it.' After that, many bull-shitters came to this house to try to get the *Pilar*, and they left the house in silence. That's why Hemingway chose me to work with him, because I understand things. I want to avoid people who think I should get money from my relationship with Hemingway. I can walk anywhere."…

Fuentes was less than a year older than Hemingway. They used to celebrate their birthdays together, sharing dinner and a bottle of whiskey on both days.

"After Hemingway died," Gregorio says, "I maintained the tradition on his birthday. I would go down to his statue by the harbor. I would have one drink of whiskey for myself, and Hemingway's I pour on his head. But I haven't done it for years. Because you can't find whiskey anymore in Cuba."

> We went to La Terraza, the restaurant where Gregorio and Papa ate fish, drank, and were deep, close friends. I was very moved by Gregorio, as he is a one hundred-year-old man whose life stopped when Papa died. This man literally lives each day mourning a man who died decades ago and whom he cannot replace. There was such a sadness in him. He kept gesturing to photos of Papa, then touching his heart, then pointing at his eyes and then at mine. It was clear he felt there was a connection in the eyes between us, and I was touched by his sentiment.
>
> — Mariel Hemingway, "In the Place of My Namesake," *Mungo Park*

I say I will bring him a bottle—the tourist shops are well stocked. He gives me an *abrazo*, an embrace, and we leave the old captain to pull on his cigar in solitude, bound to the myths he had helped create.

Bob Shacochis is the author of Swimming in the Volcano, The Next New World, Domesticity, *and* The Immaculate Invasion. *His collection of stories,* Easy in the Islands, *received the 1985 National Book Award for first fiction. A contributing editor to* Outside *and* Harper's, *he lives in Florida and New Mexico.*

DAVE EGGERS

* * *

Hitchhiker's Cuba

*You never know where your next
passenger will lead you.*

ON THE ROAD OUTSIDE HAVANA, WHERE WEEDS GROW THROUGH
the train tracks, and the crumbling buildings, colors fading into a
decorator's dream, alternate with wild trees and shrubs in the most
gorgeous, postapocalyptic way, is where it first happened, when we
first got an idea of how it all worked.

We had missed a turn (we suspected) and so had stopped to ask
directions. We pulled over next to a median strip, on which stood
eight or ten people, half with shopping bags, presumably waiting for
a bus. We rolled down the window, smiled sheepishly and directed
our confusion to one of the men (tall, black, in a shiny Adidas jersey). With a swift sort of purpose, he nodded and stepped forward
from the island and toward us, in a gesture we took as excep-
tionally friendly and helpful, getting so close to better relate the
coordinates....

Then he was in the car. It happened before we knew it had happened. He just opened the door, and then suddenly he was giving
us directions from *within* the car. The smallish back seat was empty,
then full, full with this large man, his knees cramped up near his
chin. He was so nonchalant, and had not uttered any commands or
taken out a gun or any of the other ostensible signs of car jacking,

and so it dawned on us that this was what happened in Rome. In Cuba, that is. Here hitchhiking is custom. Hitchhiking is what makes Cuba move. All those other people on the median strip? All waiting for rides. Perhaps a bus, yes, if they have a few hours to lose. But until then there are cars, and occasionally the back of a bicycle, and the hope that someone will stop. So the man in our car tells us where we're going, and then we're off, eastbound, through the outer parts of Havana, along the train tracks, more and more green, past the heartbreaking roadside propaganda, ten miles, fifteen miles out of the city's center.

His name is Juan Carlos. And while he speaks a little English, thankfully in the passenger seat is a translator/navigator (T/N), and she duly interprets.

What does Juan Carlos do for a living?

He's a basketball player-coach.

Where are we taking him? Home. Is that O.K.?

Of course, sure. Is he married?

Yes. Actually, he says, his wife is the starting center for the Cuban women's national basketball team. Do we want to meet her?

Hell, of course, we want to meet her.

We passed the dirty, dilapidated worker housing that everywhere mars the Cuban landscape. The buildings are nothing but concrete pigeon-holes—six-story-high, hundred-yard-long stacks of tiny apartment boxes open on one end. "The workers made these!" said Roberto. Though, if you think about it, workers make everything. "The government gives them the construction material. Then they rent for twelve years. And then they own them!" In other words, you get a free home in Cuba as long as you build it and pay for it.

— P. J. O'Rourke, *Rolling Stone*

His building is a concrete complex overgrown with weeds and drying laundry. Neighbors stare from above, their arms draped over balconies. Through the door and inside Juan Carlos's apartment suddenly there is Judith, easily seven feet tall. Eight? She's huge. She leans down to offer her cheek for kisses. The walls are crowded with images of Michael Jordan. We say we're from Chicago. They nod politely. Juan Carlos thinks the Suns will take it this year. The Suns? We nod politely.

Judith is practicing for the Sydney Games, with her team playing against three other teams in the Cuban women's intramural league. From the four teams, the squad for the national team is chosen. Does she think she'll have any trouble making the team? She chuckles. Dumb question. No, she'll be starting.

They ask when we'll be back in Havana. We don't know. When you come back, they say, this is your home. Their in-laws live down the street, so they'll stay with them, and we can have their bed. We say fine, but for now we have to move, must get back on the road (but not before getting a quick snapshot, for which Judith changes into her uniform), because we're heading up the coast, and we have more people to pick up and move, from here to there.

That becomes the point—it had not been the plan at the outset but now is the mission, one thrust upon us—the picking up of people, because, as we learn soon enough, the most common roadside scenery in Cuba, besides the horse-drawn wagons and broken-down classic American cars, is its hitchhikers. The roads are littered with people everywhere, along the huge highways and two-laners, all strewn with mothers and their daughters, grandmothers, working men, soldiers, teenagers, schoolchildren in their white, white shirts and mustard-colored pants or skirts, day and night, in the rain or otherwise. All waiting.

They wait for hours for the occasional bus or a spot on the back of a truck, waiting on the median strips, at the intersections, sitting with their possessions or on them, along the gravelly highway shoulders, patience their essence because gasoline is scarce and expensive, cars are owned by few and function for fewer, the buses are terrible and slow and always so full. And so we are driving in our Subaru, a tiny thing but big enough for five, and we're Americans come to move the Cubans from place to place. Feel our luxury! Hear our engine's roar!

Up the coast, and in ten minutes we stop for Jorge, who gets in at a stoplight and is going toward Varadero, a beach town on the north coast. Jorge is about eighteen, in khakis and a pink shirt, with a very hip-seeming haircut, freshly gelled, a kind of haircut that makes him look half monk, half member of a dancing, harmonizing teen quintet. Jorge's father, he says, left for the U.S. years ago. He was one of the so-called *balseros*, the rafters who left in 1994 during one of Castro's periodic spurts of permitted emigration. Now he's in Miami.

T/N: What does he do there?

Jorge: I don't know. I haven't talked to him since he left.

T/N: Oh, that's too bad.

Jorge: No, no. It's O.K.

We drop the subject of Dad of Jorge. We pass miles and miles of oil pumps along the ocean, some pumping, their bird heads rhythmically dipping their beaks, others inanimate, the surf spraying over. We ask Jorge what he does for a living. He says he's a student of astronomy.

"Oh, so what does that entail?" I ask the rearview mirror. T/N translates.

"Oh, you know," he says. "*Cervezas, sodas, comida...*"

Oh. Ha. Not astronomy. *G*astronomy. Big laughs all around. The sky is watercolor gray, and the clouds hold rain. We all go over the mix-up three more times. Not astronomy. *G*astronomy. Yes. The beach comes into view, palm trees bent by a wicked ocean-borne wind. Jorge wants to know if we need some place to stay. Jorge, like every last man in Cuba, knows of just the place, the perfect *casa particular*—the Cuban version of a bed and breakfast—and he, like most, is very difficult to convince of one's lack of *casa particular*-based need.

No thanks, we say.

I know just the place, he says.

No thanks, we say.

Very nice place.

No thanks but—

Clean, very cheap.

Thanks, no.

Have your own kitchen, very private.

No, no.

Only $18.

You are too kind but—

You want me to show you?

We drop Jorge at the beach at Santa María del Mar and get back to moving down the coast. Minutes later we pull over for two girls, each carrying a cake, each about twenty, giggling to themselves in the back seat. Sisters? No, just friends. They're on their way home, to the next town, Guanabo. We pass a photo shoot, by the water: a skeletal blond woman, a photographer, a band of Cuban men, grinning in matching shirts, all standing in front of a mid-'50s Chevy, powder blue. We all wonder who the model is. Anyone we know? The girls giggle more. We're suddenly pals, they and all hitchers instantly familiar, completely at ease—as if we've picked up classmates on the way to the minimart. Safety here is assumed, trust a given. Where is there danger in Cuba? This is unclear.

Sand covers the road. We almost get blindsided by a mural-burdened van from Pastors for Peace. Bumper stickers thereon: END THE EMBARGO! *¡VAMOS A CUBA!* Terrible drivers, these guys.

> ───────────※───────────
>
> To the list of Cuba's para-doxes, add the following: no one in Havana has a telephone but everybody's neighbor has one.
>
> —TM

We drop the cake-bearing girls on the corner just past Guanabo's main drag and pick up a much older woman, sixty or so, who's been visiting her mother and needs to go just a little ways out of town. Ten minutes later—*¡Aquí, aquí!*—she gets out. She smiles thank-you, and we smile goodbye—and again we're empty. We don't like to be empty. Through the Cuban countryside we feel ashamed to have the back seat unpeopled—all this room we have, all this fuel. It's getting dark, and as the roads go black, what was a steady supply of hitchhikers, punctuating the roads like mile markers, quickly disappears. Where they go is unclear. What happens

when night comes but a ride hasn't? It's a problem of basic math
we cannot fathom: always there are more riders than rides, a ten-to-
one ratio at best, so what are the odds that all riders will be trans-
ported before sunset?

At Varadero, there is money. Resorts and busloads of European
tourists waiting impatiently in lobbies for their bags to be ported to
their private beachside cabanas. There are buffets and games of
water polo organized in the main pool—a ridiculous sort of comfort level for about one hundred dollars a night. (Best yet, the help
is obsequious and a fifty-cent tip would do just fine!) After being
turned away at the daunting gates of the massive Club Med, we
drop our luggage next door and set out to the area's most fiery hot
spot, the Café Havana, a huge disco/Hard Rock-style fun provider.
The place is overflowing with tourists from around the world, come
to see how the Cubans entertain.

We sit at a table by the stage, and after some fantastic salsa-danc-
ing action—women wearing little beyond sequins and feathers—
there is a magician, ponytailed, with two ponytailed assistants. And
this magician's specialty is doves. Everywhere he is making doves
appear. From his sleeve, a dove. From a newspaper, a dove. A balloon
is popped, and a dove appears and flaps wildly. The crowd loves it.
The doves appear, each one flailing its wings for a few seconds of
chaos and quasi-freedom. Then the magician, with fluid noncha-
lance, grabs the dove form the air, two-handed, making from the
explosion of feathery white a smooth inanimate sculpture of a bird.
Then in one swift motion he shoves the doves into a small cage,
with little steel bars, on a stand by his waist. Once inside, the doves
sit docilely, staring ahead through the tiny silver bars. Though there
is a hole just behind them, they sit, cooing—one dove, then two,
three, four, five, six, all in a row. When he is done, the magician is
applauded. We all love him. The birds in their cage, content and so
pretty. How does he do it? He is fantastic. Then the band comes on,
and everyone dances.

The next day we're off, Varadero to Cienfuegos. First passengers,
from the roadside crowd of fifteen or twenty: a mother-and-child
duo, the mother skinny and snaggle-toothed, the baby prefect and

in pink, eleven months old, little black shoes, shiny; they're headed
home. We roll with them past horse-drawn wagons and slow, lanky
cows. Egrets skim over the road, perpendicular. Air warm, sky overcast. The car screams.

They get out near Jovellanos, and we never get their names. In
Jovellanos, a medium-size adobe town of narrow streets, we get lost,
quickly and irrevocably. At a street corner there appears beside us a
man on a bicycle. He knows where to go, he says—just follow him.
We rumble behind him and his bike at fifteen miles per hour, the
streets full of onlookers watching our parade—left turn, right, left,
left, right, left, ten minutes and there we are, back on the main road.
He points ahead, toward the on-ramp. Aha.

We pull up next to him. He is sweating profusely and grinning.
We slip him $5—for many, we're told, that's almost a month's
salary—because we are wealthy and glamorous Americans and we
appreciate his help. So easy to change the quality, the very direction
of Cubans' lives! It seems possible that, between our ride sharing
and tip giving, we can single-handedly redress whatever harm has
been done. Oh, if only!

Just outside Jovellanos there's Estelle, chatty, about thirty-five, and
her ten-year-old Javier, who jump in at a dusty corner. Estelle sighs
and laughs as she gets in and says hello. Had they been waiting long?
Yes, yes, she says, they'd been waiting an hour and a half. They're
going to a town called Australia, twenty minutes away. "Why is
there a town in Cuba called Australia?" we ask. Estelle doesn't
know. She turns to Javier. Javier has no idea. She shrugs and smiles.

We dodge more wagons, their drivers frequently asleep, the
donkeys as sad as donkeys insist on appearing. There are men in
uniform waiting for rides. There are women with groceries and
babies waiting for rides. Some of the hitchers raise their hands to a
passing car, but most don't. Some express frustration when they feel
that a passing car could fit more people (i.e., them), but most don't.
Most just watch you pass, squinting beyond you, for the next slow-
ing car or truck. But when a car stops, never is there competition
for the ride. Never is there shoving or even the most mild sort of
disagreement. Each time we pull over, whoever's closest simply

walks to the car and gets in. There is no system in place for the rewarding of longest wait, or oldest, or most pregnant. It's both perfectly fair and completely random.

We drop Estelle and Javier in Australia and pick up a family just outside of town. Grandfather, mother, daughter. They had been visiting a friend at the hospital and are going where we're going, to Playa Girón, home of the Cuban monument to the heroes of the Bay of Pigs. Our merengue tape, bought at a gas station, tinkles quietly from the speakers. We offer them—we offer everyone—water, cookies, crackers. They decline, and like most riders, this family says nothing unless we speak first; they don't even talk to one another. They watch the countryside pass. Content. We are surprised, with them and most riders, that they do not want to know where we're from. Why are they not curious about us, the Americans here to save them? At their house, a bent-over salmon-colored ranch on a brown-dirt street, they ask us if we'd like to come in for a cold drink. We decline, must move. They scoot out. In the process, the daughter's shoe catches on the seat and loses its heel. She looks up, embarrassed, horrified. "New shoes too," says Mom. We all chuckle and then sigh. *Kids.*

After Girón, we're headed to Cienfuegos, through more fields of tobacco, then bananas. When night comes again, there are no streetlights, no lights anywhere, and on the winding two-lane roads, the avoidance of donkey carts and tractors and people requires tremendous, arcadelike hand-eye coordination. All is dark, and then things will suddenly be in front of us, lit as if by a camera's flash; swerving is an essential skill. Up ahead a car is parked, hazards blinking. There is a group of people around the car. Obviously an ambush. We should not stop. In the United States, we would not stop.

We stop. Four people are standing around a white, early '70s Volvo. They're out of gas; can we help? Yes, yes, we say, of course. They want to siphon from our tank. They have an actual siphon right there. We don't have enough, we say, noticing that we're almost out ourselves. We'll take them to the next town. Another man, Esteban, about nineteen, gets in the back seat, as does Marisa, twenty-four, petite, in silk blouse and black jeans. They hold the gas container on their laps. It's fifteen minutes to tiny-town Roda and its one-pump gas station.

As we wait, we talk to Marisa, who we learn is studying English; she wants to get into tourism. She is married to an American, a photographer from Los Angeles. She was just coming back from Havana, as a matter of fact, where she was seeing him off at the airport.

So who are the others in the car?

She doesn't know. It's a taxi.

A taxi? A taxi running out of gas?

Big laughs all around.

The taxi was taking three passengers the three hours from Havana to Cienfuegos; the driver had grossly miscalculated how much fuel that would require. They had left at three that afternoon. It was now at least nine. We fill up their container and are ready to go.

But the Subaru won't start. It won't even turn over. In a flash, Esteban is out of the car and pushing. I'm driving, and he's barking orders, which need to be translated instantaneously by T/N. I have no idea what we're doing. We stop. Esteban, sighing loudly, takes my place, and then I'm pushing. Down the road, and before long we're out of the town and into the dark fields. The road is red from the taillights and slippery and I can't get a grip, but then boom, Esteban pops the clutch and the Subaru whinnies and I get in while it's moving and we're off, Esteban at the wheel. Like a getaway car! In a minute Esteban's doing eighty miles per hour. He's veering on and off the road. "*¡Flojo! ¡Flojo!*" Marisa is saying, urging him to slow down, but young Esteban has something to prove to her and to T/N, so eighty it is, the engine hitting high notes with full vibrato.

We get to the taxi. They fill up the Volvo while we wait. We meet the third passenger, Dale, an English-speaking med student from St. Kitts, who decides he's sick of speaking Spanish, so he'll ride to Cienfuegos with us. He's studying Spanish there, the first year of seven he'll spend in Cuba on his way to a medical degree. We follow the taxi into Cienfuegos, drop off Dale at his barbed wire-surrounded dormitory, check into a hotel with red lightbulbs and a lounge singer plowing through the high points of the Billy Joel songbook, and we're done for the night.

In the morning, on the way to the town of Trinidad, it's all rolling hills and farms, and the people have been waiting for us. At an intersection ten miles out of Cienfuegos we stop at a gathering of twenty or so, mostly young men, some in uniform. One gets in, followed by a woman, running—she's just jumped out of another car and into ours. Her name is Maela and like the vast majority of Cuban women, Maela, is a devout spandex enthusiast. She's in a black-and-white bodysuit, bisected with a belt, and she's laughing like mad at her car-to-car coup, the soldiers tossing her a wide variety of obscene gestures as we drive away. The soldier we've got is named Jordan; he's doing the mandatory military service—two years—and is heading home for the weekend. Maela was in Cienfuegos with friends and is going home too. He's quiet, but she's bubbly, and through the countryside we roll....

Halfway to Trinidad, while we are passing La Güira, something recklessly symbolic happens. At the bottom of a small valley, there is a split second when a huge, bulbous green army truck passes us, heading in the other direction. At the same instant,

---

Cuba has a power and a draw like a wonderful faded beauty. Her streets house buildings that recall a time when flourish, detail, and color dotted the landscape. Beaches hug every angle of Cuba's coast. On occasion I locked gazes with old women, probably themselves great beauties in their heydays. They were women in search of elusive tomatoes, or waiting in line for rationed round brown rolls. They found my gaze and seemed to inquire if all the struggle was worth the full population in school, the high number of doctors educated and working in crumbling hospitals without medicines to prescribe because pharmaceuticals and building supplies are embargoed. For me it was a space between spring and summer, between taking care and looking.

—Wickham Boyle, "Cuba Between the Worlds"

we are passing on our right a straw-hatted farmer on horseback and, to our left, a woman on a bicycle. Symbolism contained: each of our vehicles represents a different element of what makes Cuba Cuba. The bicycle is the Cubans' resourcefulness and symbiosis with their Communist brethren (about a million bikes were donated by the Chinese, a decade ago). The army truck is the constant (though relatively sedate and casual, we'd say) military presence. We are the tourists, perhaps the future, our dollars feeding into Cuba's increasingly dominant second economy, largely inaccessible to Cuba's proletariat; and the horseback farmer represents, of course, the country's rural backbone. All caught, for one split second, on a single linear plane.

Fun!

Dave Eggers is the editor of McSweeney's, *a quarterly publication and web site, and the author of* A Heartbreaking Work of Staggering Genius *and* You Shall Know Our Velocity. *He also runs 826 Valencia, a writing center for students ages eight through eighteen in San Francsico.*

PART THREE

GOING YOUR OWN WAY

ENRIQUE FERNÁNDEZ

* * *

Party Time

The author's ancestral home embraces him,
and he returns the warmth.

MY FAMILY MOVED TO THE UNITED STATES WHEN I WAS THIRTEEN, and like most Cuban-Americans, they never went back. Raised in Havana, I had been a city boy, used to apartment buildings, buses, trolleys and the general bustle of the metropolis. But at least once a year, we piled into the car and drove to Zulueta, where there were far more horses than cars, where the houses had wooden portals in front and mango and avocado trees out back, and where the men were mustachioed peasants who wore wide-brimmed straw hats and riding boots, and had sharp machetes slung from their waists. I played with my country cousins on the porch of my great-aunt's spacious house and watched the horsemen leave their mounts tied outside my great-uncle's country store next door, to step in for a drink of rum.

Now, finally, I am returning to my father's dreamscape. I have chosen the end of the year, the time when, traditionally, Zulueta's errant children return for the *parrandas*, or parties, wild year-end revels that are exactly one century old. Visiting Zulueta will also afford me a chance to see what I like to think of as the real Cuba, the backwater Cuba, the Cuba that is not the subject of constant journalistic exposure and political analysis. Mostly, though, I want

169

to see for myself if the town's romance is overblown by nostalgia—
my father's and my own. I want to walk into the storybook and either
feel its pages crumble when reality hits or get lost between its covers.

I remember the *parrandas* well from my childhood. Celebrating
the New Year, the townsfolk divide into two historic camps, vying
against each other to see who can produce the best parade float and
the most spectacular fireworks for New Year's Eve. Excitement builds
during the preceding week, as each neighborhood stages impromptu
parades and minor displays of fireworks, all to the accompaniment
of beating drums, singing, and dancing. Dawn on December 31 is
ushered in with a conga line that weaves through town; later in the
day, final touches are put on the floats, and the fireworks are set up.
Come nightfall, the wild heart of the *parrandas* is unleashed, as the
two neighborhoods take turns parading their floats—immense, fan-
ciful contraptions meant to go only up and down the main drag—
and setting off massive fireworks displays. From then on, all through
the night, there will be more fireworks: no one sleeps and the rum
flows. In the morning, the winning neighborhood dances through
the streets again in a triumphal march.

Arriving in Zulueta one night in late December, I head for the
house belonging to Mercedes Garit, the sister-in-law of a friend of
my family's, who has kindly agreed to put me up. Located on Parque
Armona, the town's main square, her home is a perfect spot to catch
the festivities. As soon as I have unpacked, Mercedes' thirteen-year-
old daughter, Yesi, and her friends escort me around the town. The
preparations for the *parrandas* are feverishly going on; we poke into
warehouses and homes where floats are being built, costumes are
being sewn, and fireworks have been stored.

Considering that the Cuban economy is in the worst slump of
its history, it's a miracle that something as festive and impractical as
the *parrandas* is going on. By my calculation, the hundred-year mark
of the celebration means that the annual festival has survived the
Spanish colonization, a shaky republic, two right-wing dictators, and
decades of Communism....

Zulueta prospered as a sugar mill center until early in this century, when the Carretera Central, a two-lane highway that ran the

full length of the island, bypassed the town. Isolation set in, turning the town into a microeconomy with limited opportunities for its native children, such as my grandfather, a small entrepreneur who was forced to migrate to Havana in the 1940s. Isolation meant that the same families would often intermarry, so that by the time of my childhood everyone there was my "cousin." And isolation also shaped Zulueta into a magical, eccentric world....

During the *parrandas*, politics takes a backseat, and even though the celebration date coincides with the anniversary of the Cuban Revolution—on January 1, 1959, Batista fled Cuba and the revolutionaries took over—it is scarcely mentioned. In this town around New Year's, whose side you are on has little to do with ideology and everything to do with whether your heart belongs to La Loma or to Guanijibes, the rival neighborhood terms.

For nothing it seems, can stop the *zulueteños'* passion for partying, pyrotechnics, and friendly, if intense, competition between the uphill and downhill neighborhoods. Indeed, as I tour the town with Yesi and her friends, fierce-looking men block my way when I try to cross into either of the competing sides—only to allow me in and invite me to join them in a drink after I explain that I'm an impartial journalist.

Later that evening, my teenage guides and I walk back to Parque Armona, in the center of the La Loma neighborhood. Like any typical, small-town Latin American plaza, it is ringed by important buildings, such as the church, the movie theater, the police headquarters, the home of the town's most distinguished citizen—a doctor—and the assembly hall where, in my father's time, Zulueta's "society" events were held. After describing some of my family's houses to my young friends and being told they are around the corner from the church, I set out on my own, telling them, "I'm off in search of my childhood."

Back then, my family would stay with my grandmother's sister, América, who had married a prosperous merchant and lived in a spacious house next to my great-uncle's store. Under the starlight, I recognize the store. The house next to it looks somewhat rundown, but I figure this must be it. When I knock, a sliver of an old man answers, and I tell him I'm looking for Rosa, América's daughter.

"We knew a grandson of Concha [my paternal grandmother] was coming to write a story," says an old woman I instantly recognize, although the last time we met she could not have been more than thirty. "I knew it had to be you."

The house has weathered inside as well as outside, quite different from the days when my great-aunt América kept it shining and full of the porcelain figurines both she and my grandmother loved. But its spaces are still big and noble, and its ceiling, like those of other old Zulueta houses, is incredibly high. "Enriquito, don't you know who I am?" a voice behind me asks, using the diminutive of my childhood. I turn to see a stocky man about my age in jeans and a baseball cap. "It's me, Julito."

Julio, Rosa's son and my playmate during my Zulueta sojourns, is now a sugar mill technician during the sugar season and a soccer trainer the rest of the year. Later, we're joined by another cousin, "Tin Tin," who arrives from the provincial capital of Santa Clara, where he lives today. Tin Tin is really named José Agustín, after his grandfather, but since the latter's nickname was "Tin," the grandson's was doubled; I remember him as a skinny kid always riding a borrowed horse. Neither of them has changed much since we were children, and they become my companions during my days in Zulueta—the country cousins and the city cousin reunited as playmates once more.

The week of festive preparation doesn't prepare me for the hectic sweep of events when the *parrandas* finally hit. Well before dawn on the morning of New Year's Eve, I am awakened by the conga line snaking through town to officially start the festivities. Led by musicians playing conga drums and cowbells, it stops at the houses where homecoming *zulenteños* are staying, inviting them to join the dance. As I shuffle gracelessly to the drumbeat, trying to wake up and not stumble in the dark, a lithe black man scolds me, "You haven't danced a step. Enjoy yourself, sonny boy. Life is short. Ha!" He's right. Surrounded by hypnotic rhythm and euphoric people, I effortlessly lose myself.

After a couple of hours, I hear the beat of the music change to a rumba. The drummers have stopped leading the conga line and are now sitting on a stoop on the town's main street, the Calle Real. Merging with the growing crowd, now moving in unison to the rumba beat, I see the drummers for the first time. They are all black; in Zulueta, as in the rest of Cuba, the African heritage is strong. Excitement mounts as La Loma and Guanijibes rivals set off fireworks and yell out for their neighborhoods:"*¡Viva La Loma!*" "*¡Viva Guanijibes!*" Then, huge banners for each neighborhood are waved on the street, each swing of the colors equally met by cheers and shouts of derision.

Suddenly, the La Loma standard-bearer climbs to a second-story rooftop above the drummers, triumphantly waving his neighborhood's red flag. He is a white *guajiro*, as Cuban peasants are called, with a big mustache and dreamy eyes. Judging by the effort it costs him to climb up and wave the heavy banner, it's obvious that he's had too much rum.

The black-skinned Guanijibes flag-bearer, the muscles of his bare torso gleaming, climbs after his rival with the agility of a circus acrobat. To the joy of his supporters, he reaches a rooftop above his adversary and waves his blue flag even higher than La Loma's, a broad grin on his face. Flustered, the *lomero* scampers on the rooftops with an unsure step to an even higher spot, carrying the big, heavy flagpole and the La Loma flag. He is waving it there when someone next to me, putting rivalry aside, says, "I just hope he doesn't fall and hurt himself. It's happened before."…

The Parque Armona is ringed twice by sawhorses studded with fireworks, with more fireworks-laden sawhorses stretching for one full block at each of its four corners. Down in Guanijibes, another park is similarly armed. That doesn't include the countless hand-held fireworks. Nor the "mortars," cannon loaded with fireworks that produce a double explosion, one when the explosive is fired and another when it bursts in the air.

We're talking sheer firepower here. It's not the elegance of the display that will win points for the competing neighborhoods, but the relentlessness and volume of the bombast. *Zulueteños* are hooked on it. My cousin Tin Tin has been saying all week, "I can't wait for the fireworks to start." And my old aunt Rosa, who has a broken hip, floods with tears whenever she thinks about not being right in the middle of the fireworks this year. A tough, muscular *guajiro*, whose soiled t-shirt and work pants are the result of his round-the-clock hard labor building his neighborhood's float, takes me aside to tell me that the authorities have set a limit on the fireworks each side can set off. "When you go back," he confides, "tell my people that I would die for my neighborhood, and that if these policemen don't let us use all we have, I don't know what I'm going to do. I don't know." And he breaks into tears.

As the night of December 31 falls, the town of Zulueta is literally ready to go off. The La Loma float begins its stately descent down the main street. Its theme is an elaborate Russian fairy tale— Slavic folklore has slipped into Cuba via the Soviet influence— about beautiful princesses, gallant princes, evil wizards, and the metamorphosis of magic animals into people and vice versa. It has all been elaborately staged, with papier-mâché elephants, dances, and acted-out dramatic sequences that follow a narration under-scored by a musical track....

The Guanijibes float is no less elaborate, though its theme, "tri-umphant backdrops," is not as exotic. On the platforms of various heights there are characters who recall the themes of floats that have won previous *parrandas* competitions: Helen of Troy, Swan Lake, the Emperor and the Nightingale, Romeo and Juliet. This one is a crowd-pleaser, more successful than the dense narrative of the La Loma float. When it reaches the crossroads, a trapdoor opens and a figure all in white (representing the African goddess Obatalá, it is later explained) rises from the depths of the float. She is merely a mannequin, but veiled in smoke and darkness she is enlivened by a huge fireworks display—beautiful lights, not just bomb blasts— released in perfect timing so as to rise behind the float like a heavenly crown.

"Tasteful," everyone agrees when the cheering subsides. After the flag incident and the clear advantage of the Guanijibes float, the *guanijiberos* seem to have the edge. But the fireworks display is yet to come. And it does come. For the next several hours—all through the night, in fact—the exhilarating explosions never cease. The sawhorses that ring the Parque Armona are refilled no fewer than three times. My clothes are impregnated with the smell of gunpowder, and for the next couple of days the whole town reeks of it....

Who wins the 100th Zulueta *parrandas*? As always, it's popular sentiment that decides. If the elegance of the floats and costumes were the true criterion, Guanijibes would be the winner this year. But, agree the zulueteños (the lomeros loudly, in public; the guanijiberos quietly, in private), Lo Loma out-boomed Guanijibes. The following day, in a gesture of friendship and sibling solidarity, both neighborhoods dance through the town in a joint victory parade, and both flags are raised in triumph. On this, the centennial year, the winner is not a neighborhood but, instead, the spirit of unbridled imagination.

And, in a way, those of us who have come back to Zulueta are winners, too. The *parrandas* are the public celebration I have come here to witness. But I also came for something else, something locked in my father's dreams and my own memories. On the night I arrived, I was struck by the beauty of the town; the starry night served as a backdrop to Zulueta's modest one-and-two-story houses, its portals, its impossibly high ceilings, its old cobbled streets, its tropical fruit trees silhouetted against the black sky....

Perhaps Zulueta's isolation has been a blessing in disguise. Regardless of what change is coming to this country—or even what lack of change—the native children of this town will always know who they are: *zulueteños* all year round, but *guanijiberos* and *lomeros* at year's end. Having come back here after so many years, some of that ease has rubbed off on me, and at least part of me also knows now with great certainty who I am. I have found my childhood. I have come home.

Enrique Fernández did not know how much his lifestyle had deteriorated since early childhood. The features editor for The Miami Herald, *he is working on a collage of dreams, monologues, recollections, and current experiences about Havana, a city he plans to live in as soon as* Zig-Zag, *a twenty-two-year-old no-holds-barred political satire magazine terminated by the Castro government in 1960, is published again.*

✴ ✴ ✴

You Beautiful Doll

She didn't feel she was home
until she was home.

I HAD BEEN IN HAVANA LESS THAN THREE DAYS AND ALREADY I WAS arousing curiosity. The taxi driver kept glancing over his shoulder at me as we rumbled along a crowded downtown street, wondering how such an obvious foreigner could sound so Cuban.

"Where did you learn your Spanish?" he asked.

He had reason to wonder. My clothing was cleaner and newer, and my skin smoother and paler than those of any of the people my age milling about on the sidewalk.

"I was born here," I explained. "This is my first time back since I was three years old."

The driver pondered this a moment. "You left when you were only three? Ah," he mused, "then you're hardly Cuban at all any more."

It was nearly dusk, and clouds of dust and diesel smoke tinted the air brown, making the crowds and the crumbling neoclassical buildings we passed look fuzzy and surreal. Through the dirty window I could see the faces of people who might have been my classmates, neighbors, friends, lovers. They hurried down the street, women sweating in cheap polyester dresses, sooty men on bicycles pedaling behind exhaust-belching buses. I tried to picture myself among them as if I had never left. Hustling home exhausted by the sheer difficulty of life with a few plantains and bit of black-market pork stashed in my shopping bag, provided I had the means.

"I've always liked to think I'm Cuban," I told him. "But I don't know."

I've never known. Children of immigrants are really two people, the one who is and the one who would have been. That other me ceased to exist when my family left Cuba ten years after the revolution, my parents complaining of long lines and little opportunity. Like most immigrant parents, they wanted to give me a comfortable life. So they came to the United States, and I became a different person in the process.

Growing up in Los Angeles, Cuba was little more to me than a myth, a shadowy world of black and white that existed only in old photographs. There were photos of our house in Havana, of me playing with my first friend next door, of my grandmother—a stranger who wrote saying she loved me—cradling a gray baby against mildewed foreign walls. I remember feeling guilty for not being able to feel sadness when she died. In my young mind, she was a black-and-white photograph, a handful of letters on thin paper, a crackling, disembodied voice calling from a remote place that I was repeatedly told had once been my home. None of it seemed real, not my grandmother, not even the child in the photos everyone said was me.

I finally returned as a tourist, eagerly bracing myself for the emotional impact that I knew would inevitably come when I arrived. I would see the same weathered building I had seen in the photos, the same flat rooftops, the same narrow streets, and finally feel a connection. I would cry with relief, home at last. The morning after I landed, I excitedly flung open my hotel window and gazed out past the weathered rooftops at the Caribbean, repeating, "I'm here, I'm here," like an incantation.

Nothing happened. Faded laundry fluttered in the moist breeze, horns honked below, the clouds shifted overhead. I could have been anywhere.

So tonight in the taxi, I carried a few old photos with me, determined to breathe life into them. The streets grew darker and emptier as we moved away from downtown, past deserted intersections where burning oil cans glowed in the thick brown dusk, serving as rough street-lamps. We eventually turned off the main thoroughfare onto a narrow street lined with decaying colonial houses, all of them huddled close. In the remaining light I could see that some had not been painted in decades. Their once-stately facades were pocked with crumbling plaster, their graceful iron gates rusted through. The driver stopped in front of one painted a faded green. I had seen this house a million times, but no one had ever told me it was green.

"Calle Lacret, number sixty-five," the driver announced. "This is where you wanted to go, right?"

Old women stared from their front porches as I got out. Maybe they had watched me as a baby, but now I was a stranger, someone to eye with suspicion. I stood in front of our old house for a long time, holding a wrinkled photo of my family posing outside, all of us gray. It was hard to imagine that this was the same house, that I had existed here.

> Most of the yard was completely overgrown; manicured lawns with shrubs, pretty tropical landscaping and flowers all around had given way to an arid, dusty yard, and most of the front of the house was obscured by out-of-control trees and vines. The house itself was in remarkably good shape, as it was all plaster, cement and tile construction. Nothing had been painted or repaired in thirty-eight years. The main outbuilding had been turned into a chicken coop, and there were old car parts, axles, and what looked like the bed of an old truck rusting on one side of the yard. Where globes had once been for lights at each rise in the wall were nothing but rusted spikes with wires hanging out of a few of them. All in all, the place was a mess, but I was home, and glad of it.
>
> —Tom Mosby, visiting the Cuban home of his youth

No one seemed to be home tonight. But there were lights on next door, and I recognized this house, too, from photographs. I knocked on a heavy door flanked by dirty marble columns, and it soon creaked open, revealing a heavy, older woman, her hair in curlers.

"*Buenas noches*," I started uneasily. "I don't know if you remember me, but I lived next door when I was little. My name is Leslie. My family moved to the United States."

The woman stared at me intently. "Leslita? You're Leslita?"

I nodded, producing a photo of her daughter and me as toddlers on a seesaw. The woman covered her mouth. She began crying.

"*¡Ay, Dios mío!* Leslita!"

With that she flung her big arms around me. A younger woman rushed out to see what the commotion was. She was chubby, with long black hair and a cherubic face the color of nutmeg.

"Lolita," her mother cried, flopping me around like a doll to face her. "Do you remember your first friend? Leslita, from next door?"

Lolita looked dumbfounded. "Is it true?" I nodded. Her mother kept sobbing.

"Can you believe it?" her mother cried. "After all these years, she has come home! That same little girl who left so long ago has come home!"

These last words settled on me like magic dust. I suddenly took notice of the bright-yellow tile on the front porch where we had played as babies, the lush green of the tropical plants surrounding us, the glitter of the marble columns beneath their coating of soot. Lolita stared at me in what looked like disbelief, then rubbed her eyes for several seconds. Her cheeks were wet when she took her hands away.

"You're not going to believe this," she said. "Your mother gave me one of your dolls when you left. My sister and I named her Leslita, because we missed you."

I glanced down quickly at the photograph in my hand, then back at Lolita's face, smiling at me for the first time since early childhood. It was soft, brown, warm, real. A lifetime's worth of gray myth was coming alive all around me in vivid color. The little girl in the photographs still existed for these people, still Cuban, still one of them. She was real. And she was me.

Leslie Berestein grew up poring over National Geographic *magazines until she was old enough to hit the road, and hasn't stopped traveling since. Between trips, she has written about immigrants for the* Los Angeles Times *and the* Orange County Register. *She wrote about people who aren't famous for the English and Spanish editions of* People, *and is now a staff writer for the* San Diego Union-Tribune.

TOM MILLER

* ✱ *

Remember the *Maine*?

*The longest running whodunit started in Havana Harbor
one Tuesday night more than a century ago.*

TO LEARN THE STORY OF THE USS *MAINE*, PULL UP A RICKETY
wooden chair at Dos Hermanos, a dockside bar on Avenida Del
Puerto in Havana's sprawling harbor district. If you had been out
with pre-Lenten celebrants at the Dos Hermanos on February 15,
1898, you would have seen a shiny American battleship dominating
the Bay. Cuba, then fighting for its independence from Spain, had
drawn the world's attention for the tenacity of its guerrilla forces
against a sophisticated European power. Off and on for three
decades the notion of Cuba Libre, a free Cuba, had motivated the
country's intellectuals, *campesinos*, and former slaves. The intermittent war attracted a youthful Winston Churchill, an aging Clara
Barton, and a host of other foreigners for a firsthand look at insur-
gency and its ghastly consequences.

The harbor was busy in early 1898. Since its arrival three weeks
earlier, the *Maine* had been moored to buoy No. 4 between a
Spanish ship, the *Alfonso XII*, and a German cruiser, the *Gneisenau*.
Earlier that February 15, the *City of Washington*, a Ward Line steamer
full of Americans, had arrived and anchored about three hundred
yards away. Bars like the Dos Hermanos were full of sailors, dock-
hands, international traders, and the *habaneros*—Havana residents—

181

who catered to them. Spain had recently given a measure of auton-
omy to Cuba, a move that satisfied neither the liberationists who
demanded full independence, the Spanish merchants who benefited
from colonialism, or the occupying army, which ceded power reluctantly. General Ramón Blanco, who had been installed by Spain as
Cuba's governor-general only three months earlier, had a thankless
task. He and his underlings received the *Maine* with politic cordial-
ity. His men gave Captain Charles D. Sigsbee and his officers a case
of Spanish sherry, locally rolled cigars, and box seats to the bull
fights. At Dos Hermanos and other bars, Spanish wine flowed.

On board the *Maine* that Tuesday night, sailors danced to an
accordion in the starboard gangway; elsewhere a crewman plucked
the strings of a mandolin. Shortly after nine o'clock you might have
heard C. H. Newton, the *Maine's* bugler from Washington, D.C.,
blow taps. The handsome ship bobbed listlessly, its nose pointing
slightly northwest, its imposing 100-yard length visible from stem to
stern for all Havana to see. The three-year-old vessel, despite its rank
as a "second-class" battleship, was well-known within the military
establishment. "I wish there was a chance the *Maine* was going to be
used against some foreign power," Assistant Secretary of the Navy
Theodore Roosevelt had written a month earlier, "by preference
Germany—but...I'd take even Spain if nothing better offered."

At 9:40 P.M. the *Maine's* forward end abruptly lifted itself from
the water. Along the pier, passersby could hear a rumbling explosion. Within seconds, another eruption—this one deafening and
massive—splintered the bow, sending anything that wasn't battened
down, and most that was, flying more than two hundred feet into
the air. Bursts of flame and belches of smoke filled the night sky;
water flooded into the lower decks and quickly rose to the upper
ones. Some sailors were thrown violently from the blazing ship and
drowned in the harbor. Others, just falling asleep in their ham-
mocks, were pancaked between floors and ceilings fused together by
the sudden, intense heat. Still more drowned on board or suffocated
from overpowering smoke. In all, 266 of the 350 men aboard the
Maine were killed, including bugler Newton.

From Dos Hermanos you could feel the explosion. As the air

thickened and lights went out, people instinctively streamed toward the dock. The explosion hit with such force that Havana's power plant was temporarily knocked out. Firemen rushed to the harbor. The foreign press, a chummy and highly competitive bunch, emerged from its lair at the Hotel Inglaterra coffee shop and raced to the waterfront. Two of them got by harbor guards by claiming to be ship's officers.

Captain Sigsbee, who had been in his cabin in the aft section of the ship at the time of the blast, groped his way to the deck, assessed the damage and ordered all hands into the lifeboats. When he finally stepped into one himself, he was the last to leave the sinking ship. The dreadful explosion had taken place less than one hour earlier, but the aftermath seemed to hang in time. Sigsbee went straight to the *City of Washington*, where Spanish officials rushed to offer help. There he scribbled a telegram to Washington, with the most important words of his life: "*Maine* blown up in Havana harbor at 9:40 tonight and destroyed. Many wounded and doubtless more killed or drowned.... Public opinion should be suspended until further report...." The captain tried to sleep on the Ward Line steamer, but moans from injured sailors in a makeshift sick bay and explosions from his own ship's magazines kept him awake most of the night.

The *Maine* was in Havana harbor, officially, on a mission of friendly courtesy, and incidentally, to protect American lives and property should the need arise. Yet the visit was neither spontaneous nor altruistic; the United States had been eyeing Cuba for almost a century. "I candidly confess," wrote Thomas Jefferson in 1809, "that I have ever looked upon Cuba as the most interesting addition that can be made to our system of States." The following year President Madison warned Great Britain to keep its hands off the island. And in the late 1820s, John Quincy Adams declared that Cuba had become "an object of transcendent importance to the commercial and political interests of our Union." He likened the island to an apple that could fall from its native tree and "gravitate only towards the North American Union."

Cubans were wary of the *Maine*'s presence in their harbor. For many, then as now, the ship came to symbolize unwarranted intrusion. But the islanders already had the Spanish to contend with. Spain's strategy in 1896–1897 under Governor-General Weyler was simple: round up everyone in the countryside and herd them into military townships. This, Weyler reasoned, would deprive the insurgents of support. The results of his plan were catastrophic. Cubans lived in concentration-camp conditions—severe crowding, almost no food, and rampant disease. Untended crops throughout the country went to waste as thousands starved; many died. Americans learned of this inhumanity with increasing horror and sympathized squarely with Cuba Libre. Despite Weyler's ruthless approach, however, the persistent Cuban insurgents were close to exhausting the superior Spanish land forces when the *Maine* arrived on its "friendly" mission. Spain's shameful strategy, coupled with our longstanding lust for Cuba, produced ideal conditions for the United States to enter the fray. Our destiny was manifest; the apple finally looked ready to fall.

The sheer magnitude of the explosion and its aftermath, coupled with Captain Sigsbee's admonishment that the public not rush to judgment, created a bubble of suspended opinion in the States. Newspapers initially reported the catastrophe with-out elaboration, leaving blame and lurid details for another day. At first, President William McKinley and Secretary of the Navy John Long considered the possibility that the ship's destruction was due to an accident. It could well have been an internal problem; explosions from faulty wiring

> Cuba seems to have the same effect on American administrations that the full moon once had on werewolves.
> —Wayne S. Smith, retired U.S. diplomat to Havana

and self-igniting coal had plagued the Navy for years. But the bubble of suspended judgment soon burst. On February 17, William Randolph Hearst's *New York Journal* headlined: "THE WAR SHIP *MAINE* WAS SPLIT IN TWO BY AN ENEMY'S SECRET INFERNAL MA-

CHINE." It showed drawings revealing how an explosive device had been planted beneath the *Maine* and how it was detonated from shore. Joseph Pulitzer's *New York World* gave readers a choice— "*MAINE* EXPLOSION CAUSED BY BOMB OR TORPEDO?"—and immediately sent divers to Havana "to learn the truth." The *New York Herald* and the *Journal*, which offered a $50,000 reward for evidence of a mine, were eager to send their own underwater investigative teams. Reporters in Havana were on top of the story, and their editors in the States were determined to squeeze every drop of tragedy possible from their coverage.

The United States had not fought on foreign soil since the Mexican War in the late 1840s. All the catalysts that bring on war were in place—land to be grabbed, money to be made, diplomatic trump cards to be played, wrongs to be righted, influence to be widened, evil to be avenged, and a military ready to be mobilized— all these the *Maine*'s explosion galvanized. President McKinley— "spineless as a chocolate éclair," wrote Teddy Roosevelt—wanted to wait until his formal inquiry into the tragedy was concluded before calling for war against Spain, but he was about the last American with that much patience. The families of sailors killed on the battleship urged the president to jump into the fracas. Throughout America, eager teenagers asked where they could enlist. Newspapers fed the fever as congressmen were deluged with letters calling for revenge on Spain. Governor Culbertson of Texas sent Rangers to guard the Mexican border against an invasion by "Spanish sympathizers." Maine's Governor Llewellyn Powers, fearing attack by Spain, asked for Navy cruisers to defend his jagged 4,500-mile coastline. Behind the scenes Spain refused to sell Cuba outright to the United States. In Cuba, U.S. Counsel General Lee called for eventual annexation, beginning with occupation. Havana could sniff the foul scent of impending war.

Reaction to the *Maine*'s destruction took many forms. Americans grieved, opened up their hearts and their wallets to *Maine* widows and orphans, sought solace in religion—and came up with money-raising schemes. Even before the U.S. investigation concluded the explosion was not accidental, that a mine laid by unknown parties had blown up beneath the ship, a Johnstown, New York, business-man suggested breaking up what was left of the *Maine* into memen-tos. "The wood," he wrote, "could be made into canes." The Siegel-Cooper department store asked the government for the *Maine's* scrap to cut into "souvenirs, buttons, scarf pins, watch charms, medallions…and many other attractive trinkets"—all income to be turned over to *Maine* widows and orphans.

"Remember the *Maine!*"—a slogan first given notoriety by the press—became the five most common syllables in America. It was printed on peppermint lozenges, buttons, and posters; it appeared in theaters on Friday night and churches on Sunday morning. Newsstands sold toy *Maine*s made of highly inflammable material; one light and whoosh! "Shop windows and family sitting rooms," noted historian Margaret Leech in *The Age of McKinley*, "enshrined pictures and models of the lost battleship." In Havana, the menu at the Plaza de Luz restaurant included "chicken fricassee à la *Maine.*"

It was impossible to forget the *Maine*; its carcass lay in Havana Harbor protruding above the water, a grisly tourist attraction and a macabre reminder of the explosion and the lightning-fast war that followed it. Over the years a stream of suggestions flowed into the Navy Department regarding ways to dispose of the ship's remains. The Cuban government told the United States in 1903 that the *Maine* was a menace to navigation and requested that it be removed. Finally Congress, in 1910, authorized the Army Corps of Engineers to dispose of the twisting hulk. Their plan was really quite inge-nious: they built an immense cofferdam around the *Maine* and then dewatered the ship itself. Next, they made the *Maine's* skeleton sea-worthy, and finally they flooded the cofferdam so a tugboat could haul the carcass into international waters. By the time they were fin-ished examining the wreckage, they had found parts of skeletons from seventy more of the *Maine* dead. They also discovered Newton's bugle.

Captain Sigsbee's effects seemed to withstand the years well. Workers came up with his inkwell, derby hat, typewriter, and shav-ing mug. They also located his pipe, overshoes, chamber pot, and handcuffs. The ship's mainmast is at Arlington National Cemetery perched next to the burial site of 229 *Maine* sailors. Its foremast stands thirty miles away on the waterfront at Annapolis. For this reason, Navy people like to say that the *Maine* is the longest ship in the world.

Cubans had lived under three flags—the Spanish, the American, and their own—between the *Maine*'s explosion and the effort to raise the ship. The postwar U.S. military occupation lasted until May 1902, but a treaty called the Platt Amendment, forced on Cuba by Congress, allowed the United States to send in troops whenever it wanted. It did on several occasions, and the Platt Amendment wasn't abrogated until 1934. Meanwhile, as shipbuilding became more sophisticated and analysis increasingly exhaustive, more and more postmortems acknowledged that the *Maine*'s destruction could have been self-inflicted. An earlier investigation, this one by the U.S. Navy, looked at the *Maine* as it sat in the muck in Havana Harbor before being towed to sea. It said the explosion had been external.

If you had returned to your seat at Dos Hermanos on March 12, 1912, you would have had a ringside view of the Maine cabled to the tugboat *Osceola*, beginning its final voyage. Beginning at sunrise a cannon boomed every half hour from La Cabaña fortress at the entrance of the harbor. At 2:30 P.M. the seaward procession began. The hulk of the *Maine*, roses covering what remained of her deck, was towed in front of an estimated 80,000 *habaneros*, past private yachts, and out into the Gulf of Mexico. Beyond the three-mile limit, the *Osceola* drifted to a halt and the crew boarded the *Maine* to prepare it for burial. Johnny O'Brien, a local port captain, was the last to leave the sinking ship. "Some thought that the *Maine* appeared to struggle against her fate," he later wrote, "but to my mind there was not only no suggestion of a struggle but in no way could she have met a sweeter, more peaceful end."

But the story of the *Maine* did not end three miles out at sea. Although the explosion came to represent our entry into the Spanish–American War, it has become clear to historians that had the *Maine* not blown up, some other reason would have catapulted the United States into the struggle for supremacy in Cuba. Over the years, a succession of Cuban governments paid tribute to the victims of the *Maine*, and in the 1920s they built a monument to those who died, complete with an American eagle. Cuba celebrated "*Maine* Day" every February with the U.S. ambassador speechifying about what close ties bind the two republics.

That would wrap up the *Maine* story were it not for two men of enormous ego, both bruised by the American military establishment—Cuban President Fidel Castro and U.S. Navy Admiral Hyman Rickover. In the closing weeks of the Eisenhower administration, just after the United States broke off relations with Cuba, the Castro government called for "the imperialist eagle with all its tragic symbolism, vassalage, and exploitation" to be taken down from atop the *Maine* monument. A new inscription would go up, dedicated "To the Victims of the *Maine*, Sacrificed for Voracious American Imperialism in Its Efforts to Take Control of Cuba." The night of May 1, 1961, two weeks after beating back a U.S.-sponsored invasion at the Bay of Pigs, the Castro government sent a crane out to topple the Maine monument eagle. After a night of huffing and puffing, the crane had dislodged only half of the bird. The next day it managed to get the rest of the eagle, but before the bird could be hauled away someone made off with its head. Its body is displayed at Havana's Museum of the City. As for the eagle's head, it is mounted on the wall of the snack bar at the U.S. Interests Section, our unofficial embassy in Havana. In 1970s Washington, Admiral Hyman Rickover, intrigued with the ship's fate, gathered together a panel of first-rate historians and engineers. After an exhaustive search and reexamination of the evidence, the team reached a definitive conclusion: the *Maine*'s death was self-inflicted. This unintentional suicide was likely the result of a coal bunker fire, they found, but whatever its cause, it was absolutely clear that an external force—a mine or torpedo—was not responsible. There are still some who take issue with that conclusion, maintaining that an external blast was to blame. The plausibility of that and the explanations, cobbled together by a fact here, an assumption there, keeps the ultimate truth of how the *Maine* blew up elusive.

Granma, Cuba's main newspaper, published by the Communist Party, claims that the United States exploded its own warship as a pretext for intervention in the War of Independence, and that a majority of the dead 260 sailors were black, and the all-white officers were all conveniently on shore at the time of the explosion. This has become, over the decades, Cuba's conventional wisdom. The fact is, however, that only twenty of its victims were black, and that all but four of the twenty-six officers were aboard.

Over slow, strong coffee at Dos Hermanos, retired Cuban navy commander Gustavo Placer offered a more rational point of view. "Could it have been the Spanish?" he asked rhetorically. "I rule that out because no one puts mines in their own port. There were military and cargo ships at anchorage and there was no state of war. There was no advance notice the *Maine* was coming, and you must remember, the United States was not Spain's enemy, Cuba was. It would have been suicidal for Spain to plant a bomb beneath the *Maine*. Could it have been Cuban insurgents? Well, why? How? They didn't have the technical ability, and they were busy fighting a war of independence. They wanted military aid from the Americans, yes, but not military intervention. Also, the Spanish Navy was all over the place.

"Could the United States have done it? The *Maine* was one of the biggest of its fleet. America was already prepared for war; it did not need a pretext. Could someone have hidden a bomb on board without it being discovered or anyone knowing? That conspiracy is extremely unlikely." Placer spoke like a prosecutor summing up his case. "No one has ever claimed responsibility or motive, from any side." Placer had read the Rickover report and agreed with its conclusions about the accidental cause of the fateful blast.

Leaving Dos Hermanos, the retired commander and I walked through Havana's narrow downtown streets to a shop where I could buy a nautical map of the harbor. I told him about the eagle's head at the U.S. Interests Section and quoted the end of the printed account next to the head: "Let us hope that some day this battered head can be again joined with its body and wings in a gesture of friendship." At this Placer broke his military bearing and let out a laugh of irony. "They just don't understand what the eagle represents, do they?"

When I screened film footage of the *Maine* going down for the last time, I turned the knob to change its speed, then reversed history by making the ship, with its enormous American flag, come back out of the water. Tinkering with the *Maine*'s role in history has given it prominence for more than one hundred years now. And now in the second century following the explosion, controversy has not yet abandoned ship.

When Cuban Customs officers see the title of Tom Miller's book, Trading with the Enemy: A Yankee Travels through Castro's Cuba, *they recognize the words "enemy," "Yankee," "Castro," and of course "Cuba." On more than one occasion, Miller, who has visited Cuba regularly since 1987, has been taken aside and interrogated about his book based on the title. "Customs officers worldwide," Miller notes, "are not trained in irony."*

$\star \, ^{\displaystyle \star} \, \star$

The Revolution's Cradle

An inquisitive writer finds a wider range of
opinions than you might expect.

FIDEL CASTRO SPENT MOST OF HIS LIFE MAKING TROUBLE. BY THE age of six he had stretched the patience of his Spanish father, who exiled the boy from the family's farm. Fidel landed in a boarding school in Santiago de Cuba, the biggest city in eastern Cuba. There he cheated on math tests, beat up schoolmates, and punched a priest. Transferred to another school, he falsified report cards. During summer vacations he tried to coax his father's cane cutters to resist their boss.

Somehow he learned to read and write. The latter came in handy when, as a teenager, he wrote a letter to U.S. President Franklin Roosevelt: "I am a boy, but I think very much... if you like, give me a ten dollars bill green american in the letter, because I have not seen a ten dollars bill american and I would like to have one of them."

A Jesuit college in Havana brought Castro under control. At sixteen, he astounded classmates with displays of memory. Feats in basketball, baseball, and track won him the title of Cuba's top schoolboy athlete. Improved work habits made him one of his class's top ten students. The priests noted that the towering teen had the stuff of greatness.

Fidel found more time for trouble at the University of Havana.

As a freshman studying law he joined the Anti-Imperialist League and the Committee for the Independence of Puerto Rico. He kicked off his second year with an antigovernment rant that became page one news. Fidel's extracurricular activities picked up in year three, when he trained for an invasion of the Dominican Republic. Back on campus, the big man's verbal attacks made the government cringe. The police tried to get physical with the critic, who packed a pistol. An ambush failed. Castro the troublemaker graduated in 1950.

Castro the lawyer favored hardship cases and political causes. The latter gave him more exposure. So did the bribery accusations he leveled against Cuba's president. Running for election to congress, he ended his campaign when the poll was canceled following a coup d'état in February 1952 by a former sergeant named Fulgencio Batista.

Castro saw red. At twenty-five, his goals were to oust Batista and revolutionize Cuba. He organized a band of like-minded patriots. One of the movement's members began to train the group to use guns. Meanwhile, Fidel crisscrossed the country to recruit and prepare other commandos. Short of guns, seeking a spark for nationwide revolt, he aimed to solve two problems with one attack.

The target was the Moncada barracks in Santiago de Cuba. On July 26, 1953, Fidel Castro and more than a one hundred fighters assembled in a farmhouse outside the city and disguised themselves as soldiers. Their convoy included a Pontiac, a Buick, and a Chevy. Their weapons were a grab bag of shotguns and hunting rifles. Real soldiers shot back with better guns. Eight attackers died. Another sixty-one were hunted down, beaten bloody, and shot dead. The rest surrendered or were captured and tried. Bit players were sentenced to three years in prison. The ringleader, whom many Cubans considered a loudmouthed loser, got fifteen.

Nineteen months later, Batista released the prisoners. Castro went to Mexico to prepare another offensive. Scores of Cubans joined him. So did an Argentine doctor, Ernesto "Che" Guevara. About a year of training, planning, and fund-raising culminated when the heavily armed rebels set sail for eastern Cuba in a boat called *Granma*, whose previous owner, an American with fond memories of his grandmother, couldn't have imagined the later uses of his sentimentality.

Strong winds slowed the boat. A choppy sea sickened the passengers. The ship sprung a leak. An engine faltered. The yacht fell two days behind schedule. Food and water ran out. Worse, the rebels missed their rendezvous with supporters waiting on the shore to drive them to hideouts in the mountains. The navigator fell overboard but was saved. Nonetheless, the captain lost his bearing when *Granma* did reach Cuba's coast.

The journey ended at daybreak on December 2, 1956. At low tide, cruising near the shore, *Granma's* hull stuck in the mud. Castro ordered his men to grab their gear and get in the water. "This wasn't a landing, it was a shipwreck," was how Che Guevara summed up the rebels' arrival near Las Coloradas, a village on the western edge of eastern Cuba.

"Fidel landed out there," said Francisco, raising an arm to indicate an area about a one hundred yards from the concrete platform beneath our feet.

I squinted at the aqua surface rippled by the faintest of breezes. The calm made easy work for the shirtless men moving across our sight line. One took leisurely pulls on the oars of a weathered rowboat. His mate reclined. Beyond the fisherman lay the Caribbean, more Caribbean, and a swollen sun suspended thirty degrees above the horizon.

"And he went that way," said Francisco; his arm spun a semicircle from its first heading.

I tracked the gesture to the edge of a swamp. My eyes met a wall of mangrove trees. Trunks no fatter than a fire hose sprouted leaves the shape of paddles. Each shaft devolved into an amalgam of crooked roots that disappeared into a tea-colored murk. A mesh of vines connected the trees. Without a boat, there would have been no way around the seamless tangle before the construction of a man-made strip that penetrated nature's mess.

The monument on the platform reminded me that others hadn't enjoyed the luxury of a walkway. Propagandists had spray-painted WE WILL CONQUER on the stone marker. They hadn't erased the scrawl of the amateur who had added, DOWN WITH IMPERIALISM. A plaque embedded in the marker explained the significance of our position in Granma province. It was here that Fidel Castro and eighty-one fellow rebels launched their war against Batista.

The roots of my own journey to Las Coloradas were more tangled. Frustration was part of the story. By skipping the film festival, Fidel had drenched my dreams of a rendezvous. I spent weeks devising other ways to meet, or at least see, El Máximo. None panned out. Then the leader flew to Paris. I didn't expect a speedy return.

There was little to keep me in Havana. I spent afternoons visiting friends. A typical day included visits to Rodolfo, and Osmani, an engineer who owned an art gallery. Sometimes I ate dinner with Eduardo the painter. For rum, I could always count on Diego, the moviemaker. Like the Cubans, I spent a lot of time staring listlessly ahead. I waited for inspiration.

"Why don't you travel?" said the French journalist.

The suggestion made sense. Trying to meet Fidel had raised broader questions about Cuba. Was it a rich island fallen on hard times or a poor place returning to its natural state after the loss of its sugar daddy, the Soviet Union? Given their poverty, how did the locals keep smiling and dancing? Say Fidel died and recommended capitalism in his will. Would the country prosper? Maybe a road trip would provide fresh grist.

The east, said the Frenchman, was the Revolution's cradle. It was there that Castro concentrated his early efforts. Popular support grew. So did the size of his army. Only when the eastern foothold felt firm did the guerrillas begin to work their way west. Following his steps from Las Coloradas to Havana wouldn't get me an audience with the president. It might, however, amount to a meeting, albeit a metaphorical one.

Francisco glommed onto my plan the moment he overheard my sketch in the living room of Boris, his nephew. Wearing glasses and a baseball cap that covered a bald pate, the fifty-year-old exploded with enthusiasm. A road map of creases appeared on his burnished face. A thick black mustache couldn't disguise the yellow of his toothy smile. He immediately invited me to start the expedition with a visit to his family in Santiago de Cuba.

A week later, Francisco met me at the airport in his hometown and insisted on driving me to Las Coloradas. An engineer, he dismissed my concerns about his missing work. "It's more important for me to help you learn about Cuba," he said. Sensing my doubt, he added, "Don't worry, Cubans are always taking a vacation from work." Francisco spent the first eight hours of his vacation steering a Lada to the tip of Granma province.

"*Vamos,*" said Francisco, casting an eye on the setting sun.

"Let's go," I replied.

"Those poor guys," said Francisco as we reentered the swamp.

"Which poor guys?"

"The rebels, they didn't know where they were or how far they had to go. Their boat was ruined, so they couldn't go back. And they were in a swamp. The environment here is very…" He paused to find the right word. "Aggressive."

Francisco understated the case. Up close, the maze of mangroves was even more daunting. Sweeping away clouds of mosquitoes, I saw nothing but gnarled trees and twisted vines. The diabolic foliage hovered over shallow water and a gruesome bottom of mud. "Imagine," said Francisco at the end of our fifteen-minute stroll to shore.

> The drive paralleling the Sierra has stayed with me not because it was especially dreamy but rather because it was ordinary. Hitchhikers were traveling no more than twenty kilometers each, to and from school, family, work. If the country's failings were leaking through its irreparable cracks, its strengths were visible through its incandescent air. The people of the Oriente had a tempo, steady and unyielding. They were part of their land, fluid enough to fill contours, slow enough to accommodate its heat.
>
> —Tom Miller, *Trading with the Enemy*

The insurgents had taken longer to clear the swamp. Weighted down by supplies, Castro's men sunk to their waists in ooze. The water reached their chests. Extrication from one obstacle led to confrontation with the mesh of trees, roots, and vines. Leaves and branches ripped uniforms and slashed faces as the rebels stumbled through the swamp. Insects feasted on their flesh. Hours passed before the first of the filthy, bloody, exhausted army reached firm ground.

Francisco and I stopped at the shapeless building beside a deserted concrete plaza. He looked for a bathroom. I wandered toward a roof covering a boat. Only on spotting *Granma* painted on the ship did I recognize the replica. Less than fifty feet long the wooden vessel couldn't accommodate a keg party. Anybody willing to load *Granma* with scores of invaders, plus their supplies, had to be gaga.

Three Cubans were standing near the stern. One held a brush, which he used to freshen *Granma's* white coat. A coworker was minding a bucket of paint. Arms folded, the third man must have been in charge of quality. The human still life brought to mind a Cuban friend's evaluation of labor relations on the island: "We pretend to work, and they pretend to pay us."

"Which way did the rebels go?" I asked

The team took a break. The painter pointed across a narrow concrete road toward a line of low bushes and coconut trees. He said that the rebels had headed east, toward the Sierra Maestra. His mates noted that there were no roads linking their town to the mountains, not then, not now. They also told me where to find a man who had met the rebels when they left the swamp.

The man was out. Or so it seemed when we passed the black pig tied to the tree in front of the small concrete house. Francisco's repeated knocks on the weathered door brought no response. Nor did his shouts. Out back we found only a barren yard populated by a half dozen scrawny hens and a pair of piglets. Their squeals aroused a gray-haired woman wearing a long dress.

"Is this the home of Pablo Luis?" asked Francisco.

"PABLO," shouted the woman through the rear door before leading us back to the front.

The man holding the front door open with a callused palm

looked well past his seventieth birthday. Lines crossed every inch of a face the color and texture of a baseball mitt. Scars and scabs marked other parts of his skin, which hung loosely from his bones. Whiskers reminded me of Bowery bums. So did his baggy shorts, a patchwork of blue cloth, black stitches, and brown soil. A soiled shirt retained only its top and bottom buttons. From his belt hung the trademark of the *guajiro*, a Cuban peasant, a scabbard carrying a two-foot machete.

"Come in. This is your house," he said in Spanish slurred almost beyond recognition. Asking neither our names nor our business, the old man gestured to two wooden chairs and seated himself in a third. He leaned forward to hear what we wanted.

While Francisco explained my interest in the *Granma* landing, I surveyed the home. The shelves carried no books. There were photographs of several children, three giant seashells, and a blowfish. A Soviet television resembled a safe. A chicken pecked for food in the cracks of the tile floor. A black-and-white shot of Pablo and Fidel Castro confirmed we had come to the right place.

"In 1956 I didn't know anything about Communism," said Pablo. "I had heard of Fidel Castro. He was the young lawyer who went to jail after attacking Moncada. But that was all I knew." When I asked how he recognized Fidel, the chatty old man turned serious. "I wasn't the first one to see Fidel Castro. It was my neighbor, Angel Pérez Rosabal."

"How did he recognize Fidel?"

"Fidel said 'Have no fear, I am Fidel Castro, and we came to liberate the Cuban people.'"

Pablo continued after reiterating that he was the second, not the first, local to sight the rebel leader. What he saw was a group of four or five men. The old man confirmed what I had read and Francisco had said: the guerrillas' uniforms were torn and dirty. Streaks of blood and scratches lined their arms and faces.

"I felt sorry for them," said Pablo, leaning down to scratch a piglet who had wandered indoors. "I asked if they wanted food but they said no. I asked if they wanted coffee. They said they had no time. They had to move on.

"Later I saw more men. One group was carrying a big machine gun and a lot of bullets. I offered to get them two trucks and to take them wherever they wanted to go. They said they couldn't accept because they didn't know me." Pablo paused, slipped his hand inside his shirt, and rubbed his ribs. "It's too bad they didn't know me. They would have had an easier time."

The leader stuck out from his group, said the old man. At thirty, he was older than most of the others. More striking was his size. "He was big, impressive," said Pablo, stretching his hand over his own head to demonstrate the height. The peasant remembered a handshake, followed by an embrace. "Fidel thanked me, even though I did very little."

"When they left, did you hope they would win?"

"Fidel hugged me. After that I was always on his side."

Christopher Hunt survived a childhood in Beirut and New York City and went on to the London School of Economics and the staff of The Economist. *He is the author of two books,* Sparring with Charlie: Motorbiking Down the Ho Chi Minh Trail, *and* Waiting for Fidel, *from which this story was excerpted. He lives in New York City.*

JON LEE ANDERSON

✦ ✦ ✦

Havana Journal

In the early 1990s, the author enjoyed
the contradictions of life in Havana.

OUR BALCONY IS A FRONT-ROW SEAT IN AN OPEN-AIR THEATER. Every day at sunrise, a group of elderly Cubans in faded clothes marches down to the sea, and fanning out in a geometric pattern, they do callisthenic exercises before plunging into the water. Then, just as inexplicably, they leave again. One day recently I awoke to the sound of waves crashing and went outside. There on the pitted gold blanket of the dog's tooth rock at the sea's edge were two people dressed entirely in white, wearing turbans. They picked up shells and threw other objects into the raging surf. It was an initiation ritual of Santería, the Afro-Cuban religion that, bizarrely, carries on unhindered in Cuba. Each evening at dusk, a man in a wheelchair is pushed down to the water's edge by a friend. There, as the sun sinks into the ocean and the night fills the sky, the invalid sings spine-tingling arias into the nocturnal void. At about the same time of day, a Cuban naval gunboat usually appears, cutting a rapid swath across the horizon as it patrols the coast. I have begun to think of the country as a surreal blend of official coercion and stubborn individualism. Much like the sea that extends to the world beyond while hemming the island in, its atmosphere is both lyrical and melancholic, liberating and imprisoning at the same time.

✳

In the late afternoon in José Martí Park the voices of black men rise in billows, apparently angry, audible even from the balconies overlooking the square. Every afternoon these men gather there, in the shade around a particular stone bench, to argue about baseball. In the same park, military cadets and their brides, dressed in white, arrive in buses for collective weddings, to pay homage to Martí. They walk to the white marble plinth to lay a wreath, then proceed gracefully back to their bus. Colleagues blow trumpets.

Habaneros tell you about the time drunken American Marines climbed on Martí's statue and pissed on it, they seem indignant even now at the arbitrary affront, as if such as act were an example of just how degraded Cuba's dignity had become in the years before the Revolution. Martí is to Cubans what Gandhi is in modern-day India: a historical touchstone whose visage is everywhere. His declamatory catchphrases are signboarded by the regime to establish a kinship between his rationalistic patrimony and that of the institutionalized Revolution.

In Vedado, there is a corner lot overgrown with weeds and some tropical vegetation, and an exposed wall of coral rock. The whole thing is strangely caged in by wrought iron. Here, preserved for all to see, is the spot where Martí, as a prisoner of the Spanish, was forced to break rocks as a common prisoner.

Cubans speak proudly about the syncretism of Afro-Cuban culture, but the label also applies to Fidel's institutionalized socialist revolution. It, too, is syncretic. It has learned to be in order to maintain power and to reach the increasingly apathetic new generation of Cubans. "Fidelismo" has pragmatically incorporated Christianity (e.g., the best-selling book *Fidel and Religion*) and Martí's nationalist mantle, with its attendant religiosity (Martí is "the Apostic"). And by merely pointing to the threatening, bullying United States, the regime has mostly managed to contain the restlessness of Cuba's increasingly youthful population by providing an external focus for dissent. As a reinforcement, it has also co-opted—if mostly in exhortatory fashion—the legacy of Che Guevara, the ultimate icon of youthful rebelliousness.

Nationalism, anti-Americanism, Communism, and Third World-ism have all shared the stage with Fidel, who is Cuba's *babalawo* (witch doctor), willing his people yet again to acquiesce as he does his next fetish dance from behind an ever-changing series of masks.

Old Mederos, the housepainter and Party militant, is back in our house painting the walls for me, only three months after we moved in. Already they had begun to bear the surface geography of our children: a phantasmagoria of infantile family history, a wall map of our brief residence.

I could have lived a little longer with the walls as they were, but the week before last he visited me and told me that they were eating only boiled cabbage and vinegar at home. His two good-for-nothing sons have been laid off from their jobs, and his large black wife, Silva, has begun to excoriate him for his insufficiency as a breadwinner.

Sofia despises Mederos for being old and sly and always arriving, as if by instinct, right around lunchtime. She silently refuses to do a thing for him, so usually I have to whisper to Erica to fix the old boy a sandwich, take him some water, a cup of coffee, and at the end of the day a swig of rum. It's true that he's a terrible painter: he spills paint everywhere, and leaves brush bristles, dust, and dirt embedded in the walls. It isn't, I've come to realize, so much that he's sloppy as that he's simply old. And the paint he brings is bad: just quicklime mixed with kerosene.

I can't bring myself, despite all this, to tell him to stop. I like his presence, his munchy toothless face and his pride. Usually once a week or so he will tell me about his undying fealty to the Party; but he is seventy now and his family is hungry, and his wife is increasingly truculent. She was once a good cook, and before the Soviets pulled the rug out they would buy a pig and have parties with real Cuban rum about every two months, back when his pension was worth something and there were things to buy with it. But now she feels useless and frustrated.

He is the head of the Committee to Defend the Revolution in his apartment building. It used to be that this position gave him some respect. There would be an audience of sixty-five people at the weekly committee meetings. Now he is lucky to have six or seven people show up. And these are mostly friends who come to help him save face and avoid ridicule. The Party has told its militants that the lack of food is going to continue, and become worse, but that the plan is to reactivate the stalled industrial production of goods by year's end, after the new supplies of Colombian oil that have been arranged begin arriving this summer. Just how this will be achieved in time to fill empty bellies and pacify despondent minds they aren't told.

At its last meeting, the committee discussed its obligation to keep an eye on all Party members receiving money or food from relatives abroad. The purpose of this vigilance is to curb "excesses of ostentation." In other words, it now is legal for people to have dollars, and to receive money from abroad, but they should not flaunt their good luck. This is to prevent the resentment of hungry neighbors who do not receive such consignments.

"Cuba has a way of following you around," says Jon Lee Anderson. After living for nearly three years in Havana at the height of the "Special Period in Time of Peace," the setting for this selection, Anderson moved with his family to southern Spain. They live in a house overlooking the sea and a sugar-growing valley which, as it turns out, used to be known as "Little Cuba." Anderson is the author of several books, including The Lion's Grave: Dispatches from Afghanistan, Che Guevara: A Revolutionary Life *and* Guerrillas. *He is now a staff writer for* The New Yorker *specializing in foreign stories.*

STEPHEN BENZ

✦ ✦ ✦

Our Mailman in Havana

Neither sleet, nor hail, nor the back
alleys of the old city....

ON MY LAST EVENING IN HAVANA, I WAS STANDING AT THE SEAWALL
along the harbor when the mailman came along and put a completely different spin on my visit to the city.

I had spent three days shuttling around on tour buses to the city's
famous sites: Hemingway's old haunts, the centuries-old Spanish
forts, the Tropicana cabaret, the hotel strip built by the mob during
Havana's heyday as sin city. But almost every moment of those days
was prearranged, leaving me little opportunity to explore Havana
on my own.

That's when he appeared at my side, a young man wearing a
New York Yankees shirt. He carried a satchel. For a moment, he
stared at the sea and said nothing. But I knew what was coming. In
an hour's time a few dozen just like him had approached me with
the same pitch: You want cigars? Girls? What you want, mister?

"I don't want anything," I told him. "I came to see Havana,
that's all."

"Come on then, I will show you Havana. You can join me on
my rounds."

Rounds? He patted the satchel. "I am a mailman."

We started off down a main street, then turned onto a side street and turned again. Soon I lost all sense of direction in the narrow maze. As we walked, the young man kept up a steady monologue in Spanish. His name was Vladimir, but he wanted me to call him Eddie. English names were better than Russian, he said. Normally he didn't deliver the mail this late—evening had fallen and the unlit streets were now dark—but his bicycle had broken down and he was forced to proceed on foot.

As we entered different buildings to deliver the mail, Eddie told me something of their history. A famous archbishop's residence, a viceroy's house, the place where Cortés stayed—all of them dating to the sixteenth or seventeenth century, and all of them teetering, on the verge of falling down. The United Nations had declared this part of Havana a World Heritage Site, but so far little attempt at preservation was in evidence.

Each building, no matter how glorious its past, was now a tenement where several families lived in dilapidated flats. By the light of dim bulbs, I saw old but tidy furniture, faded floor tiles, peeling paint, shrines to Catholic saints and Santería deities. I smelled boiling rice, mildew, dust, and crumbling mortar.

It was soon clear that Eddie was showing me off. In building after building, he introduced me to the tenants. "This is my friend," Eddie said. "An American." Everyone seemed unduly impressed. People shook my hand, offered me glasses of murky water, showed me pictures of cousins in Miami. Entire extended families gathered at the threshold to stare and ask questions. Often Eddie had nothing to deliver but knocked anyway. He wanted everyone to witness his windfall.

In one dark passage, an impossibly old man heard Eddie's boast, then grabbed my arm and pulled me into his flat. I couldn't understand his cackling. He led me to a corner where candles burned before the blackened statue of a saint. There were folded pieces of paper and little plastic animals arranged around the base. With great panache, the old man reached behind the statue and drew forth a small paper rectangle. He handed it to me. In the candlelight I saw it was a postcard, a much-handled postcard of—I squinted—Cinderella's castle in Disneyland. Mickey Mouse waved from the foreground.

The old man rummaged through a wooden cigar box until he produced a stubby pencil. His speech was animated and constant. I looked to the mailman for interpretation. "He wants you to sign the picture," Eddie said.

The request baffled me. I couldn't think of any reason why he would want my autograph on the postcard. But I couldn't very well refuse. The old man rattled off another long sentence and tapped the card to indicate where I should sign. When I had done so, he snatched the card, cackled, and returned it to the altar.

Back on the street, I said to Eddie, "That was strange."

He nodded. "Well, you wanted to see Havana," he said. "Havana is strange. Now you have seen Havana."

When we finished with the mailman's rounds, we made our way back to the tourist district and my hotel. I invited Eddie in for a drink at the hotel bar, but an armed guard was posted to keep Cubans out. So I bought two bottles of beer and we sat on the plaza outside. Scores of girls in spandex promenaded on the arms of the European tourists. Someone somewhere was playing a violin. A cigar-smoking crone sat on a stool and waited to read fortunes. A bored girl dutifully occupied her assigned post at a corner pizza stand that no longer had pizza to sell. A man passed by carrying a squawking, upside-down chicken. Across the plaza, the lambent moonlight cast shadows on a former convent's facade of saints and angels.

When the mailman took his leave, he hit me up for a few dollars—medicine for his baby girl, he said.

Hours later, I stood at the window of my hotel room, ten stories up, and stared down at the city. In three days I had gathered twenty pages of information for an article on what to do and where to go in Havana.

I now knew just how inadequate that article would be.

Stephen Benz is the author of three travel narratives, Guatemalan Journey, Green Dreams, *and* Essays En Route. *He lives in Atlanta.*

WILLIAM LEE BRENT

✦ ✦ ✦

High Top, Low Stubble

The author volunteered to cut sugarcane in 1971,
two years after he hijacked a plane to Havana.

THE MERCILESS PA SYSTEM SHOCKED US AWAKE AT DAWN WITH taunting Latin rhythms. We dressed hurriedly and went to the mess hall for bread and supersweet coffee with milk. After breakfast the director gave us an animated pep talk. Then he ordered us to climb aboard the waiting canvas-covered military trucks, which immediately took us off to the cane fields to make our contribution to the revolution.

Ravelo, a tall, rawboned *campesino* in his late fifties had cut cane most of his life. ICAP [The People's Friendship Institute of Cuba] had selected him to teach the new volunteers the correct way to work in sugarcane. Ravelo called our small group over and began explaining the basics of cane cutting: "First," he said, picking up a machete and holding it so we could all see his hands, "You must learn how to hold a machete. Wrap your fingers around the handle, in the same way you might make a fist, and relax your wrist. Right-handed cutters should place their right foot slightly forward and to the right of the stalk to be cut. The right knee bends a little, and the left leg is stretched back out of reach of the hungry machete. From this position, take the stalks of cane in your free hand, lean forward, and bring the machete around in a downward arc. This motion cuts the stalks low to the ground without letting the blade bite into the earth."

Ravelo held us entranced as he went through all the motions: waving the machete around above his head, gathering several stalks of cane in his arm, and in one deft stroke, cutting through them at their base. Then he threw the stalks onto the ground behind him, to his right.

"After you cut the stalks," he said, "toss them behind you with the tops facing outward and move up to the next cut. When you finish a row, turn around, backtrack, and cut the tops off the cane where it lies. This will dull your machete a bit, but you will have time to sharpen it later. When you finish, pick another row and start all over again. Remember, be careful at all times because carelessness causes accidents, and we don't want anyone to get hurt out here."

Ravelo and the ICAP people coached us individually until we began to get the basic idea and rhythm of cane cutting. We then went into the field, picked out a row of cane, and started cutting. By midday, sweat ran from our bodies in rivulets. We gasped for breath like long-distance runners, and we ached all over.

All the cane in this area was cut by hand, using one of two systems: the green-cane system—cut the cane just as you found it in the fields: leaves grasses, and all—or the burnt-cane system—select a field the night before cutting, then do a controlled burning to get rid of the leaves and grasses and make cutting a hell of a lot easier. Naturally the volunteers used the burnt-cane system

Cutting burnt cane however, left our entire bodies covered with a fine black ash and gave the sensation of being covered with fire ants. The more you rubbed or scratched, the more it itched. By the end of the day, I had learned the basics of sugarcane cutting. Amazingly, Geo, James, and I managed to finish several rows on our own. Nothing could have made us feel better than Ravelo's praise for having done so well on our first day in the field.

Wearing big grins on our soot-blackened faces, we swaggered around bragging about who had cut the most cane. Pride pushed our chests out even further when we learned that some of the other volunteers had quit without finishing a single row.

"You did a good job today," one of the women said as we climbed onto the truck. "If you keep at it, you will soon become good *macheteros*."

"Yes, it's true," another added, "you all did very well, but you are going to suffer for it tomorrow."

I was already suffering. I couldn't straighten my back, and every muscle in my body ached. I looked back over my shoulder as the truck pulled onto the bumpy dirt road. The field appeared as untouched as when I'd first seen them. Son of a bitch, I said to myself, we haven't even made a dent in this mother!

Back in camp, we scrubbed down vigorously with strong laundry soap and rinsed off with lots of cold water. The icy spray stung like tiny needles and rejuvenated our tired bodies.

Rafael waited for us at the mess hall with shiny metal cups and several bottles of Havana Club. "¡*Viva La Revolución!*" someone shouted, "¡*Viva La Revolución!* We chorused, lifting our cups into the air. A warm feeling surged through me. This sure as hell beats sitting around doing nothing, I thought.

> We proceed through endless acres of sugarcane which remind me of monotonous drives through Ohio's cornfields. Except that I think of the slaves who once worked *these* fields. One thing that amazes me is that slavery ended in 1886 in Cuba, twenty years after it ended in the States. For some reason, those additional twenty years make a big difference to me. Perhaps it's the difference between being children of slaves, metaphorically, and being children of slaves, literally.
> —Roger L. Collins,
> "*Nuestro Viaje a Cuba:*
> Our Trip to Cuba"

We all congratulated ourselves on how well we had done our first day in the cane fields. I couldn't remember having felt as tired in my life. My right hand was so sore and swollen, I couldn't close it. The blisters I'd noticed at lunchtime had broken open while I was washing my shorts in the shower. Now they were bleeding.

My mutilated hands felt like they belonged to someone else.

After a delicious dinner of fried chicken with thick, creamy gravy, white rice and beans, fried bananas, and cold beer, with rich custard pudding for dessert, I felt ready to tackle the cane again. Instead, we all headed for the rec hall. Some folks wanted to dance to the almost irresistible Latin American rhythms blasting from the PA system. Others preferred to try their luck at chess, or dominoes. Still others, like me, wanted only to sit around and talk and enjoy the rum and warm feeling of friendliness characteristic of the campsite.

An hour passed. I filled my cup with Havana Club, excused myself, and went to my barracks. I set the cup on the floor beside my bunk, took off my shoes, and wiggled in under the mosquito net. I had intended to rest and think for a while before getting undressed for bed, but sleep overcame me before my head hit the pillow.

The next morning the dreaded PA system jarred me awake with the blaring upbeat sound of a popular Cuban dance tune. Pain raced through my entire body as I fumbled my way through the mosquito netting and finally got out of the bunk. My hand ached worse than ever when I tried to move my fingers.

I had to use both hands to lift the cup of rum from the floor to my lips. It burned all the way down my throat, but it helped to relieve the pain. Geo and James, mumbling to themselves, finished the cup off. Then, painfully, forcing our joints to move and our hands to open and close, we did our morning exercises.

At breakfast Rafael suggested we go into town to see a doctor. Free dental and medical attention were always available. We refused his offer but accepted some first-aid treatment from another camp official, who warned us our hands would get a lot worse if we returned to the fields without medical attention. We thanked him, gathered our equipment, and boarded the trucks with the other volunteers.

Ravelo wasn't the least bit surprised by the condition of our hands. "That's normal," he said, "especially when you use those cloth gloves with rough, uneven seams inside. What you have to do is turn the gloves inside out. They won't chafe your hands then. Also, remember to keep your wrists loose and hold the *mocha* handle firmly without squeezing it. Set a pace for yourself, one you know you can handle, and stick with it. Concentrate on how much cane you're going to cut instead of thinking about your hands. In a few days you won't even remember the pain."

"What about the blisters? " I asked.

"I'll tell you a little secret," Ravelo said with a mischievous smile. "To toughen up their hands, the professionals usually piss on them while they are cutting in the fields."

All the newcomers had some kind of problem: blisters, sore muscles, body aches, headaches. You name it and one of us was suffering from it. Some people had such severe asthma they simply couldn't continue working.

Not getting the expected sympathy from Ravelo, and skeptical about his remedy, I nevertheless strode into the field and pissed on my hands. After turning my stiff, soot-caked gloves inside out, I forced my hands into them. Then, trying hard to ignore the soreness, I grabbed two stalks of sugarcane and brought my *mocha* around in an arc that sent waves of pain up my arm as the blade sliced through the succulent stalks.

Fuck you, motherfuckers, I screamed silently as I cut a narrow swath through the impassive wall of cane before me. My gloves grew wet and slippery from the early-morning dew, but I kept at it. One row down, two, three...I lost count. I stopped only to drink water and to apply Ravelo's remedy to my hands. Within an hour I had forgotten about the pain. Nothing mattered now except my mocha and the unending rows of sugarcane.

On the way back to camp for lunch, I carefully peeled the glove off my cutting hand To my amazement the blisters had stopped bleeding and the swelling had gone down. I could move my fingers without pain. When we reached camp, a friendly Dominican woman named Toni took one look at my hands and led me to the infirmary.

Nothing seemed to get her down. She was an experienced cane cutter who could hold her own with anyone in camp. Shaking her head in disapproval and speaking rapid Spanish, she made me wince as she jabbed iodine at the ugly, raw blisters in my hand.

I couldn't understand her words, but I got the definite impression she was scolding me. When she pointed to the side of her head and made the classic "tsk, tsk, tsk" sound, I was sure she was questioning my intelligence. After lunch, everyone found a nice shady spot and stretched out to rest before the four-hour afternoon shift.

A regular workday for the volunteers was from nine to ten hours. Anyone who didn't feel up to it could take a day off and go into town. Once we had finished making hogs of ourselves in the mess hall, we had several choices of things to do: Hang out in the rec hall. Make the nineteen-kilometer trip to Aguacate and take in a movie, or visit with either the villagers or the permanent cane cutters. Nights were usually pleasant, with clear, starstudded tropical skies and a soft evening breeze. Most of the time people broke off into small groups to just sit and talk.

The majority of the volunteers came from Latin American countries. They were at odds with their governments and, sooner or later, the conversation always turned to politics. No one ever had a good word for the government of the United States—nor a bad one for Cuba. Most people revered Fidel Castro as a modern-day Simón Bolívar. At the same time, they considered the U.S. government to be the natural enemy of all of Latin America.

The Latin American women in camp were open and friendly

> The work continued at the same pace from three o'clock to seven-thirty P.M. Guevara was expert at cutting the sugarcane at its base and trimming it with clean machete strokes. When the day's work was over, he climbed into a wagon with enormous wheels, the kind used to carry cane to the factory, and gave us all a doctrinal talk. This quickly turned into a question-and-answer session. The content and direction of questions gave an idea of how far the political orientation had progressed.
>
> —Ricardo Rojo, *My Friend Che,* translated by Julian Casart

from the start. They liked to tease James and me about our bad Spanish. Margarita, an outspoken, dark-haired beauty from Central America, took a special interest in *los negros americanos.*

"You are so very big and strong," she said, squeezing my biceps admiringly. "However, you will never learn to speak Spanish well until you are holding a beautiful Latin American woman in those arms."

"And she will not only teach you about nouns, pronouns, and adjectives," said Beatriz, a small, attractive brunette from El Salvador, "she will also show you how to conjugate more than Spanish verbs."

Their friendly, contagious laughter flowed through the campsite like a fresh breeze. It mixed freely with the baying of a lonely mule on the distant slopes and with the incessant buzzing of the camp's mercilessly bloodthirsty mosquitoes.

One night, Margarita leaned over and whispered something to Geo. He turned to me and said: "She wants to know why you came to Cuba."

"Tell her I had to leave my country because the government is very racist. They treat black people worse than animals."

"Did you fight with the police?" someone asked from the background.

"Yes, I did," I answered matter-of-factly. "They tried to kill me and I fought them."

"I knew it," Margarita said excitedly. "I can tell by your eyes and mouth. You are the kind who would fight the police."

"Racism is terrible," Beatriz said. "My friends criticize me because I go out with black men. I just tell them to mind their own business."...

Within a week my hands had healed and toughened. I also learned a great deal more about cutting sugarcane and making love to Latin American women. Neither was very easy. Margarita had taken over Edna's task of teaching me to speak Spanish. First she taught me the most popular Cuban cuss words: *puta, maricón, hijo de puta, come mierda....* I also picked up a few words and phrases in the village, around camp, and in the fields. Everyone wanted to help me learn Spanish. No one, however, could do anything about my harsh, unmistakable American accent.

Not only was Ravelo a champion cane cutter, he was also manager of the general store. On several occasions, he invited Geo, James, and me to help out. Filling bags with beans, rice, and noodles gave us a welcomed respite from the cane fields and the sameness of camp routine....

In the following weeks, I became a steady, reliable *machetero* in both green and burnt cane. At first I had fought the stalks of sugarcane head-on. Now, the more cane I cut the more difficult it became for me to go on. Without knowing it, I had entered into warfare with myself. It took great effort to continue getting up at dawn every morning, and it required an iron will to put on my cold, sooty work clothes, pick up my *mocha*, and go out to do battle with those silent unending rows of sugarcane.

I knew I could leave anytime I wanted to without being criticized, and this fact made it harder to do so. The problem was with me, not the people around me. I had promised myself to stay until the sugarcane harvest was over. I would keep my promise, no matter what.

As the harvest neared its end, some of the professionals appeared to be having the same problem. Occasionally, one of them would stop in the middle of the field and lift his voice in a soulful cry: "*Ayudame, Fidel*" (Help me Fidel), before bending to the task again.

I didn't call on Fidel (I didn't know him well enough). As a child, however, I had learned a little jingle from an uncle who always talked about cutting sugarcane in Louisiana: "High top, low stubble, work real hard, and stay out of trouble." I used this jingle whenever I got really tired and started to slow down, or when I truly felt like quitting. It worked wonders for me.

William Lee Brent was born in 1930 in Franklin, Louisiana, and moved to Oakland, California, during World War II where his mother worked in the shipyards. In 1968 he joined the Black Panther Party; later that year he was involved in a shootout with San Francisco police, arrested, and expelled from the Panthers. While out on bail, he "diverted" a commercial airliner from

Oakland to Havana, where he has lived since. He has a degree in Spanish literature from the University of Havana and is currently working on a book about race relations in Cuba from the Spanish conquest to the present. His first book was Long Time Gone: A Black Panther's True Life Story of His Hijacking and Twenty-five Years in Cuba, from which this story was excerpted.

BENJAMIN TREUHAFT

* * *

Tuning with the Enemy

If only foreign policy were so easily adjusted.

A HORDE OF YANKEES ARRIVES AT THE OLD TROPICOCO RESORT. IN the background a piano tinkles out familiar Play-It-Sam-style tunes while an elderly Quebecois couple watches with amusement as the last few of us check in.

The hotel piano sounds awful, and I am drawn closer. A tall black man at the keyboard peers through gold-rimmed glasses with rectangular frames. He is ancient. I introduce myself as a piano tuner during a lull in the music and offer to tune the hotel piano for fun. A plastic ivory is missing, and I have brought along a complete set to donate to a school. The pianist, Daniel Durán, speaks good English. We agree that I will tune at 7:30 the next morning, before the guests are up. Then he asks, "My piano at home needs some of those—do you have any extra?" Without thinking I offer him the school plastics.

My tuning the next morning is less than stellar because the terrible old German grand wants to break every other string in the treble, the thin wires having rusted through after decades of exposure to the salty breezes of the hotel lobby. Luckily there are plenty of other things to fix, and the pianist will like the improvement.

That evening it occurs to me: I want to visit the elegant old musician at his home, and his missing ivories will provide an excuse to invite myself. The pianist is very kind when I collar him after a song, and he lets me know I have done a fine tuning. His job, he explains, is to rotate among the resorts east of Havana and play favorites for the tourists. He gives me his address in Alamar. We are set for early the next morning.

Alamar, city of 100,000, is visible from the highway as a mass of concrete-block housing projects left to rot for twenty years. Tropicoco resort guests have to pass it en route to Havana, and it looks depressing: does Socialist Man end up living like this? But Daniel Durán gives his address there with some pride—maybe Cubans see the block houses as bunkers from which to fight the U.S. economic hostility.

It is raining the next morning. The taxi driver has to stop five times for directions, and I descend when we reach the general vicinity. Without much Spanish it is still easy to find the house by making piano-playing motions while describing a tall, dark old man. The residents must think me quite a sight, a slightly overfed, sportcoat-wearing, straw-hatted Yankee dripping with drizzle and sweat, carrying thirty-five pounds of tools in a doctor's bag. Eventually a kid takes me to Daniel's door where a woman lets me in. I start work on the piano. I am deep into tuning when Daniel appears from an interior room. Beautifully dressed for his shift at the Tropicoco, gracious and soft-spoken, he puts me even more at ease than I already am. He arranges a delicious demitasse of muddy sweet espresso, and we talk as I tune.

He has a Wurlitzer short upright, sold originally in Havana in 1915 when Wurlitzer was producing great pianos. The ivories turn out to be real, so he can't use my plastic keytops after all. As soon as I lift the lid and remove the front door, I can see this is an excellent old instrument. The tuning pins are dark brown with corrosion as are the strings, but something in the Cuban air has kept them from getting rusty and brittle—there is only one broken string at the very top of the treble. The pitch is at least half a tone low, but the action (the keys, hammers, and all the levers in-between), is in fine

Teresa Linares greets me at the door of her elegantly colonnaded neoclassical Museo Nacional de la Música at the appointed hour of ten o'clock. María Teresa takes me on a tour of some of the Museo's pianos—three Steinway grands, a 1920 Pleyel-Wolff French grand dripping with brass ornament, and a couple of ornate European uprights. I play a few triads here and there and am relieved to hear that the instruments are in quite good shape. I am surprised to see that these Caribbean pianos soaking in Cuba for many decades have been more preserved by the film of moisture than ruined by it.

In the Museo's small concert hall/meeting room I meet Raquel Montejo Soto, a student of piano tuning in Havana. She stands with María Teresa and the PA sound specialist I have dubbed Protocol because he knows some English and can translate the odd phrase for Raquel. They watch intently as I begin tuning the rare Art Steinway L, white Louis XIV with subtly decorated side panels. The pitch is close to concert A-440: high humidity won't let the soundboard (the curved belly of the piano over which the strings are stretched) contract over the years and loosen the strings. Also I learn there was a good *técnico ruso* (Soviet technician) in years past— he must have administered several solid Russian tunings.

Unfortunately the bass strings are a little dead, or tubby sounding. The strings of the bottom two octaves of a piano are steel with a tightly wound wrapping of copper wire for added mass. Moisture and age eventually corrode these unlike metals causing the strings to stiffen up and lose their sonority. This leaves me with a few options. Best would be to restring the seventy-year-old piano from top to bottom, a weeklong job. I have one day and no strings. Second best is to remove the bass strings from the back end of the piano a handful at a time, tie them in a large loop, run the loop up and down the strings to loosen the corrosion, and reinstall each string with a full twist to tighten the winding. This process takes about an hour and results in a nearly new-sounding bass, but removing strings wreaks havoc with the tuning. María Teresa has planned a flute and piano concert for the following day, and I won't be able to return to touch up the bass. So I use option three: you briskly loosen and retune each bass string in the hope that some of the old corrosion will break up.

Now you have to see it from Raquel's point of view. Here is an American stranger violently messing with the bass strings of their extremely valuable Steinway. She murmurs something about breakage. I am paddling about obliviously, talking to myself and experimenting with removing a few of the wires. Finally Raquel puts her foot down: the piano, she avers, is in perfectly good shape for tomorrow's concert. Luckily I have my C.V. and a letter of recommendation from Steinway's prestigious New York Concert Department tucked in with my passport. I hand the documents to Protocol and ask him to present them to María Teresa. A hush descends on the hall as they all pore over the two crucial leaves. In time, a verdict. I pass. By now it is almost eleven A.M. and I set to work with a vengeance.

Raquel is in a chair by my side unable to calm down about having the weird Yankee expert for the day. I answer her questions and give occasional pointers, all the while trying to speed through the concert tuning to get to the sorely-needed action work. Occasionally Raquel sings the note I am tuning—a practice guaranteed to enrage a tuner, who has to listen carefully to the faint interference beats. "*Niños ¡no canta!*" is my broken-Spanish refrain (trying to say "Children! No singing!") I myself cannot be prevented from intermittent bursts into song, so happy am I to find myself of use to these benevolent beings on a foreign planet.

A solid tuning is just the first step in preparing a piano for concert. Hammers grooved from years of play have to be reshaped and fitted precisely to the strings. The hammer take-off point as well as the let-off point (the hammer has to "let off" a few millimeters from the string or the note won't play) must be set. Eighty-eight springs must be adjusted for maximum reliability on repeated notes.

María Teresa sets me up in an office with a desk by a window. I lug the action to the desk, arrange my tools on an adjacent table and begin the three-hour job of reshaping the excellent old hammers to the "Steinway shape" in which each hammer is given the profile of the pointy end of an egg. Raquel watches for a while and asks to take over. I refuse, somewhat alienating her. She disappears for a couple of hours.

There is a room off my workshop containing the office of Ligia Guzmán Piantini. She seems to be the Museo's archivist and musicologist. She shows me her name on the cover of a tract and I ask if the Piantini refers to her mother's name and the Guzmán her father's. She says I have the order of Spanish names right and that both her mother and father were well-known Cuban musicians, and that's as far as my Spanish takes me. For some reason I ask her about a song we hear everywhere on the island, "Cuba, que linda es Cuba." She too disappears.

I am alone in my wonderful workshop, feverishly shaping the hammers by the open window in the wet heat with the sounds and smells of Old Havana intruding from the window and the sound of an advanced guitar lesson coming from the hallway and the rustling of papers from the office of Ligia Guzmán Piantini.

Ligia enters from the side door to speak with me. She presents me with some pamphlets from the archives. The first is a history of the Museo with photographs. The second pamphlet is her own biography of Eduardo Saborit, composer of "Cuba, que linda es Cuba." Ligia's father, Maestro Adolpho Guzmán, turns out to have collaborated on many of Saborit's recordings. She has written a note in commemoration of my visit. On the back cover she has written out longhand every word of "Cuba, que linda es Cuba." It certainly is.

On our last morning, I hold back tears in the hotel lobby as our Cuban hosts present farewell speeches. Only hours earlier I got past my sheer admiration of the heart and strength of the Cuban people to finally know some of them in a personal way. Last night I got bored stiff with the farewell festivities planned for us and ended up in the room of some of the hotel staff talking about rum, politics, and work. There were three young men (one so drunk you had to tell him everything twice), two fabulous young women, and one typical American. We talked until three A.M., and in the end I traded shoes with my host, the ever-smiling restaurant worker Joe. He had told me how much he loved his job, that he was learning every aspect of the waiter's trade, but that life in Cuba these days entails miles and miles of walking every day. When he pointed out the two holes in the sides of his leather moccasins I looked down at my perfect new adjustable Birkenstocks and immediately proposed a trade. Joe's shoes didn't fit me at all and ended up getting me in a heap of trouble later with Continental Airlines when I tried to board in Cancún barefoot.

The week was a success. The Museo's piano got regulated in time for the concert, and Daniel Duran's piano got its fine tuning on Saturday. He arranged for a fine box of cigars for my father.

Ben Treuhaft began his piano tuning career at age eighteen. Soon he was working at the prestigious Steinway & Sons Concert Basement for such artists as Vladimir Horowitz and Glenn Gould. His first visit to Cuba was in 1993. He was inspired to rebuild a six-foot Weber grand piano and send it with Pastors For Peace to Havana's Museo Nacional de la Música, and to collect thousands of dollars worth of piano supplies for Cuba from colleagues. When he subsequently made several unauthorized tuning trips, the U.S. Treasury Department tried unsuccessfully to prosecute him for aiding and abetting enemy pianos. In 1994 he founded Send a Piano to Havana which he runs out of his Underwater Piano Shop in New York, and which has since been occupying all of his spare time.

C. PETER RIPLEY

✦ ✦ ✦

Heroes of Tourism

Epcot Center it's not.

WE PILED INTO THE VAN TO HEAD OUT OF SANTIAGO UNDER A SKY
so threatening that Roberto urged us to reconsider our plans for the
day. One of the things Bob and I most wanted to do in Cuba was
climb in the tropical green of the Sierra Maestra and walk the path
of Castro's guerrilla army. Numbering less than two dozen when
they arrived here in 1956, they claimed the mountains as a home
and as a base of guerrilla operations until they took control of the
country two years later.

Bob brushed aside Roberto's worry about wind and rain and
insisted we drive to the mountain, hopeful that the weather would
clear by the time we arrived. He did so despite the fact that Roberto
had failed in the one chore Bob had asked of him during the entire
trip, to get us ham-and-cheese sandwiches and bottled water, our
breakfast, and liquid for the day's effort. Roberto kept predicting that
the weather would keep us off the mountain. Then he tried to cover
himself by saying, "Don't worry, we'll find something to eat on the
road," to which Caputo responded, "Not unless we hit it."

We drove along the coast, where the muscular, thickly wooded
mountains seemed to spring up sheer and forceful from the side of
the road and reach into the blackened clouds. The road worked its

way alongside bucolic bays and harbors, each with rustic fishing villages. Periodically, from a distance, it appeared as though the road ended abruptly up ahead, appeared as though the mountains rose out of the sea so radically that there was no place for a car to pass without disappearing into the landscape.

Along the route Roberto had Eric stop here and there—to get ice for the cooler, to ask about food. He returned to the van once to announce that a professional guide was required for the climb we had planned, but mostly he just delayed, hoping for some redemptive rain to keep us off the mountain, until Bob, tight-lipped and out of patience, insisted we get moving. "Quit stalling," he told Roberto. "We've already wasted two hours and won't have any food all day if we don't get going; by the time we get back to Santiago it will be too late to find something to eat."

We were sixty miles from Santiago, where store-bought supplies were as scarce as Americans in 1991, so we began to climb on empty stomachs, with no prospects for lunch, and carried with us only one can of Coke and two cans of juice to see us through the daylong trek to Pico Turquino, at 6,561 feet Cuba's highest peak and the site of a national shrine. Eric begged off with a smile, a wise man who masked his insight about how difficult the day might be with a playful comment about duty, which, he said, required him to remain with the van. Roberto, who held on to his good humor even during the trip's most difficult moments, insisted with an exaggerated bravado a microsecond removed from chest pounding, "I'm Cuban. I'm your guide. It's my duty to go with you. I have to see you to the top if the government is going to award you guys the title of "Heroes of Tourism," citing the accolade he had bestowed on us as praise and complaint for our manic insistence on seeing and doing everything possible. "Let's get going," he said. Which we did, for a few hundred yards, before Roberto turned back, though not without uttering the self-congratulatory declaration, "During the Revolution I would have been an urban guerrilla, not a mountain fighter." Caputo turned back next, a victim of his forty pounds of camera equipment. I pushed on with Bob, who quick-stepped ahead in irritation just as the sun broke through the overcast sky.

We trudged up the low, gradual base of the mountain, past an occasional small farm with fields cut out of the forest. Horses ambled across the trail and goat bells chimed in the distance. For a time the forest was so thin we could glance up from the path to see the series of rising peaks and intervening valleys that lay ahead for the day's effort, a four-mile roller-coaster hike to the top. After an hour the trail grew narrower and steeper, the sun grew warmer, the trees and vegetation grew thicker and soon covered the trail in a tropical canopy that held us in a wrap of heat and moisture. We grew less talkative, concentrating on the climb, the beauty of the mountains, and the historic significance of the place.

We wanted to make the top despite Roberto's claim that "you can't climb El Turquino in the rainy season." Years prior to Castro's arrival in the Sierra Maestra, a freedom-minded father and daughter consecrated the highest point by placing there a bust of José Martí, the father of Cuban independence and the one historic figure all Cubans view with nationalistic pride. Over the years, true believers trusted the idea that José Martí's figure looking out over Cuba from El Turquino would inspire patriots to another revolution. Bob and I wanted to see the statue. We had paid proper respect at other revolutionary monuments and historic places, but we wanted very badly to pause before that sanctuary because, I suspect, to do so required us Americans to make the extra effort.

We climbed for two hours before the liquids were gone. After three hours the rain started, gentle at first, then harder, filling the narrow trail with moving water, transforming the path into a mountain stream that rushed against our boots and started to dilute our determination. The rain turned the trail into a mass of thick red clay that sucked at our feet with every step; rocks and small boulders caused us to slip and stumble, claiming our energy just to keep our balance, and more than once the slick, jagged trail dropped us in painful falls. After five hours we were covered with mud, bruises, and scrapes, and we sat our exhausted selves down to rest rubbery legs, indifferent to the cold rain and body-shaking chill that crept into us each time we stopped moving. We sucked rain off leaves to slake our thirst, and nursed our battered bodies.

As I sat there with my fatigue, I flashed on another country lush with tropical greenery, thick moist air, and rugged terrain: Vietnam, a country unknown to me personally, but not to tens of thousands of my generation. I put my face in my hands for a sorrowful moment trying to imagine what the days might have been like there, trying to capture the rain, danger—and death and dying. But I could not. The similarities in landscape and climate common to Vietnam and Cuba, particularly the indescribable green of the forest, were evocative, causing me to feel for that instant that I could make other connections as well, but that was a false impulse. The look and feel of a shared topography could not bridge the distance between the experience of American friends who went to Vietnam and my own experience that day in Cuba, or any other day, for that matter. That distance was too great for the imagination to travel.

I shook free of that thought to consider the idea that Cuba and Vietnam represented competing touchstones for my generation. Then I raised my head from my hands to look down the mountain, over the thickness of the trees to the base of the mountain and past the base to the point where the land meets the clean, fresh sea, just across the road from where the mountain starts its steep rise toward Cuba's highest point. Then I turned to look up to El Turquino peeking through the forest, shrouded in fog that protected the bust of José Martí.

But there was no protective shroud for our adventure that day. We turned back at 4,000 feet. The two-hour descent down the muddy trail was more solemn than it should have been, more solemn than it would have been in other circumstances. Bob and I were quiet with our disappointment. We weren't disappointed that we had failed to finish the climb, exactly, or that our physical abilities were not equal to our ambition, although that certainly did not please us. It felt more as though we had failed to meet an obligation, one too imprecise to render clearly but one that we felt keenly nonetheless.

Two days later, as we headed out of Santiago toward Havana and then home, Bob and I and Caputo let our intoxication with Cuba spin out of control. Driving over the flat agricultural landscape of the island's central plains, past yet more sugarcane fields, pineapple farms, and banana groves, and through small towns, nearly all of which had dusty baseball diamonds, we Americans struggled with the pure excitement of discovery brought on by Cuba. We had walked through Havana, drunk *mojitos* at La Bodeguita, watched dancers at Cuban nightspots, snorkeled an untouched coral reef, hiked in the Sierra Maestra, seen sobering bullet holes at revolutionary shrines, repented for America at Playa Girón, gotten swept away during the music festival at Santiago de Cuba, and crisscrossed the island. We were overcome by all of it, pushed into overload by the breakneck pace, the beauty of the country, the charm of the people, the grace of the culture, the vigor of the society. All of it. Everything. It was not just the physical demands and wonderful pleasures of those days that put us on the edge, sent us into double alert. It was something more, something we could not put into words at the time because it was too close to bring into sharp focus, to define, to even describe. We were just in it.

More than anything else, the humanity of the trip held us in a tight grip, like our experience on the balcony of the Casa Granda Hotel, only with less pressure, which made the close feeling tolerable, if still terribly intense. Roberto and Eric had played their role, as had the many Cubans, like Neddie, who welcomed us without rancor or suspicion, had asked nothing more of us than that we try to see Cuba through their eyes, to put politics and personality aside and judge their country fairly and evenly. Cubans liked us, and we liked them. Strangers one minute, sharing a coffee or rum the next. No one denied us. It was all quite extraordinary.

Roberto and Eric had become more than guide and driver along the island's highways. They had directed us through the culture and the society, never refused us an opportunity or an answer to the most pressing question about Cuba, or about themselves. Traveling in the van, the five of us—with luggage, camera equipment, the cooler of beer and soft drinks, and the case of Cuban rum—created a fellowship that continued through the day's meals and into the late night's last drink. We traded ideas and even a few confidences, the first tentative steps toward friendship taken in the most traditional fashion during an uncommon journey. Consider Eric's memories of being a young man at the Bay of Pigs, where he went with Fidel, where he collected American arms and Cuban prisoners but no bitter memories.

There were jokes and good humor and language lessons and promises to stay in touch, but late that afternoon, as the lowering sun cast the sky and the land in a bright illumination, we lost control. It started with yet another lesson in yanqui idioms, which Roberto, the faithful student of English, particularly its slang, scribbled in his notebook.

"Fuckin'A," I began, following it with examples of the expression's subtle and exact usage.

"Dickhead," contributed Caputo.

"Wiseass," offered Bob.

"Attention, please, Kmart shoppers"—and on it went, with Roberto using each term in a few sentences until we were satisfied he had the true feel of it. Before long we were giddy and laughing like fools.

It was I who sent everything off on a wrong course, without meaning to or ever suspecting it at the time, and it began when I asked Roberto, "Who is the Minister of Culture? We must speak to him as soon as we arrive in Havana. I have the answer to Cuba's future. A theme park!"

"Right," said Caputo, catching on. "If you want American tourists back in Cuba, you've got to be ready to give them what they want."

"Exactly," I said, "and what they're going to want is a Revolutionary Theme Park situated at the base of Sierra Maestra. That is the natural place, the place you Cubans refer to as the 'Cradle of the Revolution.' We can get the Disney people to come in on this; it's a natural for them. Just look at what they did for Florida."

"They can make up life-size robots of Che, Fidel, all the Heroes of the Revolution," said Bob, joining in the tasteless letting-off of pressure.

"That's right," I continued. "They can make up a really wicked Batista, and every afternoon they can put him on trial for his crimes against Cuba. Then they can shoot the motherfucker at sunset, just as the park closes. Jesus, it's perfect. Perfect!"

"Ride the Guerrilla Mountain Water Slide."

"Visit the AK-47 Shooting Gallery."

"Don't miss the Revolutionary Dance Revue—topless, of course."

"If Cuba really wants tourism, then we can help you do it right. We're Americans. We understand these things. It'll make millions, Roberto, hundreds of millions. Trust us on this. We'll make you famous for this idea."

We were laughing like madmen, holding our aching sides, tears rolling down our cheeks, each hoping the others would say no more so it would come to a painless end, until finally it did, and we slumped into quiet exhaustion, like three hysterical people after a body-racking fit of crying.

Only later, when we were alone, did Bob describe the hurt he saw in Roberto's eyes, and only then did Bob confess that Eric had wanted him to translate so he could understand what we found so funny, which Bob could not, would not, do.

We had gone too far, and I had no idea. What I had done, without understanding its purpose or offense, was to act out my concern for Cuba in a merciless skit of dark, capitalist humor. Being an American, and having fallen in love with the country, hopelessly, pitifully in love, I grieved over a future too tied to tourism, grieved from knowing that each time I returned to Cuba, as I knew I surely must, I would find a loss of qualities in the county I had come to respect and admire so much.

You don't have to measure the worth of a society by the most wicked acts of its government, unless that is your choice. You don't have to judge politics and political personalities to care about a people and a culture, revolutionary or reactionary, unless that is your choice. I found in that revolutionary place, among those welcoming people, a national purpose that had succeeded after centuries of suffering at the hands of tyrants, homegrown and foreign, Spanish and Cuban, Russian and American, by both proxy and clear purpose. I wanted the suffering—whatever its origin—to end, to stop. Then. At that very instant. In my admiration and affection, I wanted to preserve Cuba before things got even worse, and I would have done it had I the power and authority. Would, in a miracle of imagination, have lifted the American embargo and loosened the close-fitting politics at home for my new friends, our old neighbors. But I couldn't. And I recognized there was no stopping the progressive ruin that would follow the chosen remedy of the day.

Tourism, I feared, would eventually bring hordes of Americans descending on Cuba, and American tourists would surely bleed the revolutionary culture with a series of small cuts and slashes that would likely go unattended until Cuba was pale and anemic from his losses. Why not, then, build a Revolutionary Theme Park at the start, mock the Revolution and market its heroes, its purpose, its meaning, its accomplishments? It was bound to come, I was warning in my crude way, so why not just be done with it?

That afternoon, in the illumination of failing Caribbean sunlight, in exhaustion and exhilaration, in a fondness for Cuba, and in fear for her future, we created Fidel Land as a caution and as a benediction.

If Roberto and Eric were offended by our excess, they gave no outward sign of it, but it was difficult to know because we were all quiet and subdued during the rest of the drive to Havana. Only Eric, who alone among us seemed not to be searching for something on this trip, remained

Beware: If you wear a guayabera in Havana, people will think you're a *seguroso*, a state security agent.
— Regla Albarrán, Havana native

alert as he drove on into the late afternoon and evening. When he finally pulled into the curved drive of the Comodoro, back where we had begun ten days earlier, we startled awake and piled out of the van like whipped dogs.

Before we parted for the night, Roberto and Eric insisted on driving us to the airport the next day, although we assured them there was no need. I don't know then if they persisted out of duty or friendship, but persist they did, and I was glad for it; I did not want to leave them without a proper goodbye. When the time came we all stood in the middle of José Martí Airport like awkward young lovers at the end of a summer romance, not ready for it to end, but realizing it must. Surrounded by knots of loud tourists, pushcart bars with overpriced *mojitos*, and lounging immigration officials waiting for the flight to arrive that would take us back to Cancún, we three Americans said goodbye to our Cuban friends with a teary embrace. "You damn Americans," said Roberto as he turned to leave "you're going to make me cry again."

Bob and I made no attempt to sit together during the flight home. Such a hard reentry was best done alone. The wacky last day's drive from Santiago to Havana, the emotional farewell at José Martí, followed by a postmodern rush through the brightly lit Cancún airport to make our connection to the States, seemed an unusually harsh combination of sensations.

On the Miami-bound airplane, a kindly gray-haired woman, apparently determined not to let me sulk, leaned across the aisle and asked if it were true that I had just come from Cuba.

"Yes, that's correct," I told her.

"What did you think?" she asked.

"It was my best experience since Richard Nixon resigned," I answered.

Ignoring my remark, she explained that she had traveled to Havana as a teenager with her mother and two cousins, in the 1950s, before the Revolution, and remembered the trip fondly, but after so many years carried but a single image in her memory, that of young children in rags rummaging through garbage pails for food.

Too absorbed with my Cuban experiences to comment, I turned my head to the window and thought, "Oh, I wish you could see it now."

C. Peter Ripley is a native of Maine who has spent most of his adult life in Florida. Cuba has been his constant curiosity since his teenage years in the 1950s when he broke into Batista's Florida home on a bet. His curiosity turned into a romantic attachment following Castro's revolution. Trained as a historian, he has published nine books and has taught at a number of institutions, including Yale University and a federal prison.

* * *

Es Cuba

*Falling for a lover or a country can
be wonderfully irrational.*

IN ISLA DE LA JUVENTUD, A SMALL ISLAND OFF THE SOUTH COAST OF
Cuba, Alfredo and I decide to tell everyone we're married. It is a
game, a way of survival in a country where foreigners have more
rights than citizens. And on this Isle of Youth, home to Cuba's foreign scholarship students in the '80s and early '90s, something has
gone dreadfully wrong. Not only can Cubans not enter a restaurant
or club without a foreigner in tow to fork over the U.S. dollars, but
if they're with a partner of the opposite sex, they need to be married.

Alfredo and I are standing at the iron rod entrance gate to the
Patio Cabaret and the bouncer, a tall man, thick like a wall, is asking for our marriage papers.

"Why would we be carrying those around?" Alfredo asks. I'm
surprised by how assertive he's suddenly become. Usually, when
rebuffed for being Cuban, he becomes quiet. He gives a dirty look
to whomever has denied him entrance and then he stomps off to
bite his fingernails, leaving me to negotiate. Later, he will shrug his
shoulders and tell me, "*Es Cuba.*" That's Cuba.

But tonight I can tell he's excited, perhaps made braver by the
idea of our false identities, of this fantasized marital future.

"I'm telling you she's my wife and I'm her husband," he repeats to the bouncer. "We're here on vacation. We live in Havana, and no one asks for papers there."

"Well, I'm asking," the bouncer says. He stands firm, his right foot planted on the swinging entrance gate.

"Forget it," I tell Alfredo, and I shake my head at the bouncer who retreats to a circular bar in the back of the patio.

"I don't really feel like seeing a show anyway," I say. "I'd rather just walk around. Is that O.K. with you?"

"It's fine," he says. "Why are you asking?"

"Because don't you remember how it annoyed you before when we traveled and I just wanted to be mellow and you were bored?"

He looks up at me. "But that was then, Aschkenas," he says. He likes my last name and has told me that if we ever got married, he'd become Alfredo Aschkenas. "It's different now," he says. "I understand you better."

Alfredo and I have been together four months now. Although there have been so many moments of rightness in our relationship that I could never keep track of them all, the same is true of our many disagreements and cultural misunderstandings. For nearly three months, we argued about everything from food (my vegetarianism, his refusal to eat anything without meat) to politics (my romanticized vision of socialism, his grounded criticisms of it) to sex (the position, the condoms, the frequency).

Once when he slipped up and, in the middle of an angry accusation, said, "You Americans," when he was really talking about something that had only to do with me, I realized the truth. We were not just arguing, eating, sleeping together as two people, but as two nations. We were carrying with us the bitter, twisted history of an international feud that was stronger than each of us and older than both our lifetimes.

So many times I almost called things off. So many times I did call things off, but Alfredo always said, "No, let's try again." He always said, "Have some patience, Aschkenas. We're coming from two different worlds."

And so we stayed together and slowly we argued less and listened more and each argument began to feel less like a collision of countries and more like a merging of two different but complementary lives.

I met Alfredo my third night in Havana, at a bus stop in the Playa neighborhood. It was a rare, cool evening in early February, and he was wearing a white sweatshirt and gray pants, frayed at his ankles where he had attempted to alter them. His hair hung in tight Tracy Chapman spiral dreadlocks. He was kicking something around on the sidewalk and looked up nervously as I approached with my friend Heather and Alfredo's friend Gerardo.

Heather was part of the group I'd come to Cuba with, and she met Gerardo at a salsa club our first night. This evening she invited me to go out with them, but when Gerardo met us outside Hotel El Bosque where we were staying, he told us he'd brought a friend.

"Where?" Heather asked. "Is he invisible?" Gerardo laughed. He was a tall, muscular black guy, and he looked entirely out of place standing outside El Bosque, surrounded by potted palms, a moat of Japanese koi, a host of light-skinned bellboys, and an open-air entrance that anyone but a Cuban could enter.

"My friend's waiting at the bus stop," Gerardo said. I remember thinking it seemed strange at the time, but later, looking back, I would see that this fit perfectly with Alfredo's personality, with his fierce sense of pride and his outrage at what many called Cuba's "tourism apartheid." If he couldn't fully take part in the social life of his country, he would not stand on the outskirts and watch as Gerardo did that night, waiting for us outside El Bosque. Alfredo just wouldn't take part.

In 1993, to stir up the moribund economy which fell fast and hard after the Soviet bloc collapsed, Castro legalized the U.S. dollar. Most Cubans, however, are paid in pesos. "You get paid in pesos," the saying goes, "but life's sold in dollars."

Before the collapse of the Soviet bloc, Cubans lived off their ration books for food, clothing, and other goods, and could buy, in pesos, beyond that at "free markets." Today the scarce offerings of the bare-board ration stores reflect the country's own depressed economic state. To survive, in addition to their day jobs, most Cubans have *negocios* or private, illegal businesses to earn enough dollars to buy food at farmers' markets and on the black market. Cubans give Spanish lessons to tourists or sell them cigars or rum. Or they get jobs in tourism. Tourism workers and selected other job-holders, by virtue of salaries paid partially in dollars and, for some, tips received in dollars, earn more than most professionals, rupturing the socialist dream of an unstratified society.

That first night I met Alfredo, as he and I and Heather and Gerardo were walking down the cobblestone streets in the tourist neighborhood of Old Havana, we were stopped by a policeman who requested Alfredo and Gerardo's ID cards.

The officer, a mulatto with the uniform navy-blue beret and hyphen-short mustache, walked over to the street corner with the cards and started making calls on his walkie-talkie.

"What's that about?" I asked.

Gerardo shook his head.

"Shit," Alfredo said in English. "It's all shit."

The four of us waited there silently. We had just bought a bottle of Guayabita del Pinar rum and were planning to sit on the Malecón, Havana's seafront wall, and drink and talk.

When the police officer returned, he asked Heather and me what we were doing in Cuba.

"We're on a dance and language program," I told him.

"How long have you been here?"

"Three days."

"And how long have you known them?" he asked, motioning to Alfredo and Gerardo.

I could hear Alfredo inhale deeply. The night was silent except for the faint notes of a salsa band that we had passed in Plaza de Armas.

"Since we got here," I said.

"Uh huh," the officer said, eyeing me skeptically. "Well, you should just know that most of our young men are up to no good. They use the foreign women for their bodies and their money."

I expected Alfredo or Gerardo to say something but they stood motionless. Heather rolled her eyes at me.

"O.K.," I said to the policeman. "O.K." I was expecting something else to come out of my mouth, but nothing did.

"It's just a power play," Alfredo told me afterwards as we sat on the seawall. "They don't usually do anything to you."

I told Alfredo about the police in the United States, about the Rodney King riots during my freshman year of college in Los Angeles. He asked me about my life in California. I told him about the solitude of being a freelance writer. I told him about my vegetarianism and my morning runs through the mountains and the Zen center near my house and he said, "I think I'm falling in love with you."

"You hardly know me," I said. "And do you know how many times I've heard that line in foreign countries?"

"No, I don't," he said, looking down at the sea where the waves swirled in little tide pools around the coral and discarded Cristal beer cans.

"I don't know," he repeated. "Because Cubans aren't allowed to travel. You need an invitation and then special permission, and if you're young and single,

The sight of Miami attorney Magda Montiel Davis kissing Fidel Castro at a reception, coquettishly shimmying her shoulders and saying, "Thank you for what you've done for my people. You have been a great teacher for me," caused obsessive media attention in the Miami exile community. For my part, I realized how easily I might have fallen into the Madga role—unconsciously being flirtatious in an effort to catch Father Fidel's attention. For no matter how strong and conflicted our emotions about Fidel may be, there is an erotics to his domination. Women deny it at their peril. Men too, but in a different way, not daring to admit they could be seduced by a more macho man.
—Ruth Behar, "Queer Times in Cuba," *Michigan Quarterly Review*

it's usually denied anyway because you're considered a possible immigrant. This island is like a prison."

And then, in a perfect, seamless switch, Alfredo told me why he was proud to be Cuban.

"We don't have violence," he said. "Health care's free. Education's free. We're masters in music." He told me about his drumming lessons and his job at the symphony where he worked on the light- and sound-system and got to hear musicians from all over the world. He said last year Fidel visited and gave everyone a raise so now Alfredo earned the peso equivalent of $15 a month.

"That was the only good thing Fidel's done recently," he said. "That and his standing up to the U.S. But once he implemented the dollar, everything fell apart."

As we talked that night, I recognized something in Alfredo's words, in his body language and flourishing hand gestures. It was that odd mix of melancholy and optimism that mimicked what, by just my third day, I had come to recognize as the determined yet contradictory character of his country.

Weeks later, Alfredo would ask me repeatedly, "I know you thought I wasn't sincere. You thought, 'It's not possible to love someone so quickly,' and maybe you were right. But why did you agree to see me again?"

I always told him that there was something, but I didn't have the words yet.

"How can that be?" he would ask. "You're a writer."

I saw something in Alfredo, as I did in Cuba as a whole, that both saddened and inspired me. I saw signs of hope in places where, on the surface, it appeared that there should be only despair. I experienced kindness that, despite that police officer's premature warning, demanded nothing in return. I felt something I could only identify as the arrival of a long-awaited happiness when I woke early every morning, refreshed after just five hours of sleep, excited for the new day. In Alfredo, I found the same inexplicable force that drew me to Cuba and made me, at the start of each month, extend my ticket once more until my planned one-month trip turned into two months and then three and then four.

*

In my mind, these four days in La Isla, as Cubans call the Isla de la Juventud, will be the final test of our relationship. I will be leaving Cuba in a week to return to the United States. And the outcome of this long weekend will determine what I will say when we say goodbye, what plans we will make for our future.

Our first night on La Isla, after the Cabaret Patio incident, Alfredo and I walk around Nueva Gerona, the island's capital.

There are fewer potholes here than in Havana. The streets are cleaner and the air fresher. I point this out to Alfredo and he breathes in deeply and laughs.

"Yes, you're right," he says.

Earlier in our relationship discussions of the city versus the country had been another source for debate. I've spent the majority of my twenty-six years living in the country or suburbs, and he's lived the entirety of his twenty-six years in Havana.

But when we stepped off the ferry at La Isla yesterday, he told me, "I think I'm changing. I think you're changing me. I feel healthier already, and I like that the sky's bluer."

As we walk, I begin to feel tired, exhausted from the ordeal of getting tickets to come to La Isla. Although I inquired about the ferry a week in advance, there were less than a handful of seats available in Cuban currency, and to get them, you had to reserve them two weeks in advance and then stand in line for several hours. So I agreed to pay US$10 for each of our tickets. I gave Alfredo the $20 to buy them since he passed by the terminal on his way to work, but no one would sell them to him. He called me from work during the day to tell me. When we met up in the evening, I was hoping he would return the money on his own. But he didn't and as the night wore on, I grew angry with him for making me have to ask for the money back. Before we went to sleep, I took a deep breath and asked, "Alfredo, why is it that you didn't give me back my $20?"

It was the wrong way to ask. I realized this immediately after the words escaped my mouth. Alfredo looked at me with a pained expression as he reached for his wallet and practically threw the money at me.

"Why did you ask me like that?" he said, his voice wobbling. "I just forgot. What do you think, that I'm trying to take your money? That I'm a *jinetero?*" *Jinetero*, or hustler, was a common word in Cuba. "You still believe what that policeman said that first night," he said. "How could you think that, after all we've gone through together, I'm just using you for your money?"

He looked at me like he no longer recognized me and added, as he got into bed and turned away from me, "I'll always love you, but this is never going to work if you can't trust me."

I said I was sorry, and I wanted to say that I hadn't meant to say what I did, but I knew it wasn't fully true. With so many inequalities, with so many stories circulating about foreigners who fell in love with the Cubans only to learn that the Cubans were in love with their wallets, I always felt on guard. That night after Alfredo fell asleep, I lay next to him in bed, watching the blanket rise and fall with his breathing, wanting to trust him completely and, at the same time, afraid to do so.

The sun sets a brilliant red on our first night in La Isla. We watch it drop behind a deep-green, marble-topped mountain in the foreground and then we walk back to the house where we're staying in Nueva Gerona.

Not long after Castro decriminalized the U.S. dollar, he legalized some private businesses such as boardinghouses. When we got into Nueva Gerona, Alfredo called the phone number for one of these houses. We'd heard that the woman who owned it wouldn't ask for our marriage papers. On the phone, Alfredo explained our situation and then I heard him say, "No, no, that's not necessary. She's my girlfriend."

"What happened?" I asked when he hung up the phone.

"She said it's $10 a night," he said, "but she said if I wanted, I could tell you it was $15 and keep the commission."

I looked at him in disbelief.

"But I told her our relationship's not like that," he said.

"I know that," I said. "It just makes me feel weird that she would try to rip me off like that, that she would imagine our relationship was like that."

"Aschkenas," he said. "She doesn't know us. In her mind, you're just another rich foreigner."

Celia's house is on the third story of an apartment complex a few blocks from the main drag. It's small but comfortable, full of the luxuries afforded those who earn dollars. There's a medium-sized color TV, a couch, a little balcony with rocking chairs and a coffee table. The bathroom has a prerevolutionary bathtub, not just a drain in the floor.

In the living room, Celia's seven-year-old daughter Leila runs around in a leotard with a pacifier in her mouth.

"She refuses to grow up," says Celia, a stocky *mulata* with long wavy hair.

We all laugh and Celia offers us some butter and oval-shaped, saltine-like crackers minus the salt. Slowly, my premature resentment towards her begins to fade, and I realize that prejudice swings both ways—against those who have no money and against those who are presumed to have too much.

That night I dream of a small cabin in the woods in Northern California. I dream of a garden encircling the house, a room where I write and one where Alfredo can practice his drumming, a place where he can earn enough to buy drums so he won't have to practice his rhythms on his bed anymore. I imagine him working days at some sort of Latin American cultural center. He'll tell people about Cuba, and in the evenings, we'll have English classes. There will be no embargo, no capitalism, no socialism, no animosity.

In the morning, we catch a bici-taxi or bicycle-powered carriage and ride through the open fields of the countryside, and when we return to Celia's in the afternoon I ask Alfredo if he would like to see my guidebook.

"We can read about Nueva Gerona, and you can practice your English," I tell him. Alfredo started classes last month and uses English phrases whenever he can, his favorites being "Oh, my God" and "Are you my neighbor?"

We sit in the rocking chairs on the balcony, and it takes nearly two hours to translate five pages from my guidebook. Still, I'm surprised by how much English Alfredo has learned. He gets excited each time he comes across a new word and jots it down in his notebook. Afterwards, as the sun begins to drop, he sits rocking and looks over at me.

"This is the most beautiful relationship I've ever had," he says. "I don't want to talk about you in the preterit. I don't ever want to say, 'I *had* this girlfriend.'"

I nod, and we sit rocking like that, silent and still, not needing to say anything else.

The next day we hike up the marble-topped mountain, at one point getting on our hands and knees to climb the raw marble towards the top.

On the way back, we stop by the ferry station to ask about tickets.

I'm prepared to pay the full $20 this time but, just like the marriage ordeal at the Patio Cabaret, everything's even more difficult outside of Havana.

Now it's no longer enough to offer to pay Alfredo's way. If we can't produce the marriage papers, he can't have a ticket in dollars, and we're about two weeks late to get on the waiting list to book passage in Cuban currency.

There are two ferries tomorrow, one at seven and one at noon. If we come at six, the ticket seller says, and someone doesn't show up for a reserved seat, we can take it. As a foreigner, I of course won't have a problem buying my ticket last minute.

We stay in again this evening. I chat with Celia, and Alfredo reads a book I brought with me, a biography of Leo Brouwer, a classical guitarist, composer, and the director of Cuba's National Symphony Orchestra. Alfredo paid $5, one-third of his monthly salary, for the book. He had the author and Brouwer write "For Lea" on the first page.

When we arrive at the ferry terminal at six the next morning, the line to board has already begun and it's obvious not everyone's shown up for their tickets. Alfredo heads off to ask what we can do.

I sit on a slab of the marble staircase and wait. Seven passes and then 7:30, and a little before 8, Alfredo returns breathless, sweating.

"Do you have $10?" he asks and rushes off again. I wait an hour, then ask someone to watch our stuff and head off to search for

Alfredo. But I have no luck. At 10 he returns looking dejected but with one ticket in hand.

"The guy in charge is a *pesado*," a jerk, he tells me. "There is one ticket in pesos left for the noon ferry, and this other guy told me the guy in charge was going on break soon. He said when he left he would sell me a Cuban ticket for the foreigner price. What a rip-off," he says.

"*Es Cuba*," I say.

"*Ya tú sabes*," he says. Now you know.

"So," I say. "We've got two hours to kill."

Alfredo looks around and then reaches up to a flowering red flamboyant tree above us and returns with some seedpods.

"A Cuban kids' game," he says, offering me a seedpod. The game, called war, consists of us each using our seedpod to try to knock the head off the other. I lose every time.

"No offense," Alfredo says, smiling, "But I think I'm better at this. How can it be that an American doesn't know how to play war?"

In retaliation, I pull a powdery flamboyant petal off the tree and, before Alfredo can figure out what I'm doing, crush it over his head, sprinkling a fine, red polleny dust all over his black dreads.

At a quarter to noon, we get in line. As we approach the front, I hear Alfredo draw in his breath. "*El pesado*," he whispers to me and I see the head ferry chief walking over to us. He comes up to Alfredo and says, "Can I see you in my office?"

Alfredo follows him up a series of stairs and disappears into the office. A few minutes before twelve, I see him walk down the office steps alone, shaking his head in disgust.

He found out about the other ticket-seller, he tells me. "And he wanted me to be there while he yelled at the guy who took the bribe. Of course, I didn't get the money back."

I put my arm around his shoulder to console him as we walk onto the ferry. It's an ancient Soviet hydrofoil called *El Kometa,* and as I settle into my seat, it reclines so far back that I practically end up in the lap of the man behind me. I turn around to apologize, but he shrugs his shoulders.

"*No hay problema*," he says. "*Es Cuba*."

Alfredo laughs and offers to switch seats with me. His is a little more upright.

"No, it's O.K.," I say.

Earlier in our relationship Alfredo would have resented this. He would have asked why I could never accept his help, and he would have equated my innocent refusal with some larger affront against Cuba, against him. I would have, in turn, become defensive and told him he was *muy machista* for not acknowledging my independence.

Now though, I see the kindness in his offer, and he smiles and rests his hand on my leg. He closes his eyes, and I try to relax into my recline as *El Kometa* lurches forward, sending us into the clear blue Caribbean, tranquil and steady for the moment.

Lea Aschkenas is a freelance writer whose work has appeared in Salon.com, Outside *magazine,* The Washington Post, *and the collection* Two in the Wild. *She and Alfredo are now married and living in Northern California.*

PART FOUR

IN THE SHADOWS

S. L. PRICE

* * *

The Conflicted Tourist

The author confronts the dark side of tourism.

I AM STILL FIGHTING MYSELF HERE. BY THE FOURTH OR FIFTH DAY, usually, the battle is over; I've given in completely to what the island does to people like me and get lost. But this time I'm determined to ride out the romance, the dizzying feel of being in a movie populated by overactors and second-rate clichés. There's a scene in *Lawrence of Arabia* where King Feisal sizes up Lawrence and, recognizing his dangerous naïveté, calls him "one of those desert-loving English." Exiles despise my type: the Cuba-loving Anglo, the foreigner jazzed by the old cars and crumbling buildings, the Communist rhetoric and dissident struggle, the thrill of skirting a four-decade trade embargo and tasting the denied. Much of their disgust rises from fear that my cash keeps Castro alive, but more unsettling is the fact that I have nothing at stake, no memories of home and childhood taken. For too many people like me, down-at-the-bone Cuba is neither war nor depression nor a place where liberty and repression wrestle every day. It's a safe trip to crisis, a story to tell. It is a place where you can get out clean.

This is, I think, despicable. I know better. I have seen too many friends here living on the margin; I've heard too many stories of people passing bloated bodies in the surf. Photographers adore

Cuba because of the buttery light and antique air, but I know that every picturesque jalopy is cursed daily by its owner because it is hell to keep running, I know the nutritional bankruptcy doled out by the weekly ration book. Hepatitis, AIDS, pneumonia, the proportion of underweight babies—all are on the rise in Cuba. Castro has locked up at least 381 political prisoners. The suicide rate is the highest in the Western Hemisphere. What writer Andrei Codrescu says is true: Cuban faces have the gaunt El Greco beauty, the eyes so luminous and alluring, because everyone is slowly dying. American sports fans scoffed at Livan Hernández's McDonald's habit, but it is a fact that every ballplayer who jumps to the States instantly gains fifteen pounds. They aren't fat. This is what they should've weighed all along.

Yet it is precisely such desperation that draws me to Cuba. I am not used to a world where people grapple with issues huge and real and simple: life, death, freedom, love, country, escape. I come from a place where health, lib-

No one in the little wooden house in Cumanayagua expressed any desires or dreams. Is such passivity normal? During a long encounter, won't certain anxieties surface, the dream of attaining something remote, a longing to be elsewhere? Were we not weighed down by a tombstone, a conclusive event, a situation in which everything was predetermined? Cuba seems like a consummated situation, and I feel that in some important sense I failed this girl. It would have been hard, but even in Cuba, in that remote, wretched place amid green tropical hills, I should have found some way of shaking off the passivity, of enriching the monotony, of casting a bottle into the sea, of issuing a warning, of establishing some connection for them with the outside world.

They asked for nothing, I offered nothing, no link was established despite the fact that the three of us, that afternoon, loved one another.

—Jacobo Timerman,
Cuba: A Journey

erty, and the future of the republic are taken for granted, and at times such comfort can leave an abiding emptiness. Riding a bus into Havana from Varadero last weekend, I sat in front of a thirtyish Brit making his third trip here in three years. He spoke of this girl he'd met once on the bus to Santiago, how her family welcomed him and his buddies to their farm. One Sunday, not knowing it was their only day to use the local tractor, he brought a bottle of scotch: everybody stopped working and, under the blazing sun, got beautifully drunk. The story, of course, had no point beyond that—which was precisely his point. As he spoke of that, or of the many times the old taxi broke down and everyone had to pile out and push to get it started, his face assumed this expression of mystified joy because he was sure he'd broken through and caught a glimpse of the authentic. Never before, he said, would he have dreamed of wasting his vacation on the same place twice. This time, he left his buddies behind.

I have acquaintances back in the States, middle-class white boys like me, and every time I hear of their latest sex tour in Havana, their cool little week of cocktail culture, I'm overtaken by a spasm of dismay. But I understand them too, and hate that understanding, because I know we share the same dirty fear that Fidel will fall and it will all be gone. Cuba will have Starbucks and answering machines in every house; Cuba will be like anywhere. Never mind that every Cuban wants change, *now*. For us, Cuba has been merely an exotic outlet for terror and lust: Our grandparent's generation honeymooned, gambled, and gazed in awe at the Superman sex shows; our parents saw it as the fulcrum of near-nuclear war. For us it is a cage containing the brutalized remains of a discredited faith.

S. L. Price has been a senior writer at Sports Illustrated *since 1994 and has written extensively about sports in Florida and Cuba. A graduate of the University of North Carolina, he previously worked as an award-winning columnist and feature writer for* The Miami Herald *and* The Sacramento Bee. *He now lives in Washington, D.C. This story was excerpted from his book* Pitching Around Fidel: A Journey into the Heart of Cuban Sports.

RUTH BEHAR

* * *

A Strawberry and Chocolate Goodbye

Go to the movies and change your life.

NIURKA TAKES MY SWEATY PALM INTO HER OWN BEAUTIFULLY manicured hands, and together the two of us push through the crowd. Gracefully, she weaves us both around to the center of the Cine Chaplin, and we leap upon two perfect seats facing the screen. In the blink of an eye, every seat around us fills up. Suddenly, someone yells, "Get up, old guy, don't you see that seat isn't yours?" Hundreds of people stop their conversations to watch and listen. "*¡Mira, una bronca!*" someone says. The man in the seat refuses to budge. "He took the girlfriend's seat! What nerve! Look at the poor woman standing there," a vehement voice exclaims.

"The show has already begun," Niurka says to me, laughing. The audience becomes an instant jury and concludes that the man has unjustly claimed his seat. "Stand up! Stand up! That seat isn't yours!" people yell out to him from all over the theater. A policeman arrives on the scene, and before he's had a chance to say a word, the man reluctantly gets up. People applaud. There's a sense of giddy excitement in the air that feels as wild as kids getting out of a long day at school. Niurka and I also feel liberated. We've both left behind our husbands and children. Rey, the owner of a cerulean-blue 1956 Chevy with red upholstered seating, whom I've hired with dollars to drive me around Havana, waits for us outside the theater. When the movie is out, he'll return us to our families, waiting in Niurka's neighborhood in Miramar.

While we wait for the film to begin, I realize how strange are the turns of destiny, immigration, and reunion which have brought me, a white Cuban-born woman, and Niurka, a black Cuban-born woman, together to the movies. Niurka is the daughter-in-law of Caro, the black woman who was nanny to my brother and me until we left Cuba in 1961 when I was four-and-a-half years old. When I first returned to Cuba in 1979, I feared that Caro would not want to see me, that she'd view me as a middle-class white girl to whom she'd turn her back in a gesture of defiant revolutionary pride. Instead, Caro welcomed me and told her entire Miramar neighborhood about me. In that once-posh neighborhood of suburban houses and three-story apartment buildings, where today blacks and whites live next door to one another, I am known as *la hija de Caro*, as Caro's daughter. Caro's twin sons Paco and Paquín and her daughter Adriana, who are only a few years younger than me, also treat me with affection. Our mutual trust transcends race and class boundaries, even if we don't forget that those boundaries have everything to do with my position as the one who comes and goes and their position as the ones who wait for me to return. Thanks to Caro and her family, returning to Cuba has become for me an act of faith in the possibilities of spiritual kinship. Since none of my blood relatives remain in Cuba, Caro's family is my only family on the island now....

With Niurka, a lawyer and committed Communist Party member, there is the deep bond that comes from feeling you have found a soul sister you never expected to find. I first met Niurka in 1991 on the day she returned from a two-week stint doing volunteer labor gathering tomatoes in the countryside. I'd heard she was a Party member and imagined she'd be grim and humorless, attired in baggy pants and shapeless work shirt. Niurka, it turned out, was stunningly beautiful and vivacious. She wore a tight t-shirt and very short shorts. In her hands she carried a bunch of ripe fruity tomatoes, which she happily passed around, as if she were distributing party favors. Her long nails were painted bright pink. She didn't despise me, as I'd feared she would. From the start, she engaged me in intense conversation. That very same night, while we talked and compared notes about our lives, she sat in the patio of her neighbor's house having her hair dyed black because she said she'd gotten too much sun out in the fields. Like me, Niurka is a vain woman, an ambitious woman. Like me, she has chosen to only have one child. Like me, she thought nothing of telling her husband to watch their child as we took off for the movies. ...

We are about to see *Fresa y chocolate* (*Strawberry and Chocolate*). Directed by Tomás Gutiérrez Alea, who in the early 1960s defined another key moment in Cuban history with his film *Memorias del subdesarrollo* (*Memories of Underdevelopment*), and Juan Carlos Tabío, *Fresa y chocolate* has drawn huge crowds and won a string of prizes, including best film, at the Festival. The writer Senel Paz, on whose prize-winning story "The Wolf, the Forest, and the New Man" (1991) the film is based, has also written the screenplay, which portrays the unlikely friendship of two men—Diego, an outspoken gay art critic, and David, a young, sexually repressed, Communist activist.

As the film begins, Niurka squeezes my elbow. "That's a posada," she explains. "Where couples go to have sex. They pay by the hour. People don't have enough privacy in their own houses, so they go there." David is with his girlfriend, who chastises him for bringing her to such a rundown place. "Sex is all you want from me," she says. While she goes to the bathroom, sweet-faced David looks through a peephole in the room and sees a woman screaming as she reaches her climax. His girlfriend returns, naked and ready, but he tells her he'll wait until they're married. Next scene we see her getting married, but not to David. Niurka whispers into my ear, "She's chosen a bureaucrat, someone who will make it possible for her to live well and to travel. She's not marrying for love." Disappointed, David looks on, reduced once again to being a voyeur. It is after this failed heterosexual romance that Diego enters David's life.

"Look, that's Coppelia," Niurka tells me, as the film moves to the famous ice-cream parlor in the park in the Vedado section of

Havana. Diego and Germán, a gay artist friend, decide to play a joke on David. Diego flamboyantly joins David at his table, and when David stands up to leave, he discovers that the only other table has been taken by Germán. With disgust, David watches as Diego savors his strawberry ice cream, which he's chosen over chocolate. Seductively, Diego tells David about the books, including some that are forbidden and unavailable (by Vargas Llosa and Cabrera Infante), which he could lend him at his apartment. David follows along, mainly out of a sense of revolutionary duty. He finds Diego a polit-ically suspicious character and plans to gather more facts to be able to report on him.

Instead, as the story unfolds, David finds himself increasingly attracted to Diego as a friend and mentor. David, from a rural *campesino* background, feels he owes the privilege of his Havana education to the revolution. But it is Diego who truly teaches him about his own Cubanness, introducing him to such classical figures of Cuban literary and artistic culture as the writer José Lezama Lima and the composer Ernesto Lecuona (both of whom were gay), as well as to the popular Catholicism and Santería once taboo in a secular Communist state. David gradually comes to understand Diego's gayness and to appreciate and even admire his political out-spokenness. For, indeed, Diego's gender subversion is inseparable from his political subversion. Diego, in turn, who'd made a bet with his friend Germán that he would get David into his bed, ceases to view David as merely the object of his frustrated desire and begins to love him enough that he fears he has tarnished the innocence of his once homophobic friend. As the movie comes to a close, Diego, who kept from David the knowledge of his decision to leave Cuba, finally announces, "I can't stay, there's nothing left for me here," and asks David to please hug him goodbye. A hug representing no demands of any kind; a hug of forgiveness, friendship, redemption, and hope.

With that last hug, the audience of the Cine Chaplin rises and applauds. As we leave the theater, no one pushes anymore. Outside, Niurka and I find Rey just waking from his nap in the backseat. "How was it?" he asks. "Excellent," Niurka responds. "It was full of truths that needed to be expressed." Rey nods his head. "Exactly what my wife said."…

The Coppelia ice cream parlor of *Fresa y chocolate* takes on a poignant set of meanings for me when I learn that our neighbors in the Vedado apartment building where we used to live are having a couple of scoops of ice cream for breakfast every day for lack of milk. Despite the hard times, they insist on preparing a fancy dinner for us. But you have to let us know a day in advance, O.K.? So we can get everything. What do you prefer, pork chops or lobster? I tell them that rice and beans are really fine, that at home we eat neither pork nor lobster. They don't believe me. That can't be true. They insist I choose. So I take the lobster. Are you sure this won't be too much of a sacrifice, I ask, a few too many times. I'd be happy to take everyone to dinner, I say. Her green eyes ablaze, Consuelito responds, "So it's all right for you to sacrifice yourself to come here, and we're not allowed to reciprocate?" To remember is to live, she says, and gives me the swizzle sticks she's saved from the 1959 New Year's party at the Hotel Riviera. Keep two for yourself and give two to your mother. Ask her if she remembers how happily we spent that night…. Christie, my counterpart, a white woman like me of middle-class origins, puts a topaz stone into my hand when she learns that we share the same astrological sign. Make a ring for yourself, Ruti, she says, so

> Let us talk of the "special period," the permanent emergency we Cubans have lived, the daily tension, the rebuilding of the spirit, the daily decency. Of the solid mortar of which the cane cropper is made, the sensuousness of the generous hips perfumed with musk, these eyes that no longer avoid the other's glance, but that, on the contrary, look for it, pin it, challenge it. What to say then to the one who asks me why I live in Cuba? I have no answer.
> —Miguel Barnet, in *Cuba y Cuba* by René Burri

you'll remember me.... In the two-bedroom apartment with the pink bathroom tiles that is a mirror image of the one I grew up in, I eat lobster in a creole sauce with rice and fried green bananas. It all tastes strangely delicious. The lobster is a touch salty, seasoned with old memories and farewell tears....

Just before I left Havana in December, *Fresa y chocolate* moved to the Yara theater, directly across from the Coppelia ice cream parlor and a block away from my hotel. In the mornings, as I headed for the breakfast buffet on the twenty-fifth floor of La Habana Libre Hotel, I'd watch the crowds forming in front of the theater. By nightfall the lines would extend for many long blocks. My heart rose to my throat, seeing the number of people in Havana—estimated at a million—who in the midst of a staggering crisis were willing to wait hours to witness for themselves the possibility of friendship between Diego and David. Like Diego, I longed for a hug goodbye because I knew I was leaving.

Ruth Behar has traveled to Spain, Mexico, and Cuba as an anthropologist, writer, and poet. She is the author of Translated Woman: Crossing the Border with Esperanza's Story *and* The Vulnerable Observer: Anthropology That Breaks Your Heart. *The winner of a MacArthur "genius" award and a Guggenheim Fellowhsip, she returns frequently to Cuba, the land of her birth. She is widely anthologized, and was the editor of* Bridges to Cuba, *from which this story was excerpted.*

LYNN DARLING

✦ ✦ ✦

Havana at Midnight

*Sex tourism from the other
side of the equation.*

IT IS MIDNIGHT AT THE HOTEL RIVIERA, AND THE PALACIO DE LA Salsa is finally in full swing, its entrance besieged by young women begging for admission to the disco's dark interior.

They spill into the lobby, languid girls with golden ringlets, creamy *mulatas* with spindly arms and long legs, and big-breasted, big-assed black girls, their heads thrown back as if a harsh hand held them at the napes of their necks. The women wear neon-orange biking pants and black spike heels and ruffled, off-the-shoulder shirts. They wear Daisy Mae-style checked shirts and tight spandex pants laddered with cutouts all the way up the sides, from ankle to waist. They wear shirred fifties-style conga dresses and black-and-white-striped anything. Their hair is pulled back or swept up or cascading over one eye or erupting in frizzy fountains and dyed all manner of blond. To walk through the strobe-lit darkness of the disco is to inhabit several simultaneous decades of hand-me-down Hollywood: Veronica Lake and Marilyn Monroe; Betty Grable and Whitney Houston. But there are no Madonnas; her taunting power trip has no place in this garden of pliant goddesses.

The men the women want to meet wait inside the Palacio de la Salsa. The men are older and pale and fat, and they walk with their shoulders hunched and the backs of their hands forward, Nuevo Neanderthal style. They are little men, the kind who get pushed around twice for every shove they get to give. They come from Mexico and Spain and Italy, Canada and Germany, and though the women hate the Mexicans for their drunkenness and cheapness and laugh at the Canadians for their inhibitions, they tell you that they are all just men. Many are here on business, investing in Castro's dollar daze. Others are tourists who have heard Cuba advertised as the latest stop on the international sex tour: the Mexicans come by the planeload now, much as Japanese men go to Bangkok, but without, so far, the same AIDS-steeped sense of danger.

In Cuba, these women—the ones who go with the tourists to their rooms in the newly renovated hotels—are called *jineteras*. The word comes from the Spanish for "jockey" and in its masculine form applies to all the small-time hustlers trying to cling to the neck of the tourist trade on which Fidel Castro has placed all of Cuba's bets. But it is the feminine form that arrests attention.

The women in the disco are not typical whores, if such a thing exists outside the minds of men: Cuba is not Thailand, where destitute peasants sell their twelve-year-old daughters to the Bangkok brothels. It is not New York, where underclass addicts ply their trade under the watchful eyes of the men who manage them. Not yet.

Those types are out there, of course. You can find them along the Malecón, the seawall, after sunset: the twelve-year-olds, the drug addicts, the girls with blackened eyes and frightened faces, the whores we have always with us. But prostitution in Cuba is still something of an amateur affair. Many of the *jineteras* are middle-class women—former teachers, former translators, women with university educations who work the weekends and go back to their middle-class neighborhoods in the morning. They are not prostitutes, they say, because they would not be doing this if the money earned at their day jobs could buy anything.

Not all of the men make such distinctions....

When I said I was going to Cuba to write about prostitutes, there was always the same question: why Cuba?

The easy answer was the tired irony, the way in which the revolution had come full circle, the corruption of Batista's Cuba, the trampled dignity, the mocking mirror embodied now in the women who crowd the discotheques and the men who make use of them.

But there was more. Cuba is a country at the end of its hope, and whatever you might think of the revolution that brought it there, even if its failure does not break your heart, there is still the detritus of its promise to contend with, shards still sharp to the people who must walk among them.

This is the deal in Cuba today: The state pays the people in pesos. The stores accept only U.S. dollars. This is official policy, and the official policy means that a doctor earns the equivalent of about $20 a month and a prostitute earns $50 in an evening....

Please understand, the Cubans say, everything in the country is for sale. There is no moral center to life now. Once, the moral center was the family, but the families are scattered from here to Miami, divided by dollars, made crazy by the lack of living space. Love is hard to come by; people get married for the celebratory keg of beer provided by the state, beer that they then sell on the black market for dollars. The revolution was meant to replace the family as a moral center, but the revolution has had to make a few concessions. It has invited the foreigners and expelled the people.

"We are living in a time of no kindness," says one of the *jineteras*. "That doesn't exist here. Everywhere there is envy, and people value things that are not true, and everyone is very selfish now, and it is very scary in my heart."...

There was this that brought me to Cuba, a kind of titillating *aperçu* of the dicey, disturbing morality of it all, an observation offered by a foreign correspondent who has seen a thing or two:

"It doesn't matter what a man tells himself when he goes to a prostitute," he says. "On some level, he thinks he's going to fuck his high school sweetheart. He won't find her on Forty-second Street. But in Cuba, he still can."

Her name is Laura. The first tourist who wanted her told her she had a face like a doll. She is just eighteen, still a high school student. Small and finely built, she is beautiful in the imperious way of the baby of the family and of that time in a woman's life when she first discovers the megaton power of her sexuality. She looks about her with a prairie dog's wired attention to her surroundings. She is dressed in long-sleeved, flowing white linen, and she has loosed her shining, straight brown hair in a meticulous tumble down her back. She is sitting with her friend Camila in the lobby of the Riviera, talking to a couple of sun-burned Danes, who light the girls' cigarettes before heading, a few moments later, for the elevators, without them.

It is an off night at the Riviera, the anniversary of the death of some martyr to the revolution, and the disco is closed. I sit there with my stepdaughter, who is fluent in Spanish, watching Laura. We are new to Cuba, my step-daughter tells her. We are interested in what it is like for women here. We ask, in a studiously casual way, what they are doing here. They look at each other uncertainly. It is Laura who begins. "*Mujer a mujer*," she says. "Woman to woman." I have to smile....

It is so difficult, Laura is saying. She is sitting with Camila on the bed in my step-daughter's hotel room, studying herself in the mirror as she

Inside the halls of the Federation of Cuban Women, which prides itself on having rehabilitated 100,000 of the prostitutes from Batista's days, I ask two of its officials how they feel about the resurgence of prostitution. "There's a *big* difference between the prostitutes of those days and the prostitutes now," snaps Alicia González. "They are different in their quality. Before, they had no schooling; they had health problems. These young women are healthy and educated. Before, they did it to feed their children. Here, there are economic problems, but they are not of the same magnitude. Here, their children go to school, go to the doctor. They are not going to starve to death. Look even at what they are called, *jinetera*, because it is she who dominates the animal," says González almost with pride. Thanks to the revolution, these are empowered prostitutes.

—Silvana Paternostro, "Sexual Revolution," *The New Republic* talks. She is wearing tight blue jeans, a denim shirt, and canvas mules. She smokes a cigarette with the darting motions of a bird. One has to be so careful, she says. In the neighborhood, there is nowhere to go, there is nothing to do. No one has any work. Everyone gossips to kill the time, and everyone knows your business.

The neighbors are always asking questions, she says. The questions reach like tentacles into whatever privacy you had stored away for yourself. The neighbors will say, "Where did you get that dress, and how much did you pay for it?" And if you tell them it cost a $100, Laura says, they know that a tourist bought it for you, and they will call the police.

And while the police may turn a blind eye to the women in the lobbies and on the streets, they listen to their informants. A woman convicted of prostitution can go to jail for a year or two—Laura and Camila say they have a lot of friends behind bars. Prostitu-tion, after all, is illegal in Cuba, despite the fact that some of the $40 a tourist pays at the front desk of the Hotel Riviera to bring a Cuban woman to his room goes to the state. The contradiction barely casts a shadow over Laura's perfectly arched eyebrows: the cynicism that such government-sanctioned hypocrisy engenders is as much a part of Cuban life now as rum and Coke in the afternoon.

We ask her why her neighbors call the police. Isn't life hard for everyone in Cuba? "The older people believe in the revolution," she says. "The revolution has given them a lot, Fidel has given them a lot, and they need to believe in him, and they say what we do is against the revolution, that everyone is supposed to have the same."

Camila—slower, softer, quieter—gently interrupts. Her grandfather, she says, fought in the Sierra Maestra with Castro. Since she was a child, she has heard the stories, but "ever since I was little, I haven't liked this system. I would listen to Radio Martí, and he would say, 'Turn it off, Camila. I didn't fight for this trash.' The old people fought for an illusion—something that was never there in the first place."

Before they began, Laura and Camila looked down on the *jineteras*. It seemed so gross, the idea of going to bed with a man for money. But she didn't want to dress in rags, says Laura; she wanted to dress nicely, to have soap and be clean. One night, when she was sixteen, she met a man, an Italian, at a discotheque, and he invited her over to his yacht. It was he who told her she had the face of a doll, and before she left, he gave her some underwear, a pair of jeans, and a hundred dollars. She says he didn't touch her.

But then she met another man, at another disco. This time, it was the Havana Club at the Hotel Comodoro, the one where the most beautiful women go and the competition is keenest. He was Mexican. It wasn't a difficult decision to sleep with the man. While he was inside her, Laura just thought about the money and how she would spend it. She didn't think about the discos again until the money he gave her ran out. Gradually, it became a regular thing, to go to the discos twice or three times a week, because the money always ran out.

Most of the money goes to clothes and makeup, even though Laura keeps a lipstick long after it has become hard and cracked, reviving it with a few drops of cooking oil from the kitchen. She lives at home

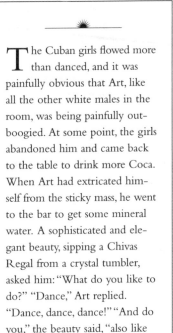

The Cuban girls flowed more than danced, and it was painfully obvious that Art, like all the other white males in the room, was being painfully out-boogied. At some point, the girls abandoned him and came back to the table to drink more Coca. When Art had extricated himself from the sticky mass, he went to the bar to get some mineral water. A sophisticated and elegant beauty, sipping a Chivas Regal from a crystal tumbler, asked him: "What do you like to do?" "Dance," Art replied. "Dance, dance, dance!" "And do you," the beauty said, "also like to fuck, fuck, fuck?" Art beat a hasty retreat to our table, told his story, and said his goodbyes.

"He doesn't like us?" one of the teenagers asked.

"Very much, but it's past his bedtime."

"We are good in school, we really are."

"When we go."

"What do you study?"

"Economics, of course."

—Andrei Codrescu, *Ay, Cuba!*

with her mother, a chemical engineer, and her brother, who is studying engineering in college. No, they know nothing of what she does. She says she lives in fear of her mother finding out.

"You look different from the others," I say, thinking of how her white linen stood out in the lake of Lycra.

"You have to have intelligence to do this," she says disdainfully, with that painfully brittle self-confidence intrinsic to eighteen. "You have to go out with a purpose, with an idea of what you want, that you're going out to make money to buy a TV, for example. The other women are not intelligent, and they do not respect themselves. You have to be in control."

They look for older men, the ones with Rolexes or, at the very least, leather shoes. The younger ones want only sex, she says. The older men want company; they spend more time talking and buying you things.

"I treat them like dogs," says Laura, thrilling to her own scorn. "I treat them like that because I have a strong character. One has to demand respect as a woman. You have to say, 'It's like this, we're here for the moment, you give me the money and I go home, no kissing, no hugging in front of people, because what people say matters to me.'" And in the way she pats down a strand of hair, straightens her back, and purses her lips, she is such a proper little bourgeois wife-in-waiting that it is hard to imagine her in bed with a man for love or for money.

In bed, she says, you have to think quickly. She insists on condoms. If a man wants to have sex more than once, you have to say, "Once is $100, and again is $100 more." Most of them won't pay for a second time, she says, and so she leaves. I look at her slight body, think about her in a dark hotel room with a surly, fat-bellied drunk, and wonder....

Besides, she says, she will be leaving soon. There is an uncle in Sacramento, and one day he will send for her and she will go to the States, and in the States she will become famous. She will be like Whitney Houston—and she is young enough to believe this.

It is a haunting picture. She looks so young, so lovely, so fragile, innocence setting out for the world, as if she were riding in a limousine. If you were a man, you might wish it were you who was going to have her next; if you were a woman, you might remember what it was like to be that age, when you really thought it was all under your control, and knowing what you know now, it might make you wince. But the picture haunts as well because of the look in Laura's eyes: willful, considered, and utterly blank.

The *jineteras* become the target for the envy and anomie that have filled the vacuum left by the collapse of socialism's egalitarian promise, even when the promise only ensured that everyone had nothing. It's why a lot of Cuban women hate the *jineteras* for their long hair: You need dollars to buy shampoo. No dollars means short hair, the sacrifice of a cherished sexual talisman, and that does not come easily in a country where women wear four-inch heels to wait three hours for a bus that may never come....

Betty is twenty-nine, dressed in cutoff blue jeans and a diaphanous black shirt over a lacy black bra. She has short auburn hair and large eyes and a lovely mouth set in a face still wincing from the latest slap of fate. Seven months ago, she was married, possessed of a degree in French and a job in the Ministry of Communication. But 198 pesos a month is not enough to put food on the table for herself, her mother, and her seven-year-old daughter. Behind the sleepiness etched in her face is a kind of stunned quality that steals any sexiness it might have gained from the transparent shirt and the lacy black bra.

Margot is the tougher of the two—black-haired, narrow-eyed, with a permanent scorn ironed into her lips. She is wearing blue jeans cut off haphazardly at the knee, a denim work shirt, sneakers. She is openly gay—a rarity in Cuba—but her clients are men.

Betty and Margot are ten years older than Laura and Camila; they can no longer muster the energy that illusions take. The first man with whom Betty had sex for money was an Italian she had met through friends. He had taken her to a fancy restaurant for dinner. He told her he wanted to sleep with her, and she asked for a hundred dollars. "Too much," he told her, stung to discover that this was not a romantic encounter. "In Cuba, you can get any whore you want for thirty dollars."

After that first time, Betty says, she was very depressed. "It was very hard. Until then, I had had a normal life: I loved, I got married, I had a baby. There are people who do this because they like it or just for the discos and the restaurants; they are with a man, they wash themselves off, and that's that. But when you have led a normal life, then you know what you have done, and it's very depressing." How long did it take to get over the depression? Betty shrugs. "You put in a cassette and you erase it," she says. "You're not going to die from it, because you are prepared to do what you have to do."…

Martha notices that Betty's father has come down the stairs. There is an embarrassed pause, but in fact he wants to join the conversation. He serves everyone dark rum, neat, in small glasses, and then sits down on the sofa next to my stepdaughter.

How does he feel about the men who sleep with his daughter? He is forty-eight, a shambling, weak-mouthed man with another family to support—he is the father of a two-month-old son. He understands the men's side of it, he says. A young, clean girl is such a bargain in Cuba—he understands they're very expensive in New York. Recently, he was at the Marina Hemingway, he says, and a sixteen-year-old girl came up to him and said, "Do you want me? Because if you have me and don't like me, you don't have to pay me." He seems rather pleased to have been asked by the girl, clearly considering it a credit to his innate attractiveness. "But to go back to your original question," he says, "how does it make me feel? It makes me feel sad."

I wonder how sad it makes him feel when my twenty-three-year-old stepdaughter tells me later that he asked her out, telling her how much he likes younger women.

At times, it is grotesque, watching the women brush their breasts against some doughy man in a bad shirt as they ask him for a drink, counterpointing the request with the overripe rhythms of an obviously forced laughter. Other times, it is comedy, just another song about the same old story: A beautiful tall blonde in a tight red dress is dancing with a short fat guy who is so blissed out he's barely breathing, his arms wrapped around her, his eyes closed, his lips parted—a newt gasping for air. During one of their slow revolutions, the blonde watches me watching her, takes note of my expression. She laughs, raising her eyes to the ceiling in rueful acknowledgment, and I begin to laugh because, after all, there is something so ludicrous and timeless about the delusion she is indulging, and I know that she, at least, will be all right.

Lynn Darling is a New York-based writer whose work frequently appears in such publications as Elle, Us, *and* Esquire.

ANDREI CODRESCU

* * *

Cemetery Blues

Sometimes the dead can tell you
more than the living.

PROFESSOR LOHANIA ARUCA, FORMER DIRECTOR OF THE CRISTOBAL
Colón Cemetery, treated us to orangeades and rum. She thrust a
thick book of photographs of the cemetery into my hands and disappeared into the bathroom of her small, modern apartment to put
on her makeup. She had an appointment with a Dutch television
crew later that morning. The professor had written the text accompanying the photographs, but before I could read any of it, she reap-
peared, looking pretty much the same. She was ready to show us
what she called lovingly, "the fourth-most-important cemetery in
the world."

The streets around the Cristobal Colón were jammed because, I
was surprised to find out, it was Havana's predominant cemetery
and was very much in use. Four funerals were going on simultaneously, with gangs of mourners following behind hearses, trying
not to follow the wrong one. It was hard to see how they kept it
straight. Doubtless, many of these people were going to end up at
the wrong funeral. We dashed across the boulevard and paused before the imposing gate to the necropolis. Professor Aruca stopped
dead center before it, causing several streams of grieving *habaneros*
to part. Pointing to the top of the arch, she drew our attention to

details. There were inverted torches, symbols of death; branches of myrtle tied with ribbons, symbols of resurrections; and a child, representing a soul newly arrived in heaven, as well as a profusion of other symbolic figures, over the inscription "*Junua Sum Pacis*" (I am the doorway to peace). There wasn't anything Cuban about this Byzantine-Romanesque monument, but it was impressive.

There was some very Cuban confusion about the visitors' fee at the entrance, though, because former cemetery director Aruca, after warmly hugging the girl at the ticket counter, had given us to understand that, being her guests, we didn't have to pay. This was, of course, an entirely unreasonable assumption on my part, based on capitalist museum directors I had known. Cuba needed dollars, the cemetery needed dollars, and the director could do only so much. We had but penetrated the stately boulevard of death that stretched, flanked by great monuments, to a domed chapel in the distance, when the ticket girl caught up with us, demanding dollars. This unnerved David, who was in the process of snapping a noble sugar merchant's tomb, but didn't faze the professor, who continued lecturing intensely on the ages of the cemetery and its grand architecture. I paid the gatekeeper, without taking my eyes off Lohania. She was passionate about her subject, to the exclusion of most earthly matters. David huffed, annoyed at the slow pace of the proceedings. He and I had plans to go that afternoon to the Malecón to photograph and interview the conga line of miniskirted *jineteras* hitchhiking. I could see how that appointment could claim some priority over the extraordinarily detailed description of funerary art by the world's foremost expert on Cuban graves. We were shallow Yankees. In describing her cemetery, the professor was speaking about much more, of course. There was no subject in Cuba that did not jump at some point into history and politics.

"The cemetery is organized like a city. And it has a structure, a class structure. In this side of the cemetery, there is the zone of monuments of the first category. Wealthy industrialists, politicians, generals. So, in this zone, you will find historical characters, individuals who are very important to Cuba."

"In Romania," I said, "I used to go to the cemetery to think. There was no room in my house."

If Lohania made a connection, she gave no sign. But is was true. In crowded countries, cemeteries are great for escape. I had also first made love in a cemetery. A Polish artist who'd led a high school strike had taken his classmates to the Warsaw cemetery to study "the real history," not the lies they were taught in school.

We inched past grand mausoleums of Revolutionary heroes interred beneath bombastic verses, forgotten generals weighed down by purple tributes, captains of industry in architect-designed houses, sugar barons in royal tombs, heavily eulogized writers and artists. Had I been more familiar with Cuban novels and romances, I'd doubtless have recognized the characters of their dramas. Professor Aruca could easily have spent a day with each tomb, but she remembered her appointment with Dutch TV and picked up the pace a bit. Still, she was visibly annoyed by Art's suggestion that she show us "the three most important graves in the cemetery."

"Three?" she snapped. "What is it with Americans? The bottom line? The best of? The ten best-dressed people? You are very impatient."

> Edith Monterde let me examine the original record books with the names and dates of burials carefully handwritten in the ledgers. The first burial was in 1944, the last in 1993. There were fifty baseball players buried in the section. The only player who appeared in the major leagues was Armando Marsans—the first Cuban in the big leagues—an outfielder with Cincinnati, the St. Louis Browns, and the New York Yankees between 1911 and 1918. Born in Matanzas in 1887, Marsans died in Havana in 1960. In a way, the monument is one to professional baseball in Cuba, which died less than one year later.
>
> —Milton H. Jamail, *Full Count: Inside Cuban Baseball*

We came to a relatively modern monument. A white, art–nou-veauish angel held a flowing body in her arms. The figures floated out of a black marble background. This striking sculpture called *Piedad* (Pity) adorned an empty tomb. Noticing a birthday chiseled in the marble, but no death date, I asked: "When was this tomb built? What period?"

"In 1959."

"So the family fled Cuba, and the tomb is unoccupied?"

"Unoccupied."

"I don't understand. What happens if they come back dead? Do they get buried here?"

"If they leave the property in Cuba with some family or some friends, they have the right to be buried here. It's no problem, because there are many people in the United States who send their family to the cemetery of Havana. But you have to have the property in advance."

"I see. So it would be a shame if they came without any papers and just hung around in front of their own tomb."

"You leave the property, then you leave everything. You see? One thing I reflect on many times is, how rich could be a person that can leave everything? It's just fantastic. You have to be very sure of yourself and your life and everything to leave everything."

"I certainly left everything in Romania when I was nineteen years old. We couldn't take anything with us. Not even photographs that my mother took, because she was a photographer and we couldn't take that. I couldn't take the early poetry that I wrote. It was everything. So it was really a very painful process of being born again."

"Anyway, I don't think I wouldn't fight for something I love. When the Revolution came, I said, 'I will give my life to this country.' I have given my life to my country, my people. It's very difficult for me to understand. I know those on the other side, I know they may not understand me."

The bitter truth of Cuba was quite plain here before the empty tomb of the Aguilera family. Cuba was like a heart torn in two. An image carved on many of the funerary bas-reliefs around us. People had left their homes and gone into exile, but their dwellings had stayed behind to be inhabited by another generation, many of whom had also left in second and third waves of emigration. But the idea that the bodies of the Aguileras could arrive here at their burial place and be refused entry was even more awesome and absurd. They had fled alive but could not return even dead. There was no *piedad* here, history'd had no pity on anyone. I thought of Coyulo's model of Havana—a world of buildings through which humanity washed in and out like the sea, its waves lifted by history.

What Lohania Aruca had just told me was complex. On the one hand, she'd let me know that she was patriotic, a supporter of the Party and Fidel, who would never think of abandoning the Revolution or Cuba. On the other hand, she had put the question in purely material terms. Professor Aruca had not assumed automatically that we were friendly Yankees, already sold on Castroism, like most Americans who visited the island. Professor Aruca had sensed, quite correctly, that our group had two poles, an antistatist Eastern European and an all-American boy (David), who had to have things put to them in the simplest terms. Art, she had probably thought, was more sympathetic, and she must have trusted Ariel implicitly. Of course, David paid no attention at all to her profession of faith before the Aguileras' empty grave, while Art was professionally sympathetic and privately a classic liberal and no friend of Castro's. Only Ariel, the former *ideológico* and guerrilla fighter, would have been Professor Aruca's match in a real debate. But this was no real debate, and we merely skimmed the surface of the vast necropolis built around the missing body of the white discoverer of the Americas. We flitted, like bats, and the girls on the Malecón beckoned. On the other side of this seawall, ninety miles and a world away, was the whole other Cuba of the Aguileras, waiting to get back into their old homes and graves.

Andrei Codrescu, a Romanian-born poet, arrived in the United States in 1966 penniless and without knowledge of the English language. Within four years he had learned to speak English well enough to publish his first poetry collection. Today, he has more than forty works to his name, including The

Blood Countess, Hail Babylon!: In Search of the American City at the End of the Millennium, Zombification: Stories from National Public Radio, *and* Ay Cuba! A Socio-Erotic Journey *from which this piece was excerpted. He lives in New Orleans.*

PATRICK SYMMES

✴ ✴ ✴

Hasta La Victoria Sometimes

*The author's inner Che emerges on
their final trip together.*

WE ROLLED EAST FROM HAVANA AFTER BREAKFAST, MISSED THE exit, and spent the morning wandering back and forth, asking directions, chatting with bicyclists and horsemen, and police officers and patiently waiting would-be bus passengers. Eventually we got the rental car pointed in the right direction and sat back for the ride to Che's funeral.

They had found him, or at least some of him. A year after I passed through Vallegrande, the Argentine-Cuban forensic team had returned to the grassy airstrip with new funding. They'd dug and dug some more, and eventually, in June 1997, they had found enough bones to fill a small coffin. The arms lacked hands; these, then, were the bones of Ernesto Guevara de la Serna, known at various points in his life as Little Ernesto, the Shaved Head, the Sniper, the Pig, Big Che, Mongo, Fernando, Fernández, Adolfo Mena, El Puro, and El Che. It wasn't the whole Guevara, only an elusive portion, but it was enough to construct a symbolic extravaganza. The remains of six other guerrillas who fell in the battle at La Higuera were also, at least theoretically, identified.

Che had been bundled off to Cuba just in time for the thirtieth anniversary of his death, in October 1997. The remains of the seven were put on display inside the José Martí Monument at the heart of the vast Plaza de la Revolución in Havana. They put a flag identifying the nationality of each guerrilla on the appropriate box. Che was draped in the red, white, and blue flag of Cuba. He might have renounced his Cuban citizenship and died an internationalist Argentine fighting in Bolivia, but he was going to be buried a Cuban.

Thousands of people were in line to see the remains when I walked toward the plaza at night in the company of a *Newsweek* reporter and a bottle of rum. Havana is a dark city; we held hushed conversations at intersections with invisible men who did not identify themselves. The uniformed police deferred to these civilians, who extracted a pull from the bottle and let us pass their outposts in the night.

The line stretched from beyond the edge of visibility, up a long avenue, over a bridge, alongside the plaza, and then curled around the vast parking lot that was the heart of official Cuba. The line passed beneath the electric gaze of a six-story neon Che blazing from a blank wall. The same little groups of mysterious civilians stood around, supervising everything via radio. We approached, seeking permission to poke and prod the public for comment. By the light of Che, I could see that these men with their cloaked authority wore tiny lapel pins reading BRIGADA ESPECIAL. The special brigades are the enforcers of the revolution, the plainclothes police who specialize in pounding Cuba's square pegs into round holes. They scolded us for drinking rum while observing the "act of homage."

> While rumors full of gloom and foreboding about the fate of the vanished Guevara continued to fly, pouring into Washington and other capitals, a fascinating new type arose. Essentially, these were Guevara "sightings," and for the better part of two years, they occurred around the globe, causing Martín Guevara to observe aptly, "Now, my brother is like the white horse of Zapata: he is everywhere."
> — Henry Butterfield Ryan, *The Fall of Che Guevara*

The line of mourners continued around the plaza, moving at a quick march and never stalling for even a moment. After passing beneath the illuminated Che, it snaked right and ascended a gentle, lengthy staircase into the base of the monument itself, a tasteless stupa erected by the Soviets. The uniform line that entered in a compact, speedy thread emerged from the other side as a disordered throng. Little clumps of families and dots of solitary people wandered out of the viewing chamber, moving at different speeds in various directions, as though lost. In death, Che converted the Cuban masses back into individuals.

I thought about joining the hour-long line and marching up the stairs and into the monument to see the box holding his bones, but I didn't. It was all too much. Loudspeakers overhead blared with Socialist-Realist music that seemed, at a distance, indistinguishable from the liturgical tones of a Holy Mass. The disembodied voice of Fidel Castro echoed from the heavens, reading Che's farewell letter to the Cuban people in an endless loop interrupted only by Che songs "Hasta Siempre" and Che poems "Thus, Guevara, strong-voiced gaucho...." Forty-four years ago, a young Ernesto had scribbled a final warning in his notebook that revolution is impersonal, that it consumes the innocent and guilty together, and then manipulates the memory of the dead as an instrument of control.

The Cubans in the queue did seem deeply moved. A lean black man told me that Che was "one of the men of the twentieth century, of the twenty-first century." He pointed to his twelve-year-old son. As the boy skipped about, the father said, "He was born to come here." A woman with her two daughters said, firmly and steadily, "This is not just an act of homage to Che but an expression of solidarity with the revolution by the entire nation as the eyes of the world are upon us," and went on in that vein for another two minutes.

But away from the plaza, my Cuban friends only groaned when I described the crowds at the event as "spontaneous." I knew two brothers who lived in the old Chinatown, and they had been skewered neatly on the horns of a Cuban dilemma. Their problem was simply that they had two funerals to attend, that of

Che here in Havana and that of a grandmother who had just died in Cienfuegos. The brothers were smart young men, products of the revolution, educated and hardworking and dedicated to Cuba, if not necessarily to those who ran the island. At their job sites, the brothers explained, those who "volunteered" to go to the plaza to see Che received a check mark in their files. Those who didn't, didn't, and the consequences were clear, if unspoken. Cuban Communism is a system for micromanaging every aspect of life, and failure to earn enough of these check marks indicates a "poor attitude" toward the revolution in a society where your attitude affects what you eat, where you live, and how much gasoline and education and pay you receive. Caught between family and state, they had divided the consequences. One brother had dutifully gone to see Che—and he showed me his pay slip with a notation of his attendance. The other brother had gone to Cienfuegos.

Unlike in the rest of Latin America, where Che was a symbolic outsider, in Cuba he was the Establishment, stripped of his rebellious appeal by the coercive government demand underpinning his postmortem existence. Toddlers literally napped under his gaze in day-care centers. Children promised en masse to "Be Like Che." There were portraits of him in every school, and the officially sanctioned lessons of his life were taught on every blackboard. Anything he had done or touched was sacrosanct. He'd once spent four hours operating a cigar-boxing machine; the machine was now retired, decorated with placards, and painted silver because Che had used it. All Che's books were available in Cuban bookstores, and there were always new books about him—memoirs by others who knew him or claimed to, plus profiles of Che the guerrilla fighter, Che the economist, Che the journalist, Che the doctor, Che the Argentine, Che the photographer, and Che the traveler.

Che was everywhere, not just as political propaganda but as profitable consumer goods: there were Che posters and lapel pins, Che refrigerator magnets, Che t-shirts, Che cigarette lighters and Che nail clippers, Che postcards and Che photo albums. The Swiss watch company Swatch put out a Che Swatch bearing his photo and the slogan *"Revolución!"* The Cuban government bought the entire production run and begun flogging the watches at José Martí International Airport, outside Havana, for fifty dollars apiece....

On October 9, 1997—thirty years to the day after Che died in La Higuera—the Cuban daily newspaper *Granma* ran the headline CUBA WILL NOT ENCOURAGE TOURISM WITH THE FIGURE OF CHE and quoted Vice Minister of Tourism Eduardo de la Vega as he assured the nation, "We don't believe the figure of Che should be commercialized." I bought a pair of Che maracas and tapped out my rhythmic applause for the vice minister....

Che's final road trip began at dawn the next day. I staggered down to the waterfront with a splitting headache. I'd been partying in a bar full of whores and Germans until 3 A.M. The city was filled with European and Canadian men who didn't even know about the funeral. They bought Che t-shirts and listened to trios sing "Guantanamera" and then went off to private houses to screw the girls for twenty dollars. They slept through the mornings and then started over again.

Che's bones were going to parade out of the city in a motorcade, passing along the length of the Malecón seawall and then heading for Santa Clara, to the east. At 7 A.M. the tropical sun was already too harsh for my eyes, but a serpentine crowd had assembled along the length of the waterfront and was keeping to a respectful murmur. There were probably ten thousand people waiting, craning their necks for any sign of the cortege. Children climbed onto the pedestals of streetlamps, and some fathers held toddlers on their shoulders. A middle-aged *mulata* named Ana Portela asked me where I was from, and I told her. "Anyone who invaded this country," she promptly volunteered, "would find blood, and sweat, and rubble left in Cuba, but not one Cuban." She was with an older friend, also an Afro-Cuban. I asked this woman what she thought of Che, but she answered another question. "I am eighty-five years old," she said, "and here we are all equal. There is no racism or discrimination here. We are united."

At last the little column of vehicles approached, passing first under the shadow of Meyer Lansky's Riviera Hotel, then by the Nacional, where Capone stayed. The crowd stood straight and silent as a few motorcycle cops passed, and then came seven military jeeps pulling seven glass-topped caissons bearing seven wood boxes under seven flags. When the procession was gone, the Cubans disbanded to their schools and places of work.

The seven jeeps were headed for Santa Clara, the scene of Che's great victory over that armored troop train carrying more than four hundred government reinforcements. That was in late December 1958. After Santa Clara surrendered to Che, the dictator Batista fled the country within days. While Castro loitered in the east, Che formed a convoy of commandeered vehicles and rolled up the highway with his guerrillas toward Havana, greeted by cheering throngs along the route. In those days history was flowing in the opposite direction....

Santa Clara was where my own journey had begun. Just like six years before, you could still see the bullet holes from Che's shootout on the facade of the Santa Clara Libre Hotel. We drove in past the plaza, past the benches where the *gusano* with his home-brewed beer had expressed the conviction, "If he were still alive, none of this would be happening."

Now that statement was literally true. The funeral was already under way, and the side streets near the plaza were packed with pedestrians walking out toward the new mausoleum. I wove the Subaru gently through the bodies, tooting the horn like imperialism personified. On the radio we could hear the speeches beginning, and just around the time I found a parking space, Fidel Castro came on. I could hear his voice on the car radio; looking down the hill, I could see a crowd of perhaps fifty thousand people and on the far side a tiny green figure addressing us from the podium, The mausoleum dominated everything. It was capped with a twenty-two-foot-tall bronze statue of Che striding forward, rifle in hand. The statue rested on a high stone pedestal that was hollow. At the end of the ceremony, they were going to stick him inside it.

We pushed through the crowd, but with the event already under way it was impossible to get near the front. Policemen manned fences that cut us off from the press gallery. The sound system was breaking down, and Castro's voice boomed in kind of unintelligible abstraction. In the car, I had heard his every word; in person, I couldn't understand anything he was saying. It didn't matter; when I read it in the paper, I saw that he had declared that Marxism was advancing across the globe and that Che and the other six guerrillas in the funeral were "a reinforcement brigade" come home to bolster the revolution.

I began to panic. I had come all this way to watch Che buried, but I couldn't see or hear anything but a crowd of tens of thousands of sweaty regime loyalists. We slogged around the outside of the event looking for the press center, hoping for access to the bandstand, but had to settle for a spot behind the event and to one side, along a fence....

The words *imperialism* and *immortal* floated over us from time to time, and eventually Castro stopped talking and some cannons rattled off a salute. I saw a group of soldiers march past, turn sharply, and disappear over the little rise that separated us from the reviewing stand. More groups marched by; different types of soldiers, a phalanx of policemen in blue, more green, and finally a group of model workers who wore their own clothes and could not march in step, although they tried. Over they went, doing their best to keep together as they passed the rise and went down the other side, dropping into invisibility.

Slowly, the field emptied out. The crowd became thin, and then there were just isolated clusters of people, and after an hour all that was left was a muddy expanse of trampled grass. At long last we were all done. El Che stood alone against the tropical sky.

Patrick Symmes is a foreign correspondent for Harper's *magazine. This selection is excerpted from his first book,* Chasing Che: A Motorcycle Journey in Search of the Guevara Legend. *He lives in New York City.*

PART FIVE

The Last Word

⋆ ⋆ ⋆

Cycle of Love

A brief bike ride produces
enchanting results.

THE MOPED WASN'T MUCH TO LOOK AT, BUT IT RAN. THE TIRES were completely smooth except for the occasional patch of cord showing through. The front wheel was definitely not round. The frame was rust and blue, and I could make out remnants of a "P" and an "O." It looked Italian—I figured it had to be a Piaggio.

The agent in charge of the small stand of ancient mopeds pulled the wooden plug out of the fuel tank, peered in, sloshed the gas, and asked, "How far?"

"About an hour," I replied.

He laughed, slapped me on the back, and said, "Oh, sure. You'll make it!"

And so I hopped on and began my two-wheeled exploration of Cuba, first inland, past green fields and skinny cattle, then back toward the sea. Up the coast there was supposed to be a quiet beach, but for a few miles I saw nobody as I picked my way through sand and around potholes. Encountering an ancient flatbed truck headed the other way, I waved at the half dozen people hitching a ride aboard it. A couple of them politely waved back.

When I passed a small group of pedestrians, they laughingly hailed me in Spanish, wanting a ride. But I doubted my rattling steed could carry another pound, so I declined with a nod and puttered on.

I rounded one corner to find a strange apparition floating toward me. It looked like three farmers and a bushel basket of fruit levitating on a light-blue cushion of air. When they got closer, I realized they were all piled onto a moped remarkably similar to mine, but older and going faster. Suddenly I felt stingy about having refused pedestrians a ride in this land of poverty and gracious manners.

There was a beautiful beach at the end of the road, a deserted one—sand, sky, trees, ocean, birds, and total silence. For the hundredth time since coming to this island, I wished that I could paint. Eventually, I turned the moped around and headed back the way I'd come.

At a villa, two women smiled and waved for a ride. But between the two of them and their burdens, they probably topped four hundred pounds, so I just smiled back and puttered past.

Onward the Piaggio grumbled, and then I saw her. A white blouse, shoulder bag, sandals, and a thousand-watt smile. She was beautiful. She waved for a ride, and I stopped like what I was—a man entranced.

She laughed and ran up. I hadn't really considered where I might put a passenger on the rattling contraption, and I greeted her in masterful and eloquent English: "Hi...er...Hello...umm...I'm not really sure where you can sit...."

She laughed and chatted for a bit in the most musical Spanish. I didn't understand a word. To be honest, it didn't matter. It was the way she smiled, the way she moved those brown hands and arms while she talked, and those laughing dark eyes. I would have listened to her happily all afternoon.

She sat down on the rack and put her arms around my waist. My brain short-circuited, but I applied the throttle and set off.

I wrote those next fifteen minutes in my memory with indelible ink. I pressed on between sea and greenery with her arms around me. She laughed and waved to friends and pointed out sights in Spanish. Conscious of her precarious perch, I picked my way around the most obvious road hazards and kept the speed down.

All too soon I felt a pat on my shoulder and saw her arm point to an apartment complex festooned with laundry. I slowed to a stop, and she got off and stood beside me. She was looking for words with which to say goodbye. I took off my cap—a *Cycle Canada* cap by odd coincidence—and stuck it on her dark curly hair.

"See you later!" I said. But I never saw her again.

I don't remember the rest of the ride, except that the Piaggio made it back on whatever fueled its faithful soul.

"How was your ride?" my wife asked when I returned.

I am intrinsically an honest man, but pragmatism ruled my decision; no way was I going to tell my wife of sixteen years the whole truth about my motorcycle excursion.

"It was fun...roughly what you'd expect," I replied, trying to sound relaxed, even bored.

"Where's your hat?" she asked with uncanny perception.

Shamefaced, I told her the whole story. She laughed and teased me, and made me a tall Cuba libre with real Cuban rum. We reminisced about the year we met and the carefree summer we spent rambling around southern Ontario on my old Honda. We remembered the reasons we married and found some new reasons why we stay that way.

We left Cuba warmer, wiser, and younger. I had found a new love, lost it, and renewed an old love. And none of it might have happened without that Piaggio.

Felix Winkelaar lives with his wife and two children in Lindsey, Ontario, Canada, where he teaches writing to adults returning to high school. "In their quest for clarity," Winkelaar admits, "my students have inadvertently taught me how to write." This story was inspired by a March Break trip to Cuba in search of a place that was not white and cold.

Recommended Reading

Anderson, Jon Lee. *Che Guevara: A Revolutionary Life*. New York: Grove Press, 1997.

Baker, Christopher P. *Havana Handbook*. Emeryville, Calif.: Moon Travel Handbooks, 2000.

Baker, Christopher P. *Mi Moto Fidel: Motorcycling Through Castro's Cuba*. Washington, DC: National Geographic Adventure Books, 2001.

Barnet, Miguel. *Autobiography of a Runaway Slave*. New York: Pantheon, 1968.

Batista, Fulgencio. *Cuba Betrayed*. New York: Vantage Press, 1962.

Behar, Ruth. *Bridges to Cuba: Puentes a Cuba*. Ann Arbor: The University of Michigan, 1996.

Brent, William Lee. *Long Time Gone: A Black Panther's True-Life Story of His Hijacking and Twenty-Five Years in Cuba*. New York: Times Books, 1996.

Burri, René, Marco Meier, and Miguel Barnet. *Cuba y Cuba*. Washington DC: Smithsonian Institution Press, 1998.

Cardoso, Eliana, and Ann Helwege. *Cuba After Communism*. Cambridge: The Massachusetts Institute of Technology Press, 1992.

Codrescu, Andrei. *Ay, Cuba!: A Socio-Erotic Journey*. New York: St. Martin's Press, 1999.

Galeano, Eduardo. *The Book of Embraces*. New York: W. W. Norton & Co., 1989.

Gébler, Carlo. *Driving Through Cuba: Rare Encounters in the Land of Sugar Cane and Revolution*. New York: Simon & Schuster, 1990.

Hunt, Christopher. *Waiting for Fidel*. New York: Houghton Mifflin Company, 1998.

Jamail, Milton H. *Full Count: Inside Cuban Baseball.* Carbondale: Southern Illinois University Press, 2000.

Martí, José. *The José Martí Reader: Writings on the Americas.* Hoboken, N.J.: The Ocean Press, 1999.

McManus, Jane. *Cuba's Island of Dreams: Voices from the Isle of Pines and Youth.* Gainesville: University Press of Florida, 2000.

Medina, Pablo. *Exiled Memories: A Cuban Childhood.* Austin: University of Texas Press, 1990.

Michener, James A., and John Kings. *Six Days in Havana.* Austin: University of Texas Press, 1989.

Miller, Tom. *Trading with the Enemy: A Yankee Travels through Castro's Cuba.* New York: Atheneum, 1992; New York: Basic Books, 1996.

Pattullo, Polly. *Last Resorts: The Cost of Tourism in the Caribbean.* New York: Monthly Review Press, 1996.

Pérez, Louis A., Jr. *On Becoming Cuban: Identity, Nationality, and Culture.* Chapel Hill: The University of North Carolina Press, 1999.

Pérez-Stable, Marifeli. *The Cuban Revolution: Origins, Course, and Legacy.* New York: Oxford University Press, 1993.

Pettavino, Paula J., and Geralyn Pye. *Sport in Cuba: The Diamond in the Rough.* Pittsburgh: University of Pittsburgh Press, 1994.

Price, S. L. *Pitching Around Fidel: A Journey into the Heart of Cuban Sports.* New York: The Ecco Press, 2000.

Ripley, C. Peter. *Conversations with Cuba.* Athens: University of Georgia Press, 1999.

Rojo, Ricardo. *My Friend Che,* translated by Julian Casart. New York: Grove Press, Inc., 1968.

Ryan, Henry Butterfield. *The Fall of Che Guevara: A Story of Soldiers, Spies, and Diplomats.* New York: Oxford University Press, 1998.

Smith, Stephen. *The Land of Miracles.* New York: Little, Brown and Company, 1997.

Stanley, David. *Cuba: A Lonely Planet Travel Survival Kit.* Oakland, Calif.: Lonely Planet Publications, 2000.

Symmes, Patrick. *Chasing Che: A Motorcycle Journey in Search of the*

Guevara Legend. New York: Vintage Departures, 2000.

Szulc, Tad. *Fidel: A Critical Portrait*. New York: William Morrow, 1986.

Thomas, Hugh. *Cuba: The Pursuit of Freedom*. New York: Harper & Row, 1971.

Timerman, Jacobo. *Cuba: A Journey*. New York: Vintage Books, 1990.

Our impressions of a land come from many sources. Often, the care and research that go into a work of fiction—on the printed page or the silver screen—can tell us as much about a country as a well-crafted narrative. Here are some revealing and provocative books and movies about Cuba we thought you might appreciate. All are available in libraries, bookstores, and video stores.

Cabrera Infante, Guillermo. *Three Trapped Tigers*. New York: Harper & Row, 1971.

García, Cristina. *Dreaming in Cuban: A Novel*. New York: Ballantine Books, 1993.

Greene, Graham. *Our Man in Havana*. New York: Penguin, 1971.

Gutiérrez, Tomás, and Edmundo Desnoes. *Memories of Underdevelopment and Inconsolable Memories*. Piscataway, N.J.: Rutgers University Press, 1990.

Hemingway, Ernest. *The Old Man and the Sea*. New York: Scribners, 1952.

Mestre, Ernesto. *The Lazarus Rumba*. New York: Picador USA, 2000.

Smith, Martin Cruz. *Havana Bay*. New York: Random House, 1999; New York: Ballantine Books, 2001.

Movies

Before Night Falls. Director: Julian Schnabel. 2000.

Buena Vista Social Club (documentary). Director: Wim Wenders. 1998.

Death of a Bureaucrat. Director: Tomás Gutiérrez Alea. 1966.

Strawberry and Chocolate. Directors: Juan Carlos Tabío and Tomás Gutiérrez Alea. 1994.

Index

Index of Contributors

Acknowledgments

Literature and Cuba are two words that flow together as easily as rum and Coke. In assembling this collection of contemporary travel writing about Cuba, I have kept in mind the broader range of literature from and about the island, writing that reveals the character of the *cubano* and the contours of his homeland. For the larger picture I am indebted to my wife Regla, author Jane McManus, my literary *compañero* Jesús Vega, and historian Louis A. Pérez Jr. On the more practical side, the staff at Travelers' Tales provided long-distance guidance—firm, supportive, and necessary—through the intricate editorial and production maze, and I am most grateful to have had them show me the way.

"The Bus" by Eduardo Galeano excepted from *The Book of Embraces* by Eduardo Galeano, as translated by Cedric Belfrage with Mark Schafer. Copyright © 1989 by Eduardo Galeano and 1991 by Cedric Belfrage. Reprinted by permission of W. W. Norton and Company, Inc.

"An Elegiac Carnival" originally titled "Cuba—An Elegiac Carnival" by Pico Iyer reprinted from the May/June 1990 issue of *Islands Magazine*. Copyright © 1990 by Islands Publishing Company. Reprinted by permission.

"Simple Life" by Cristina García reprinted from the July/August 1996 issue of *Islands Magazine*. Copyright © 1996 by Cristina García. Reprinted by permission of the Ellen Levine Literary Agency, Inc.

"Finding My House in El Cerro" by James A. Michener excerpted from *Six Days in Havana* by James A. Michener. Copyright © 1989 by James A. Michener. Reprinted by permission of University of Texas Press, and Souvenir Press, Ltd.

"Communism and the Art of Motorcycle Maintenance" by Phillippe Diederich reprinted from the March 1997 issue of *Miami New Times*. Copyright © 1997 by Phillippe Diederich. Reprinted by permission of the author.

"Ticket to Ride" by Alisha Berger published with permission from the author. Copyright © 2001 by Alisha Berger.

"Picture This" by Tom Miller originally titled "A Look at…Myths of Cuba: The Image…And The Man Who Made It" appeared in *The Washington Post*, November 2, 1997. Copyright © 1997 by Tom Miller. Reprinted by permission of the author.

"Under Havana's Hood" by Charles Degelman published with permission from the author. Copyright © 2001 by Charles Degelman.

Acknowledgments

"You Beautiful Doll" by Leslie Berestein published with permission from the author. Copyright © 2001 by Leslie Berestein.

"Remember the *Maine*?" by Tom Miller originally appeared in *Smithsonian*, February 1998 as "Remember the *Maine*." Copyright © 1998 by Tom Miller. Published with permission from the author.

"The Revolution's Cradle" by Christopher Hunt excerpted from *Waiting for Fidel* by Christopher Hunt. Copyright © 1998 by Christopher Hunt. Reprinted by permission of Houghton Mifflin Co. and the Angela Miller Agency. All rights reserved.

"Havana Journal" by Jon Lee Anderson reprinted from the January 26, 1998 issue of *The New Yorker*. Copyright © 1998 by Jon Lee Anderson. Reprinted by permission of The Wylie Agency, Inc.

"Our Mailman in Havana" by Stephen Benz reprinted from the November 19, 2000 issue of *The Washington Post*. Copyright © 2000 by Stephen Benz. Reprinted by permission of the author.

"High Top, Low Stubble" by William Lee Brent excerpted from *Long Time Gone: A Black Panther's True-Life Story of His Hijacking and Twenty-Five Years in Cuba* by William Lee Brent. Copyright © 1996 by William Lee Brent. Reprinted by permission of the author.

"Tuning with the Enemy" by Benjamin Treuhaft originally titled *"Tipico Afinador de Pianos"* published with permission from the author. Copyright © 2001 by Benjamin Treuhaft.

"Heroes of Tourism" by C. Peter Ripley excerpted from *Conversations with Cuba* by C. Peter Ripley. Copyright © 1999 by C. Peter Ripley. Reprinted by permission of The University of Georgia Press.

"Es Cuba" by Lea Aschkenas published with permission from the author. Copyright © 2001 by Lea Aschkenas.

"The Conflicted Tourist" by S. L. Price excerpted from *Pitching Around Fidel: A Journey into the Heart of Cuban Sports* by S. L. Price. Copyright © 2000 by S. L. Price. Reprinted by permission of HarperCollins Publishers, Inc.

"A Strawberry and Chocolate Goodbye" by Ruth Behar originally titled "Queer Times in Cuba" reprinted from the Fall 1994 issue of *Michigan Quarterly Review*, Vol. XXXIII No.4 Fall 1994. Copyright © 1994 by The University of Michigan. Reprinted by permission of the author.

"Havana at Midnight" by Lynn Darling reprinted from the May 1995 issue of *Esquire*. Copyright © 1995 by Lynn Darling. Reprinted by permission of Sterling Lord Literistic, Inc.

"Cemetery Blues" by Andrei Codrescu excerpted from *Ay, Cuba!: A Socio-Erotic Journey* by Andrei Codrescu. Copyright © 1999 by Andrei Codrescu. Reprinted by permission of St. Martin's Press, LLC. and The Lazear Agency.

"Hasta La Victoria Sometimes" by Patrick Symmes excerpted from *Chasing Che: A Motorcycle Journey in Search of Guevara Legend* by Patrick Symmes. Copyright © 2000 by Patrick Symmes. Reprinted by permission of Vintage Books, a division of Random House, Inc., and Constable & Robinson Publishing Ltd.

"Cycle of Love" by Felix Winkelaar, reprinted from the Jan/Feb 1998 issue of *Islands Magazine*. Copyright © 1998 by Islands Publishing Company. Reprinted by permission.

Additional Credits (Arranged alphabetically by title)

the Cat Ledger Literary Agency.

Selection from "Latins Still Make Lousy Lovers" by Helen Lawrenson reprinted from *Esquire* magazine. Copyright © 1968 by Helen Lawrenson.

Selection from "Lilting Long Ball" by Alan West-Duran published by permission of the author. Copyright © 2001 by Alan West-Duran.

Selection from *"Los Jardines de la Reina"* by Jane McManus published with permission of the author. Copyright © 2001 by Jane McManus.

Selection from *Mi Moto Fidel: Motorcycling Through Castro's Cuba* by Christopher P. Baker copyright © 2001 by Christopher P. Baker. Reprinted by permission of National Geographic Adventure Press.

Selection by Miguel Barnet excerpted from *Cuba y Cuba* by Rene Burri, Marco Meier, and Miguel Barnet copyright © 1998 by Smithsonian Institution Press. Reprinted by permission of Smithsonian Institution Press.

Selection from *My Friend Che* by Ricardo Rojo, translated by Julian Casart, copyright © 1968 by Ricardo Rojo. Reprinted by permission of The Dial Press, a division of Bantam Doubleday Dell Publishing Group.

Selection from *"Nuestro Viaje a Cuba*: Our Trip to Cuba" by Roger L. Collins published with permission from the author. Copyright © 2001 by Roger L. Collins.

Selection from *On Becoming Cuban: Identity, Nationality, and Culture* by Louis A. Pérez Jr. copyright © 1999 by The University of North Carolina Press. Published by The University of North Carolina Press.

Selection by P. J. O'Rourke reprinted from the July 1996 issue of *Rolling Stone Magazine*. Copyright © 1996 by Rolling Stone. All rights reserved.

Selection from "Pilgrimage to Somewhere-Outside-Havana" by Michelle Snider published with permission from the author. Copyright © 2001 by Michelle Snider.

Selection by Regla Albarrán copyright © 2001 by Regla A. Miller. Reprinted by permission.

Selection from "Sexual Revolution" by Silvana Paternostro reprinted from the July 10–17, 2000 issue of *The New Republic*. Copyright © 2000 by Silvana Patenostro. Reprinted by permission of International Creative Management, Inc.

Selection from "Striking Chords" by Paige Evans reprinted from the May 18, 1999 issue of the *Institute of Current World Affairs Letters* (the Crane-Rogers Foundation). Copyright © 1999 by Paige Evans. Reprinted by permission of the author.

Selection by Tom Mosby published with permission from the author. Copyright © 2001 by Tom Mosby.

Selections from *Trading with the Enemy: A Yankee Travels through Castro's Cuba* by Tom Miller copyright © 1992 by Tom Miller. Reprinted by permission of Perseus Books and the author.

Selection by Wayne S. Smith copyright © 2001 by Wayne S. Smith. Published with permission of the author.

About the Editor

Tom Miller is the author of the highly acclaimed *Trading with the Enemy: A Yankee Travels through Castro's Cuba* ("it may just be the best travel book about Cuba ever written," says *Lonely Planet's Cuba*). He has been writing about and traveling through Latin America and the American Southwest since the late 1960s when he moved from his native Washington, D.C. to Arizona. An early participant in the underground and alternative press, his books include *The Panama Hat Trail*, a classic of contemporary travel writing, *On the Border*, a permanent fixture in the U.S.-Mexico frontier's literary landscape, and most recently, *Jack Ruby's Kitchen Sink: Offbeat Travels Through America's Southwest*. He is also editor of *Writing on the Edge: A Borderlands Reader*. A renowned bambalogist, Miller has a collection of some seventy-five versions of "La Bamba" from all over the world, and compiled the Rhino Records release, "The Best of La Bamba." His work has been widely anthologized, and he appears in *Travelers' Tales American Southwest*. While researching *Trading with the Enemy*, Miller met and married a Cuban woman who now lives with him and her two sons in Tucson. His articles about Cuba, which he first visited in 1987, have appeared in *Smithsonian, LIFE, Natural History,* and *The New York Times*, among other publications. Miller has led educational trips through Cuba on behalf of the National Geographic Society and the American Museum of Natural History, and since 1990 has been affiliated with the Latin American Area Center at the University of Arizona. His papers have been acquired by Special Collections at the University of Arizona Library.

TRAVELERS' TALES

THE POWER OF A GOOD STORY

New Releases

THE BEST TRAVELERS' TALES 2004
$16.95

True Stories from Around the World
Edited by James O'Reilly, Larry Habegger & Sean O'Reilly
The launch of a new annual collection presenting fresh, lively storytelling and compelling narrative to make the reader laugh, weep, and buy a plane ticket.

INDIA
$18.95

True Stories
Edited by James O'Reilly & Larry Habegger
"Travelers' Tales India is ravishing in the texture and variety of tales."
—*Foreign Service Journal*

A WOMAN'S EUROPE
$17.95

True Stories
Edited by Marybeth Bond
An exhilarating collection of inspirational, adventurous, and entertaining stories by women exploring the romantic continent of Europe. From the bestselling author Marybeth Bond.

WOMEN IN THE WILD
$17.95

True Stories of Adventure and Connection
Edited by Lucy McCauley
"A spiritual, moving, and totally female book to take you around the world and back." —*Mademoiselle*

CHINA
$18.95

True Stories
Edited by James O'Reilly, Larry Habegger & Sean O'Reilly
A must for any traveler to China, for anyone wanting to learn more about the Middle Kingdom, offering a breadth and depth of experience from both new and well-known authors; helps make the China experience unforgettable and transforming.

BRAZIL
$17.95

True Stories
Edited by Annette Haddad & Scott Doggett
Introduction by Alex Shoumatoff
"Only the lowest wattage dim bulb would visit Brazil without reading this book." —Tim Cahill, author of *Pass the Butterworms*

THE PENNY PINCHER'S PASSPORT TO LUXURY TRAVEL (2ND EDITION)
$14.95

The Art of Cultivating Preferred Customer Status
By Joel L. Widzer
Completely updated and revised, this 2nd edition of the popular guide to traveling like the rich and famous without being either describes, both philosophically and in practical terms, how to obtain luxurious travel benefits by building relationships with airlines and other travel companies.

Women's Travel

A WOMAN'S EUROPE
$17.95
True Stories
Edited by Marybeth Bond
An exhilarating collection of inspirational, adventurous, and entertaining stories by women exploring the romantic continent of Europe. From the bestselling author Marybeth Bond.

WOMEN IN THE WILD
$17.95
True Stories of Adventure and Connection
Edited by Lucy McCauley
"A spiritual, moving, and totally female book to take you around the world and back."
— *Mademoiselle*

A WOMAN'S WORLD
$18.95
True Stories of Life on the Road
Edited by Marybeth Bond
Introduction by Dervla Murphy

—— ★ ★ ★ ——

Lowell Thomas Award
—Best Travel Book

A MOTHER'S WORLD
$14.95
Journeys of the Heart
Edited by Marybeth Bond & Pamela Michael
"These stories remind us that motherhood is one of the great unifying forces in the world."
— *San Francisco Examiner*

A WOMAN'S PASSION FOR TRAVEL
$17.95
More True Stories from A Woman's World
Edited by Marybeth Bond & Pamela Michael
"A diverse and gripping series of stories!"
—Arlene Blum, author of
Annapurna: A Woman's Place

Food

ADVENTURES IN WINE
$17.95
True Stories of Vineyards and Vintages around the World
Edited by Thom Elkjer
Humanity, community, and brotherhood comprise the marvelous virtues of the wine world. This collection toasts the warmth and wonders of this large extended family in stories by travelers who are wine novices and experts alike.

FOOD
$18.95
A Taste of the Road
Edited by Richard Sterling
Introduction by Margo True

—— ★ ★ ★ ——

Silver Medal Winner of the
Lowell Thomas Award
—Best Travel Book

HER FORK IN THE ROAD
$16.95
Women Celebrate Food and Travel
Edited by Lisa Bach
A savory sampling of stories by the best writers in and out of the food and travel fields.

THE ADVENTURE OF FOOD
$17.95
True Stories of Eating Everything
Edited by Richard Sterling
"Bound to whet appetites for more than food."
— *Publishers Weekly*

THE FEARLESS DINER
$7.95
Travel Tips and Wisdom for Eating around the World
By Richard Sterling
Combines practical advice on foodstuffs, habits, and etiquette, with hilarious accounts of others' eating adventures.

Travel Humor

SAND IN MY BRA AND OTHER MISADVENTURES $14.95
Funny Women Write from the Road
Edited by Jennifer L. Leo
"A collection of ridiculous and sublime travel experiences."
— *San Francisco Chronicle*

LAST TROUT IN VENICE $14.95
The Far-Flung Escapades of an Accidental Adventurer
By Doug Lansky
"Traveling with Doug Lansky might result in a considerably shortened life expectancy…but what a way to go."
— Tony Wheeler, Lonely Planet Publications

HYENAS LAUGHED AT ME AND NOW I KNOW WHY $14.95
The Best of Travel Humor and Misadventure
Edited by Sean O'Reilly, Larry Habegger, and James O'Reilly
Hilarious, outrageous and reluctant voyagers indulge us with the best misadventures around the world.

NOT SO FUNNY WHEN IT HAPPENED $12.95
The Best of Travel Humor and Misadventure
Edited by Tim Cahill
Laugh with Bill Bryson, Dave Barry, Anne Lamott, Adair Lara, and many more.

THERE'S NO TOILET PAPER…ON THE ROAD LESS TRAVELED $12.95
The Best of Travel Humor and Misadventure
Edited by Doug Lansky

Humor Book of the Year
— Independent Publisher's Book Award

ForeWord Gold Medal Winner — Humor Book of the Year

Travelers' Tales Classics

COAST TO COAST $16.95
A Journey Across 1950s America
By Jan Morris
After reporting on the first Everest ascent in 1953, Morris spent a year journeying across the United States. In brilliant prose, Morris records with exuberance and curiosity a time of innocence in the U.S.

THE ROYAL ROAD TO ROMANCE $14.95
By Richard Halliburton
"Laughing at hardships, dreaming of beauty, ardent for adventure, Halliburton has managed to sing into the pages of this glorious book his own exultant spirit of youth and freedom."
— *Chicago Post*

TRADER HORN $16.95
A Young Man's Astounding Adventures in 19th Century Equatorial Africa
By Alfred Aloysius Horn
Here is the stuff of legends—thrills and danger, wild beasts, serpents, and savages. An unforgettable and vivid portrait of a vanished Africa.

UNBEATEN TRACKS IN JAPAN $14.95
By Isabella L. Bird
Isabella Bird was one of the most adventurous women travelers of the 19th century with journeys to Tibet, Canada, Korea, Turkey, Hawaii, and Japan. A fascinating read.

THE RIVERS RAN EAST $16.95
By Leonard Clark
Clark is the original Indiana Jones, telling the breathtaking story of his search for the legendary El Dorado gold in the Amazon.

Spiritual Travel

THE SPIRITUAL GIFTS OF TRAVEL $16.95
The Best of Travelers' Tales
Edited by James O'Reilly and Sean O'Reilly
Favorite stories of transformation on the road that shows the myriad ways travel indelibly alters our inner landscapes.

PILGRIMAGE $16.95
Adventures of the Spirit
Edited by Sean O'Reilly & James O'Reilly
Introduction by Phil Cousineau

—— ★ ★ ★ ——

ForeWord Silver Medal Winner
— Travel Book of the Year

THE ROAD WITHIN $18.95
True Stories of Transformation and the Soul
Edited by Sean O'Reilly, James O'Reilly & Tim O'Reilly

—— ★ ★ ★ ——

Independent Publisher's Book Award
—Best Travel Book

THE WAY OF THE WANDERER $14.95
Discover Your True Self Through Travel
By David Yeadon
Experience transformation through travel with this delightful, illustrated collection by award-winning author David Yeadon.

A WOMAN'S PATH $16.95
Women's Best Spiritual Travel Writing
Edited by Lucy McCauley, Amy G. Carlson & Jennifer Leo
"A sensitive exploration of women's lives that have been unexpectedly and spiritually touched by travel experiences.... Highly recommended."

—Library Journal

THE ULTIMATE JOURNEY $17.95
Inspiring Stories of Living and Dying
James O'Reilly, Sean O'Reilly & Richard Sterling
"A glorious collection of writings about the ultimate adventure. A book to keep by one's bedside—and close to one's heart."

—Philip Zaleski, editor,
The Best Spiritual Writing series

Special Interest

THE BEST TRAVELERS' TALES 2004 $16.95
True Stories from Around the World
Edited by James O'Reilly, Larry Habegger & Sean O'Reilly
The launch of a new annual collection presenting fresh, lively storytelling and compelling narrative to make the reader laugh, weep, and buy a plane ticket.

TESTOSTERONE PLANET $17.95
True Stories from a Man's World
Edited by Sean O'Reilly, Larry Habegger & James O'Reilly
Thrills and laughter with some of today's best writers: Sebastian Junger, Tim Cahill, Bill Bryson, and Jon Krakauer.

THE GIFT OF TRAVEL $14.95
The Best of Travelers' Tales
Edited by Larry Habegger, James O'Reilly & Sean O'Reilly
"Like gourmet chefs in a French market, the editors of Travelers' Tales pick, sift, and prod their way through the weighty shelves of contemporary travel writing, creaming off the very best."
—William Dalrymple, author of *City of Djinns*

DANGER! $17.95
True Stories of Trouble and Survival
Edited by James O'Reilly, Larry Habegger & Sean O'Reilly
"Exciting...for those who enjoy living on the edge or prefer to read the survival stories of others, this is a good pick."

—Library Journal

365 TRAVEL $14.95
A Daily Book of Journeys, Meditations, and Adventures
Edited by Lisa Bach
An illuminating collection of travel wisdom and adventures that reminds us all of the lessons we learn while on the road.

FAMILY TRAVEL $17.95
The Farther You Go, the Closer You Get
Edited by Laura Manske
"This is family travel at its finest."
—*Working Mother*

THE GIFT OF BIRDS $17.95
True Encounters with Avian Spirits
Edited by Larry Habegger & Amy G. Carlson
"These are all wonderful, entertaining stories offering a *bird's-eye view!* of our avian friends."
—*Booklist*

THE GIFT OF RIVERS $14.95
True Stories of Life on the Water
Edited by Pamela Michael
Introduction by Robert Hass
...a soulful compendium of wonderful stories that illuminate, educate, inspire, and delight."
—David Brower,
Chairman of Earth Island Institute

LOVE & ROMANCE $17.95
True Stories of Passion on the Road
Edited by Judith Babcock Wylie
"A wonderful book to read by a crackling fire." —*Romantic Traveling*

A DOG'S WORLD $12.95
True Stories of Man's Best Friend on the Road
Edited by Christine Hunsicker
Introduction by Maria Goodavage

Travel Advice

THE PENNY PINCHER'S PASSPORT TO LUXURY TRAVEL $14.95
(2ND EDITION)
The Art of Cultivating Preferred Customer Status
By Joel L. Widzer
Completely updated and revised, this 2nd edition of the popular guide to traveling like the rich and famous without being either describes, both philosophically and in practical terms, how to obtain luxurious travel benefits by building relationships with airlines and other travel companies.

SAFETY AND SECURITY $12.95
FOR WOMEN WHO TRAVEL
By Sheila Swan & Peter Laufer
"An engaging book, with plenty of first-person stories about strategies women have used while traveling to feel safe but still find their way into a culture."
—*Chicago Herald*

SHITTING PRETTY $12.95
How to Stay Clean and Healthy While Traveling
By Dr. Jane Wilson-Howarth
A light-hearted book about a serious subject for millions of travelers— staying healthy on the road—written by international health expert, Dr. Jane Wilson-Howarth.

THE FEARLESS SHOPPER $14.95
How to Get the Best Deals on the Planet
By Kathy Borrus
"Anyone who reads *The Fearless Shopper* will come away a smarter, more responsible shopper and a more curious, culturally attuned traveler."
—Jo Mancuso, *The Shopologist*

GUTSY WOMEN $12.95
More Travel Tips and Wisdom for the Road
By Marybeth Bond
Second Edition
Packed with funny, instructive, and inspiring advice for women heading out to see the world.

GUTSY MAMAS $7.95
Travel Tips and Wisdom for Mothers on the Road
By Marybeth Bond
A delightful guide for mothers traveling with their children—or without them!

Destination Titles

ALASKA $18.95
Edited by Bill Sherwonit, Andromeda Romano-Lax, & Ellen Bielawski

AMERICA $19.95
Edited by Fred Setterberg

AMERICAN SOUTHWEST $17.95
Edited by Sean O'Reilly & James O'Reilly

AUSTRALIA $17.95
Edited by Larry Habegger

BRAZIL $17.95
Edited by Annette Haddad & Scott Doggett
Introduction by Alex Shoumatoff

CENTRAL AMERICA $17.95
Edited by Larry Habegger & Natanya Pearlman

CHINA $18.95
Edited by James O'Reilly, Larry Habegger & Sean O'Reilly

CUBA $17.95
Edited by Tom Miller

FRANCE $18.95
Edited by James O'Reilly, Larry Habegger & Sean O'Reilly

GRAND CANYON $17.95
Edited by Sean O'Reilly, James O'Reilly & Larry Habegger

GREECE $18.95
Edited by Larry Habegger, Sean O'Reilly & Brian Alexander

HAWAI'I $17.95
Edited by Rick & Marcie Carroll

HONG KONG $17.95
Edited by James O'Reilly, Larry Habegger & Sean O'Reilly

INDIA $18.95
Edited by James O'Reilly & Larry Habegger

IRELAND $18.95
Edited by James O'Reilly, Larry Habegger & Sean O'Reilly

ITALY $18.95
Edited by Anne Calcagno
Introduction by Jan Morris

JAPAN $17.95
Edited by Donald W. George & Amy G. Carlson

MEXICO $17.95
Edited by James O'Reilly & Larry Habegger

NEPAL $17.95
Edited by Rajendra S. Khadka

PARIS $18.95
Edited by James O'Reilly, Larry Habegger & Sean O'Reilly

PROVENCE $16.95
Edited by James O'Reilly & Tara Austen Weaver

SAN FRANCISCO $18.95
Edited by James O'Reilly, Larry Habegger & Sean O'Reilly

SPAIN $19.95
Edited by Lucy McCauley

THAILAND $18.95
Edited by James O'Reilly & Larry Habegger

TIBET $18.95
Edited by James O'Reilly & Larry Habegger

TURKEY $18.95
Edited by James Villers Jr.

TUSCANY $16.95
Edited by James O'Reilly & Tara Austen Weaver
Introduction by Anne Calcagno

Footsteps Series

THE FIRE NEVER DIES
One Man's Raucous Romp Down the Road of Food, Passion, and Adventure
By Richard Sterling
"Sterling's writing is like spitfire, foursquare and jazzy with crackle...."
—Kirkus Reviews

$14.95

ONE YEAR OFF
Leaving It All Behind for a Round-the-World Journey with Our Children
By David Elliot Cohen
A once-in-a-lifetime adventure generously shared, from the author/editor of *America 24/7* and *A Day in the Life of Africa*

$14.95

THE WAY OF THE WANDERER
Discover Your True Self Through Travel
By David Yeadon
Experience transformation through travel with this delightful, illustrated collection by award-winning author David Yeadon.

$14.95

TAKE ME WITH YOU
A Round-the-World Journey to Invite a Stranger Home
By Brad Newsham
"Newsham is an ideal guide. His journey, at heart, is into humanity."
—Pico Iyer, author of The Global Soul

$24.00

KITE STRINGS OF THE SOUTHERN CROSS
A Woman's Travel Odyssey
By Laurie Gough
Short-listed for the prestigious Thomas Cook Award, this is an exquisite rendering of a young woman's search for meaning.

$14.95

ForeWord Silver Medal Winner
—Travel Book of the Year

—— ★ ★ ★ ——

THE SWORD OF HEAVEN
A Five Continent Odyssey to Save the World
By Mikkel Aaland
"Few books capture the soul of the road like The *Sword of Heaven*, a sharp-edged, beautifully rendered memoir that will inspire anyone."
—Phil Cousineau, author of The Art of Pilgrimage

$24.00

STORM
A Motorcycle Journey of Love, Endurance, and Transformation
By Allen Noren
"Beautiful, tumultuous, deeply engaging and very satisfying. Anyone who looks for truth in travel will find it here."
—Ted Simon, author of Jupiter's Travels

$24.00

ForeWord Gold Medal Winner
—Travel Book of the Year

—— ★ ★ ★ ——